CW01024587

Improving Your Relationship

FOR

DUMMIES®

Improving Your Relationship

FOR DUMMIES®

by Paula Hall

A John Wiley and Sons, Ltd, Publication

Improving Your Relationship For Dummies®

Published by
John Wiley & Sons, Ltd
The Atrium
Southern Gate
Chichester
West Sussex
PO19 8SQ
England

E-mail (for orders and customer service enquires): cs-books@wiley.co.uk

Visit our Home Page on www.wiley.com

Copyright © 2010 John Wiley & Sons, Ltd, Chichester, West Sussex, England

Published by John Wiley & Sons, Ltd, Chichester, West Sussex

All Rights Reserved. No part of this publication may be reproduced, stored in a retrieval system or transmitted in any form or by any means, electronic, mechanical, photocopying, recording, scanning or otherwise, except under the terms of the Copyright, Designs and Patents Act 1988 or under the terms of a licence issued by the Copyright Licensing Agency Ltd, Saffron House, 6-10 Kirby Street, London EC1N 8TS, UK, without the permission in writing of the Publisher. Requests to the Publisher for permission should be addressed to the Permissions Department, John Wiley & Sons, Ltd, The Atrium, Southern Gate, Chichester, West Sussex, PO19 8SQ, England, or emailed to permreq@wiley.co.uk, or faxed to (44) 1243 770620.

Trademarks: Wiley, the Wiley Publishing logo, For Dummies, the Dummies Man logo, A Reference for the Rest of Us!, The Dummies Way, Dummies Daily, The Fun and Easy Way, Dummies.com and related trade dress are trademarks or registered trademarks of John Wiley & Sons, Inc. and/or its affiliates in the United States and other countries, and may not be used without written permission. All other trademarks are the property of their respective owners. Wiley Publishing, Inc., is not associated with any product or vendor mentioned in this book.

LIMIT OF LIABILITY/DISCLAIMER OF WARRANTY: THE PUBLISHER, THE AUTHOR, AND ANYONE ELSE INVOLVED IN PREPARING THIS WORK MAKE NO REPRESENTATIONS OR WARRANTIES WITH RESPECT TO THE ACCURACY OR COMPLETENESS OF THE CONTENTS OF THIS WORK AND SPECIFI-CALLY DISCLAIM ALL WARRANTIES, INCLUDING WITHOUT LIMITATION WARRANTIES OF FITNESS FOR A PARTICULAR PURPOSE. NO WARRANTY MAY BE CREATED OR EXTENDED BY SALES OR PRO-MOTIONAL MATERIALS. THE ADVICE AND STRATEGIES CONTAINED HEREIN MAY NOT BE SUITABLE FOR EVERY SITUATION. THIS WORK IS SOLD WITH THE UNDERSTANDING THAT THE PUBLISHER IS NOT ENGAGED IN RENDERING LEGAL, ACCOUNTING, OR OTHER PROFESSIONAL SERVICES. IF PRO-FESSIONAL ASSISTANCE IS REQUIRED, THE SERVICES OF A COMPETENT PROFESSIONAL PERSON SHOULD BE SOUGHT. NEITHER THE PUBLISHER NOR THE AUTHOR SHALL BE LIABLE FOR DAMAGES ARISING HEREFROM. THE FACT THAT AN ORGANIZATION OR WEBSITE IS REFERRED TO IN THIS WORK AS A CITATION AND/OR A POTENTIAL SOURCE OF FURTHER INFORMATION DOES NOT MEAN THAT THE AUTHOR OR THE PUBLISHER ENDORSES THE INFORMATION THE ORGANIZATION OR WEBSITE IT MAY PROVIDE OR RECOMMENDATIONS IT MAY MAKE. FURTHER, READERS SHOULD BE AWARE THAT INTERNET WEBSITES LISTED IN THIS WORK MAY HAVE CHANGED OR DISAPPEARED BETWEEN WHEN THIS WORK WAS WRITTEN AND WHEN IT IS READ.

For general information on our other products and services, please contact our Customer Care Department within the U.S. at 800-762-2974, outside the U.S. at 317-572-3993, or fax 317-572-4002.

For technical support, please visit www.wiley.com/techsupport.

Wiley also publishes its books in a variety of electronic formats. Some content that appears in print may not be available in electronic books.

British Library Cataloguing in Publication Data: A catalogue record for this book is available from the British Library

ISBN: 978-0-470-68472-6

Printed and bound in Great Britain by TJ International Ltd.

10 9 8 7 6 5 4 3 2 1

WILEY

About the Author

Paula Hall is an accredited sexual and relationship psychotherapist who has worked with many hundreds of couples and individuals with relationship difficulties. Originally trained by and working with Relate she now works in private practice in Warwickshire. As well as writing about relationships she also provides professional comment on sexuality, separation and young people's issues to the national press, women's magazines, teenage magazines, websites, national and local radio and television. She also runs her own website at www.TheRelationshipSpecialists.com.

Author's Acknowledgments

It's really hard to know where to start and who to thank for helping me write this book. I first started learning about relationships from watching my parents, so thanks first to Mum and Dad for showing me the importance of love and respect in a marriage, as well as how to have an argument and make up afterwards. And whilst on the theme of personal experience, hoooge ongoing gratitude to my husband Steve who makes improving our relationship meaningful, exciting and endlessly rewarding.

In the realms of professional, I'd like to thank Relate for their excellent training and continuing commitment to improving the relationships of thousands of couples each year. I'd particularly like to thank my colleagues and supervisors who've inspired, encouraged and challenged me to improve my practice, especially Angie Purdom, Marnie Brewster and Heather Storr. I'd also like to thank my publishers, John Wiley & Sons, Ltd. for giving me the opportunity to write this book. I'd especially like to thank Nicole Hermitage, who entrusted this mammoth project to me and Simon Bell for holding my hand throughout.

Finally I'd like to thank all the clients I've seen over the years who've shared their relationship struggles with me. It is such a privilege to witness the courage and hard work so many people put into making their relationships better. Thank you for letting me join you on the journey, and for teaching me how unique and precious relationships can be.

Publisher's Acknowledgments

We're proud of this book; please send us your comments through our Dummies online registration form located at www.dummies.com/register/.

Some of the people who helped bring this book to market include the following:

Commissioning, Editorial, and Media Development

Project Editor: Simon Bell

Developer: Charlie Wilson

Copy Editor: Sally Osborn

Acquisitions Editor: Nicole Hermitage

Assistant Editor: Jennifer Prytherch

Production Manager: Daniel Mersey

Cover Photos: ©Jan Will / Fotolia

Cartoons: Ed McLachlan

Composition Services

Project Coordinator: Lynsey Stanford

Layout and Graphics: Ashley Chamberlain

Proofreader: John Greenough

Indexer: Ty Koontz

Brand Reviewer: Zoë Wykes

Contents at a Glance

Table of Contents

Part III: Improving Communication and Resolving Conflict 141

Introduction

1 wrote this book because I believe everyone who's in a relationship wants to improve their relationship. That's not to say that every couple is on the brink of divorce or living in abject misery, but most people know that in at least some areas of their relationship they could do better. That might mean improving communication, becoming better at managing conflict, spicing up a flagging sex life or becoming more intimate and romantic. No one is perfect and that means no relationship is perfect, but there's always room for improvement.

What's more, couple relationships are always a 'work in progress'. They're never complete because they're made up of two individuals who continue to grow and change, who live in a world that never stays the same. As life changes, you and your partner are forced to adjust and renegotiate the rules and roles of your relationship. What worked for you two years ago before you had children may no longer work now you have tantrum Toby in tow and haven't slept for a month because of teething Tabitha. And the obsessive fascination and constant passionate desire you felt with your partner in the first few years may be little more than a fond wistful memory 30 years on. Whatever your circumstances, relationships change and it's up to you whether those changes are for better, or worse.

In this book you can find advice and guidance on navigating through the ups and downs of relationship life hand in hand. You find help on the predictable changes of life, like having a baby, moving home and retirement, and also on the sudden shocks some people have to face such as bereavement, redundancy and affairs. You also find tips on negotiating your way through the day-to-day grumbles that sometimes challenge even the most harmonious homes, such as housework, money and parenting.

For most people, a happy and fulfilling couple relationship gives meaning and purpose to life and creates the motivation and enthusiasm to explore and enjoy their world. Strong couple relationships are also the foundation for a secure and happy family life and a healthy society. Unfortunately, I can't guarantee this book will make you and your partner live 'happily ever after', but it can definitely help!

About This Book

There are hundreds of books out there on relationships, some written by journalists, some by psychologists, some by social commentators and a few by quacks like me (or psychotherapists, as we prefer to be called). Over the past 15 years I've worked with literally hundreds of couples and individuals who want to improve their relationship and I know first hand that every person is different and every relationship is unique. I've also learnt that problems within a relationship can affect almost every area of a person's life and most people will do almost anything to make things better.

In this book you won't find easy answers or simple, guaranteed solutions, but you will gain the tools you need to analyse and understand your personal situation and lots of advice and strategies for sharing this information with your partner. I also share lots of tips and suggestions that have worked for other couples who've been in a similar situation to yours.

Unlike most relationship books, this isn't a book that promotes any particular theory or route to happiness. It's a reference book you can turn to whatever your individual circumstances and find insights, information and advice to tailor to your needs. Ultimately, you're the expert on your relationship and this book is simply an instrument to help illuminate your journey to a happier life with your partner.

What You're Not to Read

This book has been designed so you can go straight to the subject that's most relevant to your situation and get specific advice. You don't have to start at the beginning for the book to make sense, or read every single word.

Wherever you see the 'Casebook' symbol attached to a sidebar (one of the grey boxes dotted through the book) you'll find an example that expands on what you're reading, but if you're already able to make the connection between your own story, feel free to scoot past. And if you're not into following prescribed exercises you might want to ignore the 'Try This' sections. Any info you see in a sidebar is there as extra information about the topic but it's not essential reading.

Foolish Assumptions

I'm making two assumptions about you, the reader. They may be wrong, but you'll get more from this book if I'm right.

Firstly, I'm assuming you're in a couple relationship. You may be just starting out, together a few years or heading for your diamond anniversary. This may be your first relationship, your second or your twentieth, but either way it's a relationship you want to improve. I'm not assuming it's a heterosexual relationship, but for the sake of balance I've alternated 'he' or 'she' from chapter to chapter to avoid clumsy language.

Secondly, I'm assuming you're willing to change. You may feel it's your partner who has all the faults and should be reading this book, but the reality is that no one can change another person unless they want to change. All you can do is change yourself and hope that your partner is encouraged to change the way they respond to you.

How This Book Is Organised

This book is divided into 5 parts and 19 chapters. The table of contents includes subheadings for each chapter so you can see which subjects appear within each chapter. Each part contains chapters on a similar theme, as the following sections illustrate.

Part 1: Preparing for Relationship Change

Before setting out on a journey it's helpful to know where you're going and even more helpful to know where you're starting from. In this part you look at the ground rules of a successful relationship and the rules for making it work. You also have the opportunity to look at your individual circumstances and make some decisions about exactly what it is that you want to improve.

Part II: Boosting Your Relationship

A successful relationship is made up of lots of good stuff and a few unavoidable tricky bits. Part II is all about how you can create more of the good stuff by maximising your time together and ensuring you're doing things you both enjoy. You also get some tips and suggestions for getting and keeping romance alive, which hopefully get you in the mood for looking at your sex life. I'm sure you did at least a rudimentary amount of sex ed at school, but if it's too long ago to remember or was about nothing more than how not to get pregnant then this part offers lots of information and advice for you, from bedroom basics to x-rated exploration.

Part III: Improving Communication and Resolving Conflict

Good communication is essential for a happy relationship and, because differences of opinion are inevitable unless you're living with a clone, resolving disagreements is also crucial. Part III is all about communication: how to listen, how to be heard, how to fall out without your relationship falling apart and how to break free of those horrible ongoing arguments that so many couples get into.

Part IV: Working Through Relationship Issues

This is the part where you get to the nitty gritty of what makes relationships so complicated. You start with the day to day stuff that affects most of us, like running a home, managing money and dealing with the kids, and then move on to the really tough stuff like living with difficult emotions such as jealousy, anger and depression. You then find help and guidance for getting through the major changes in life, such as starting a family, moving home, redundancy and retirement, and then a whole chapter dedicated to surviving affairs, whether you were the unfaithful one or the person who was betrayed. Part IV concludes with how to recognise whether your relationship has reached the end of the road and how you might make the agonising decision to separate.

Part V: The Part of Tens

If you're a fan of 'top ten tips', you'll like this section. If you really can't be bothered to thumb through the whole book in your hour of need, turn straight to these pages for an instant hit. You find quick tips on communicating effectively, getting passionate and steering clear of an argument, and also some great expectations you can adopt.

Appendix

This is where you find some useful resources to guide you as you seek to strengthen your relationship. I've included some of the best books on the market as well as details of some of the most important relationship organisations and their websites.

Icons Used in This Book

The funny little pictures in the left-hand margin are there to draw your attention to a particular type of information.

This icon means that the little tale next to it is a real story about a client whose story you might find helpful. Names and personal details have of course been changed to protect clients' identities.

This icon tells you that there's a bit of information here that I think is particularly important for you to bear in mind.

This bullseye flags up useful tips to help you get the most out of the practical exercises and information in this book.

This little picture tells you that the exercise next to it is safe for you to try at home. And you might find it jolly helpful too.

There aren't many warnings in this book, but where you do stumble across this symbol it means be careful or be aware: possible relationship or personal danger ahead.

Where to Go from Here

This is a reference book, not a book you have to read from cover to cover, so if you already know the problems within your relationship then now's the time to look at the contents page and head straight for the relevant section. If you're not really sure what's going on, but you know it isn't right, do the inventory in Chapter 2 and then go to where your learning leads you. Wherever you start, don't stop until you've got the improvements you and your partner desire and deserve.

Part I
Preparing for Relationship Change

'I realise you're trying to cheer me up Arthur
but I just don't like the colour.'

In this part . . .

If your relationship is going through a difficult time and you want to make it better, this part of the book will give you the basics you need to get started. I'll explore how couple relationships work and what you need to do to make one survive and thrive. I also help you get ready to improve your relationship by prioritising what you want to work on, and by ensuring you have the resources you need.

The final chapter in this part contains the five essential ground rules for a successful relationship. When you put these rules in place, they will help you to build your relationship into one that makes you happy.

Chapter 1

Understanding the Economics of Love

In this chapter you get a quick overview of how to improve your relationship. You also find out about the meaning of relationships, how they work, why they work, what goes wrong and what you can do about it. And you get a glimpse at what chapters are most likely to be relevant to your current situation.

The chapter looks at the economics of love, through the relationship bank account. Every couple has one of these accounts and, like a standard bank account, it thrives when you make deposits but empties when you make a withdrawal. Your transactions are emotional ones. So each time you do something nice for your partner, you boost the funds in your account – but when things go wrong, you make a withdrawal. Using this simple metaphor, this chapter looks at the importance of regular deposits into your account and the pitfalls of too many withdrawals – and, most importantly, how to avoid going into relationship bankruptcy!

Investing in Your Relationship Bank Account

Every couple, whether knowingly or not, create something entirely new and unique when they get together. This third entity is something that they carry with them for the rest of their relationship, something very special that needs constant care and attention by both partners. From the moment you develop a relationship, the relationship will always contain three entities: you, me and us. 'Us' is the place in the middle where the two of you meet.

You also need to stay mindful of your account balance by making it a priority to build and protect your investment, so that your account is a resource you can both rely on in times of need.

Chapters 4 and 5 are full of ideas on how you can boost your relationship account.

Recognising that love needs work

When you first meet the man or woman of your dreams and fall hopelessly in love, you can't possibly imagine that anything can ever go wrong. As you gaze lovingly into each other's eyes, you see nothing but beauty and perfection. You love everything about the other person. And if love hasn't completely blinded you to the person's faults, you see those as wonderful, endearing little quirks. Temporarily, you're in heaven and all's right with the world.

These early, heady days of love are intoxicating and effortless. But unfortunately, they're also finite. And when this first stage of a relationship passes, love needs work to survive.

Writers and researchers have given various labels to this first stage of a relationship: the romantic phase, limerence, blending, bonding or simply being 'in love'. And most agree that it's a biochemical phenomenon that eventually fades. As Chapter 5 explains, Mother Nature wants you to get as close as possible to the other person, as fast as possible. So she floods your body with a chemical called PEA, which fills you full of lust and attraction for approximately 18 months (I guess by then she thinks the woman should be pregnant – job done for Mother Nature). Then the passionate feelings of love gradually subside and evolve into a deeper, long-term attachment.

While you're 'in love', you're probably blissfully unaware of your relationship bank account. This is because both of you are investing bucketloads of love into the account and, hopefully, not making any withdrawals. But as the in-love feelings begin to wear off and real life intrudes, you become more and more aware that if you want to keep your relationship alive, you're going to have to work at it.

When Tom and Rose came for counselling, they were surprised to learn they had a relationship account. They knew their relationship wasn't as healthy as it used to be and that something was missing, something they used to feel really good about. When they found out about the economics of love and discovered their relationship account, they soon realised that they hadn't made any deposits for a long, long time. They'd got so used to looking after themselves as individuals that they'd stopped looking after their relationship.

Discovering that you've got to work at your relationship often comes as a shock, especially if you were lucky enough to have a blissfully romantic phase. But that's the reality of life. Even if you and your partner are a match made in heaven, you have to do the maintenance down here on planet earth.

When real life kicks in, it puts relationships under pressure. Living together means accepting that neither partner's perfect. You have to compromise over your differences and tolerate imperfections. Children arrive with their own precious little bundle of stresses, and you've got to make a living and run a home. And few people get through life without at least one or two significant heartaches, each of which can take a toll on individuals and have a knock-on effect on relationships.

A happy relationship can be a blissful refuge from the storms of life, but you've got to make sure you keep it strong and safe. And to do that, you need to make sure you're continually investing in your relationship love account.

Making regular deposits

The deposits you make into your relationship account are emotional, and you can convey them in either words or deeds. Each time you say or do something caring for your partner, the account goes up in value. You feel loved, valued and cherished. You can make many of these deposits on a daily basis, but other deposits are bigger investments you make only occasionally or when the need arises.

Daily deposits include things like:

- ✔ Showing interest when your partner's talking
- ✔ Expressing empathy with your partner's feelings
- ✔ Demonstrating thoughtfulness with gestures such as making a cup of tea, running a bath or doing an errand
- ✔ Providing physical affection and comfort
- ✔ Sharing your thoughts and feelings
- ✔ Saying 'I love you'
- ✔ Cooking a favourite meal
- ✔ Ignoring your mobile when you're in a conversation with your partner
- ✔ Paying your partner a compliment

Agreeing on a common love language

What words and actions say 'I love you' to your partner? You have many different ways of showing your partner that you love him, and each way means more to some people than to others.

One trap that many couples fall into is that they show their love in the way that means most to them, rather than the way that means most to their partner. So you may think you're making regular deposits by saying nice things and showing affection, but what your partner really wants is to spend more time together or have some help with a task.

To clear up confusion, discuss with your partner what makes you feel loved. You may be the kind of person who most appreciates love being shown verbally, when your partner says 'I love you' or pays you a compliment. Or you may be someone who loves to receive unexpected gifts: a flower, a card or your favourite bottle of bubbly (bath or otherwise!). Then ask your partner what you can do to show your love in return.

Discovering what each other's favourite love language is can be a powerful step towards boosting your relationship love account and improving your relationship.

Bigger deposits can be:

- ✔ Doing something especially thoughtful when your partner's having a difficult time
- ✔ Buying a present
- ✔ Really pushing the boat out to celebrate a special occasion
- ✔ Going away together to enjoy some quality time

A bigger deposit is any event that really shows your partner how much you love him and boosts your relationship love account.

A healthy sex life is another way in which you build your relationship account. When a couple are able to connect and communicate with each other through their sexual relationship, they create a special and unique bond. Chapters 6 and 7 contain plenty of information on the importance of sex and how to overcome sexual difficulties.

Saving for a rainy day

When a relationship's going well, you can easily forget to make regular deposits into the love account. The cash flow seems fine, so you stop checking the account balance and start taking each other for granted. But a relationship's economic climate is an unpredictable one, so you must be ready for a rainy day.

A rainy day can hit a relationship like a bolt out of the blue. The couples who stay close throughout these storms are the ones with a healthy balance in their relationship accounts. A rainy day may be a forced period apart or enduring a particularly stressful time at work. It can be a family crisis, or bereavement or anything else that affects you as a couple. During times like this, you need more support than ever from your partner, but if your account is low, you may find you have little to draw on. So keep topping up your account at every possible opportunity.

Like a financial account, the relationship account can't have too much in it. I don't know anyone who thinks they have too much money, and no one's ever complained of having too much love. You've got no reason to stop building on your account. The more you put in, the more resources you have to draw on during difficult times, and the more confident both of you are that your relationship's strong.

Reaping the rewards of your investment

The relationship love account is a joint account: both partners can make deposits. The great thing about this account is that the more you put in, the more your partner is likely to put in. When you're nice to someone, the person is generally nice back – you get into a positive upward spiral.

But the rewards are much greater than this. When the balance in your account is healthy, you get on well with your partner. You more easily forgive little grievances and tolerate differences. You're more likely to compromise with each other and not pick up on minor irritations. In the same way that having a healthy bank balance makes life run more smoothly, having a healthy love account makes a relationship run more smoothly too.

When I see couples who are snapping at each other constantly – couples who are suspicious of one another's motives and have to question and argue about every tiny little thing the other does – then I know their relationship account is low. Not investing in the love account creates the same kind of tension that you feel when you know you have very little in the bank and you have no reliable income: it's the emotional equivalent of penny pinching. Couples become increasingly tight.

Make a commitment to start putting a minimum of five deposits every day into your love account. That may be one act of affection, paying a compliment, doing something helpful, smiling when your partner enters the room and giving your partner your full, undivided attention when he speaks.

Making regular deposits into your relationship account is an investment in your happiness today and tomorrow, whatever tomorrow may bring.

TRY THIS

Try
This

How healthy is your love balance?

To find out how good you are at making deposits in your relationship account, ask yourself the following questions:

✔ Am I regularly spontaneous with my affection?

✔ Have I done anything helpful in the last week?

✔ Do I show patience and consideration?

✔ Have I told my partner recently how much I appreciate him?

✔ When was the last time I did something thoughtful and romantic?

✔ Do I make time to share my thoughts and feelings each day?

If answering these questions leaves you feeling your account's running low, then make a resolution to start making more deposits – today.

Minimising Damaging Emotional Withdrawals

No one's perfect. Sometimes you say and do hurtful or inconsiderate things that upset your partner. You may do it because you're angry with him or angry about something else, or because you're just being thoughtless. Either way, each time you hurt your partner, you're making a withdrawal from your relationship account.

People often try to kid themselves that the little things they do that upset their partners don't really matter, but they do. If you continually take money out of a bank account, however small the amount, then you find yourself overdrawn. The same is true of the relationship love account. If you're regularly taking out more than you're putting in, then you're going to end up in debt.

Knowing why little things can hurt so much

People need to know that their partners love them. And the only way you can truly know that is by the way your partner treats you. Simply saying 'I love you' isn't enough – your partner needs to back up the words with actions and behaviours that demonstrate that love.

You know you're loved when your partner treats you with courtesy and respect, when he enjoys your company and wants to spend time with you, when he shares his life and values your opinions. You feel loved when your partner shows interest in the things that you do, cares about your happiness, is committed to resolving differences and minimising stress, and when he wants to be physically close and tender.

Any action or word that gets in the way of knowing that you're loved is a withdrawal from the relationship account. It may only be a minor withdrawal, but it takes something away. In the same way as small acts of kindness and consideration build a relationship, small acts of unkindness and inconsideration fracture it.

Couples commonly make withdrawals from their account by being:

✔ Aloof (reluctant to make time to be together)

✔ Critical or sarcastic

✔ Defensive or argumentative

✔ Forgetful

✔ Late

✔ Lazy

✔ Silent or moody

✔ Unaffectionate

Every relationship goes through times when being kind and considerate to your partner is harder, such as when you're in a particularly difficult life stage like starting a family, moving home, coping with redundancy or adapting to retirement. The additional stress is bound to take its toll, but this is when you need to find extra reserves of attention and affection, not less. Chapter 13 explores these life stages in more depth.

The day-to-day stress of living together can also put a strain on relationships. Most couples fall out, at least occasionally, about issues such as housework, money and children. But finding ways to manage these minor differences can ensure that you're not depleting your love account. Flick to Chapter 11 for more information and advice on overcoming day-to-day grumbles.

When communication is awkward between a couple and resolving even the smallest of differences feels impossible, the account can begin to dwindle. Discovering how to talk and listen with respect and empathy, and being able to manage conflict in a way that leaves you both feeling you've won are essential couple skills. For more on communication and resolving conflict, look at Chapters 8, 9 and 10.

Another common way in which couples make withdrawals is by not acknowledging the deposits their partner is making. If you feel like your relationship is all one-sided, with only one of you putting anything into your relationship account, then you can quickly become resentful. This may be understandable for a short time if one of you is under a lot of external pressure, but if it's an ongoing pattern in your relationship, then you're going to run into trouble.

A successful relationship's about give and take. You both need to be giving equally into your account and be equally committed to minimising any damaging withdrawals.

Increasing awareness of your faults

Some people seem to be naturally good at depositing, while others have a flair for withdrawals – often without even knowing it. If you grew up in a home environment with lots of open love, praise and affection, then showing love and tenderness to your partner probably comes easily. But if you were brought up in a more hostile environment, you may be completely unaware that your withdrawals are bleeding your relationship account dry.

Becoming aware of your faults is essential for improving a relationship. You can't change unless you know you're doing something wrong in the first place. In order to do that, you have to make an honest, critical assessment of your faults. And you need your partner to help you. Even if you're blissfully unaware that you're making withdrawals, the chances are your partner isn't. The best way to find out if you're damaging your relationship without even knowing it is to ask your partner.

Pick a time when you know you won't be disturbed and simply ask your partner 'I'd like to know if things I do hurt or offend you, so I can stop doing them.' Then wait. Depending on your partner, you may not have to wait long, or you may let your partner think about the question for a while and come back to you with a considered answer. If you're lucky, your partner may only think of one or two things. But even if that's the case, you're not quite off the hook yet.

Using the input from your partner, now fill in Table 1-1.

If you have lots of ticks in the 'often' and 'occasional' boxes, make a concerted effort today to change this behaviour. Parts III and IV can help you.

Another way of becoming more aware of when you may be making withdrawals is to try to tune in to your partner's moods and body language. Next time your partner goes quiet or snappy for no apparent reason, ask whether you've done something to upset him. Or if you see your partner's eyes roll or glaze over, or he folds his arms or tuts and sighs, rather than shrugging it off as some strange idiosyncrasy of his, check whether something you've said or done has triggered the behaviour.

Table 1-1	Facing Your Faults		
I Am . . .	*Often*	*Occasionally*	*Never*
Inconsiderate			
Unreliable			
Unaffectionate			
Short-tempered			
Critical/sarcastic			
Unhelpful			
Defensive			
Disrespectful			

Becoming more aware of your day-to-day faults can be a painful process, but if you're serious about improving your relationship, you need to overcome these small but powerful irritations.

Accepting your partner's definition of a withdrawal

What offends one person is water off a duck's back to someone else. Obviously, exceptions occur to this: few people are totally unbothered if their partner is two hours late without warning and still manages to forget the milk. But many thoughtless words and actions are just that: thoughtless. Or rather, you said and did them because you 'thought' it wouldn't cause a problem.

Many couples live very successfully by the 'treat others as you want to be treated' motto. But doing so only works if both of you expect to be treated the same. If sarcasm and teasing were harmless fun in your childhood family, you probably don't react to them in adulthood and are shocked if your partner goes into a huff. Or if you were brought up in a home with very strict divisions of labour, you may not expect your partner ever to lend you a hand with your chores, and therefore consider as unfair him getting upset when you don't help them out with his. Nothing's right or wrong in these matters, just different, but if you want your relationship to improve, your partner's opinion needs to come first.

If your partner is offended or hurt, no matter what your intention or motivation was, then you've made a withdrawal from your account. Whether the same thing the other way around would hurt you doesn't matter: it hurts him and therefore you need to stop.

One of the most damaging things you can do in a relationship is pretend to yourself that something doesn't matter, to try to convince yourself that your partner loves you just the way you are, warts and all, and therefore you don't have to make an effort.

The bottom line is this: if you continue to make damaging withdrawals without making an effort to change, your partner feels taken for granted and unloved. And if your contribution to the relationship account is continually lower than your partner's, you run the risk of him closing the account altogether.

Avoiding Relationship Bankruptcy

Some things in a relationship equal a massive withdrawal from your relationship account. While thoughtlessness and lack of consideration can slowly drain your account, some things can empty it in an instant. These are the relationship wreckers, the triggers that often send couples to the divorce courts. The good news is that you can avoid them all.

Identifying the relationship wreckers

Many things have changed in relationships over the years. People have new challenges to face, such as having the opportunity to cheat on the internet, and the increasingly difficult balance of work and life. Many couples are going into second relationships with stepchildren in tow, and an increasing number are trying to manage long-distance relationships.

But some things don't change. No relationship can happily survive without love, trust and respect. These are essential ingredients for a successful relationship, and when you cross the line and walk all over these, you can instantly bankrupt your account and end your relationship.

Here are the seven relationship wreckers to steer well clear of:

- **Abuse:** Whether verbal, emotional or physical, abuse is never okay in a relationship. A relationship must be a safe place where you feel cared for. If either you or your partner is controlling the other with threats, intimidation or manipulation, then at some point the other person is going to call it a day. If any kind of abuse is happening in your relationship, read Chapter 12.

- **Betrayal:** The most common form of betrayal is an affair, although any other major breach of trust counts too. Nowadays an affair can be a physical one or a relationship that one of you built online. Either way, if you or your partner is knowingly doing something that hurts the other, then you run the risk of wrecking your relationship. A relationship can survive an affair, but getting beyond that takes a lot of hard work and heartache, which you should avoid at all costs. Chapter 14 has more on affairs.

✔ **Dishonesty:** A big difference exists between privacy and secrecy. No matter how close you may be to your partner, you're still individuals and therefore you're entitled to some space to yourselves. But if you're keeping secrets and telling lies, your motivation for keeping things to yourself is to deceive your partner. Honesty is a prerequisite for trust, which is essential in any relationship. If either of you is trying to hide something like an addiction, a bad habit, a friendship or some financial matter, and you have no intention of coming clean, then you're being dishonest and you're not being true to your partner.

✔ **Jealousy:** Jealousy is one of the biggest killers of love. I've seen so many couples over the years with happy relationships that have been eaten away by one partner's inability to trust the other. The root of jealousy is low self-esteem: not being able to accept that your partner loves you and wants you and you alone. If this is a problem for either you or your partner, take a look at Chapter 3 and also *Boosting Self-Esteem For Dummies* by Rhena Branch and Rob Willson (Wiley). You can also find more on jealousy in Chapter 12.

✔ **Possessiveness:** Possessiveness often accompanies jealousy, but it can also be a problem in its own right. When one partner treats the other like a possession and feels he has the right to make the decisions about how the other should look, who she should see, where she should go and generally how she should run her life, then you don't have a relationship of equals. A successful relationship consists of two autonomous individuals who encourage each other to be themselves. If this isn't happening in your relationship, you're heading for bankruptcy.

✔ **Selfishness:** 'Me first' attitudes don't build loving relationships. When you love someone, you put the person's needs before your own, knowing that that person is doing exactly the same. In this way, you build a relationship of mutual reciprocity, both knowing that you don't have to fight for your needs to be met. If either you or your partner is more self-centred than couple-centred, then you've got the balance all wrong and sooner or later the neglected partner may choose to walk away.

✔ **Indifference:** This may seem like an odd one to put down as a relationship wrecker, but in my experience as a couple counsellor, indifference kills more relationships than any other single factor. Indifference is when you just don't care any more. You don't care whether you argue or whether you don't. You don't care whether you spend time together or talk. You don't even care if your relationship's going down the toilet. Then you've really got major problems. The fact that you're reading this book hopefully means that you're not in that place. But if you suspect that your partner is, you've got an uphill struggle on your hands.

If any of these relationship wreckers has happened in your relationship, you need to make the decision to face it head on and deal with it immediately.

You can continue to deposit positive words and actions into your relationship account and minimise the small, thoughtless withdrawals, but at the same time you need to pull your relationship back from the brink of bankruptcy. Read on to find out how.

Accepting that Snoopy was wrong

Some couples try to stick their heads in the sand, pretending the relationship-wrecking withdrawal from the love account (see the previous section) hasn't happened and hoping that, in time, they have enough deposits to make up for the deficit. The problem with this approach is that it seriously damages the security of the relationship, because neither partner is ever sure whether the issue is really over or whether it may arise again. You've got a whopping great bank charge hanging over your bank account, which can be imposed at any time. One wrong move and the payment's taken in full, leaving you completely bankrupt.

'Love means never having to say you're sorry.' That may be true if you're a dog or a cartoon character, but if you're a human being, living in the real world, wanting your relationship to work, it's a load of rubbish. The only healthy way to recover from a massive relationship account withdrawal is for the offender to apologise and commit to never doing it again, and for the injured party to try to forgive and move on.

Saying sorry

If you've experienced a major withdrawal from your relationship account, the very first thing you need is an apology that:

- ✔ Is wholehearted
- ✔ Accepts full responsibility without placing blame or finding excuses
- ✔ Demonstrates the degree of pain that's been caused
- ✔ Shows regret and remorse

 If you're the one who needs to make an apology, choose the timing so that you can have your partner's undivided attention. Slipping in a 'by the way, sorry about blah, blah, blah' as you're on your way to the shops isn't enough. You need to find a time when you're not going to be interrupted, face your partner, give him full eye contact and say 'I'm sorry.'

As you're apologising, make clear exactly what you're apologising for. That should include saying sorry for the offence you've committed and saying sorry for the pain you've caused. The sentence shouldn't contain any buts or any attempt to justify yourself or blame the event on someone or something else.

If your partner asks you for an explanation, then provide one. But make sure you give an explanation not a justification. You're trying to justify yourself if you're putting the responsibility anywhere else except on yourself, whereas an explanation provides the context but still takes full blame for what happened.

But an apology's just the start. Saying sorry is meaningless if you continue the offence and don't follow up with a sincere desire and effort to change.

Committing to change

Repentance is an old-fashioned word that's generally only used in the context of spirituality. But the English language doesn't really contain any alternative. To repent means to turn around, to turn your back on what you've done and begin to walk in the opposite direction.

If either you or your partner has made a relationship-wrecking withdrawal from your account, you need to turn your back on that behaviour and head in a new direction. You need to commit to change and work at rebuilding the trust in your relationship. This takes time and effort – things that some couples just don't want to invest. But if you're serious about improving your relationship, you must commit to never making the same mistake again.

Giving forgiveness

Forgiveness isn't a one-off event but a process, something that often takes a long, long time to complete. It's not something that you can or should offer glibly, as the effort required is often much greater than you anticipate.

Forgiving your partner for a relationship wrecker isn't the same as saying that what he did doesn't matter. And it definitely doesn't mean saying that the issue's over and in the past and you won't ever raise it again. Forgiving means making a decision that you want to move on from something. You want to let go of the pain that's been caused and not harbour a grudge. But you both need to accept that this takes time and that both of you need to work together to make the process happen – to rebuild your relationship love account to the point where both of you can feel safe and secure again.

Chapter 14 contains much more on forgiveness.

Pulling back from the brink

If your relationship love account is empty, you may be trying to decide whether you have anything left worth fighting for. Deciding whether to end a relationship or work at it is probably one of the most painful and difficult decisions you'll ever have to make in your life. And it's a decision that you should take plenty of time to consider.

As well as reading the relevant chapters in this book that relate to the issues that have brought your relationship to where you are, take a look at Chapter 15, which helps you recognise when a relationship is over. But for now, take some time to read through and consider the following:

- ✔ **Is any love left?** Love isn't only something that you feel but also something that you do. Being 'in love' is an emotion that waxes and wanes throughout your relationship, but 'loving' someone is a conscious decision that you make. Because the feeling of love can change so much, you're not wise to rely on this for making such a major decision as ending your relationship. But if you both still love each other in a practical sense and are both committed to getting the in-love feelings back, then the time to walk away hasn't arrived.

- ✔ **Is change possible?** If your relationship's going to get better, you have to know that whatever caused the difficulties can change. Sometimes, good intentions aren't enough. If you and your partner have repeatedly tried to change your behaviour and failed, then maybe change just isn't possible. You also need to have a shared commitment to change. If you can't both agree on what the problem is, you can't be committed to overcoming it. You have to reach a shared understanding of what's wrong and a shared goal for the future you want to create together.

- ✔ **Are you too late?** Without a doubt, some things do get better with time. Even the most painful betrayals can become less significant in a relationship if you have a willingness to change, forgive and move on. But if the pain hasn't eased at all or either of you is intent on bearing a grudge forever, then you may be too late. Another sign that you're too late is if one of you has already embarked on a course of action that excludes the other one. For example, if one of you has already moved out or started another relationship, then even though you haven't made a verbal decision to end the relationship, it may already be over emotionally.

- ✔ **Can you talk?** The bottom line in overcoming any relationship problem is communication. Without the ability to talk, you have no tools to fix it. Part III has lots of advice on improving communication, but if you need more, then do consider relationship counselling. If all that fails and you still feel unable to express your thoughts and feelings in a way that feels okay for both of you, you probably have to face the fact that your relationship is over.

With love, a willingness to change and the ability to talk, you can overcome any relationship problem. And indeed, many relationships that hit rock bottom do pick themselves up and become better than they ever were before. But unfortunately, some relationship love accounts have to go bankrupt before the investors realise what they've got to lose.

Chapter 2

Doing a Relationship Inventory

- -

In This Chapter

▶ Recognising the different components of a relationship

▶ Gaining perspective on relationship difficulties

▶ Establishing areas for improvement

▶ Thinking about professional support

- -

Y ou can't fix something if you don't know what's broken. Similarly, you can't improve your relationship unless you know what you want to change. So the aim of this chapter is to help you establish what's going wrong in your relationship and to get ready to improve it.

To start with, you get a look at the different components that make up a relationship. Then you have the opportunity to complete a relationship health check-up questionnaire to see what's working well and what you want to improve. You also take a look at how you can get yourself and your relationship ready for the improvements you want to make, and how you can maximise your chances of success.

If you already know what's wrong in your relationship, you can skip this chapter and go straight to the relevant section later in the book. Keep in mind, though, that you may want to have a read anyway, because what you discover about your relationship and its strengths and weaknesses may surprise you.

Defining the Different Areas of a Relationship

Couple relationships are complicated things. Unlike any other kind of relationship, as a couple you have to live together and share pretty much every area of your life. You parent together, finance and run a home together, support other family members and friends together, relax together occasionally and have sex! If you think about it, the fact that any relationship survives is a miracle. You have a huge amount to collaborate on and compromise about. But couples do succeed and have done so for centuries. They may have a heck of a lot to fall out about, but they also have a lot to share and enjoy together.

This great big bundle of confusion called a relationship has four broad aspects:

✔ **Compatibility:** This is a great starting point for a successful relationship. Sharing common interests and the same outlook on life can certainly make a relationship easier.

✔ **Intimacy:** Most couples want to feel close, to share levels of intimacy that make their relationship special and unique.

✔ **Practical day-to-day living stuff:** These are the things that when you first fall in love and are in the grips of wild and wanton romance, you think don't matter at all. But as reality sets in, they can become the things that make or break a relationship.

✔ **Communication:** This is the final and absolutely essential component of a relationship that underpins all the others.

The following sections explore each of these four aspects in turn.

Understanding the importance of compatibility

Without a doubt, compatibility is one of the most important indicators of a successful relationship. But trying to decide whether two people are compatible is not a simple 'yes' or 'no' process. Compatibility is more of a continuum, with 'very similar' at one end and 'completely different' at the other. Every relationship you have falls somewhere along that line.

Compatibility also changes over the years. As you grow and mature, your attitude to life changes and so do your preferences. So even if you and your partner were perfectly compatible ten years ago, you may not feel the same today. But if you stick with the relationship, you may be more compatible again in the future.

You also have to accept that difference is an inevitable part of being a unique human being (more on this in Chapter 3). You're not a clone, you're an individual. Obviously, the more things you have in common with your partner, the less you have to argue about. If you share the same interests, the same attitudes to life, the same dreams and goals, your life together is likely to be smooth. But it may also be very boring. Like many people, you're probably drawn to a partner who encourages you to grow and discover more about yourself – someone who's different from you but whose differences complement your characteristics.

The basis of any successful relationship is good communication (see the later section 'Recognising the centrality of communication'). When you can negotiate and compromise, you can overcome most differences in compatibility.

The incompatibilities that can be difficult to overcome are those where compromise involves too high a degree of personal sacrifice. These are the areas of life that touch the deepest part of who you are, the bits that you fundamentally don't ever want to change. These areas include:

- ✔ **Moral values:** These form a fundamental part of who you are. For example, someone who's been brought up to believe that lying is an absolute sin is going to find compromising with a fraudster extremely difficult.

- ✔ **Personal life goals:** These may include the decision whether to have children, to move around the world or to follow a particular faith or religion. If you have different goals to your partner, then at least one of you may always be left feeling deeply dissatisfied with your life.

- ✔ **Understanding of commitment and fidelity:** A shared view is essential here. If you want an open relationship where you're free to sleep with other people, that's absolutely fine, but not if you marry a monogamist.

Some difference is inevitable – and desirable – but if a couple don't share the same moral values, life goals and attitudes to commitment and fidelity, a deep distrust of the other can develop and the other person can feel as if improving the relationship is pointless.

If your differences lie in these essential compatibility areas, then make sure you read Chapter 14 on recognising if a relationship's over, and also the section 'Considering professional help', later in this chapter.

Identifying the facets of intimacy

What exactly is intimacy? It's one of those words people bandy about as being important in a couple relationship, but find very difficult to define properly.

The dictionary offers a number of different definitions for intimacy, including a 'close personal relationship', 'a quiet and private atmosphere' and 'a detailed knowledge resulting from a close or long association or study'. I particularly like the last one. In my experience, an 'intimate' relationship is one that results from close study of each other, for example when two lovers first meet and spend every moment exploring each other. Or intimacy can result from long association, such as the closeness you see in couples celebrating their 50th wedding anniversaries.

These definitions demonstrate that you need a level of effort and commitment to enjoy intimacy. They indicate that intimacy isn't something that happens automatically, but is something that couples can work towards. Knowing that intimacy takes effort is good news for people who want to improve their relationship – it means that if intimacy is missing, you can work together to create it.

When thinking about intimacy and the areas of your relationship that you want to improve, considering exactly what kind of intimacy you want more of can be helpful. The following is a description of the five facets of relationship intimacy:

- ✔ **Emotional intimacy:** Being similar in your emotional expression. That may mean crying or shouting at the same sorts of things or that both of you are equally sensitive or robust to emotion.

- ✔ **Intellectual intimacy:** Being on the same wavelength. You share thoughts and ideas and feel able to understand each other's thought processes.

- ✔ **Physical intimacy:** Being close physically and sharing a meaningful connection through mutual touch, sensuality and sexual pleasure.

- ✔ **Recreational intimacy:** Being able to laugh, relax and have fun together through similar needs and interests in non-essential pursuits.

- ✔ **Spiritual intimacy:** Being able to share the big stuff with similar levels of passion and fervour. That may be religion, politics, environmental issues, human rights, animal rights or even sharing a passionate belief in nothing at all.

Looking through this list, you may instantly recognise some areas where you want to be closer. Perhaps you've never really been close in this way and you want to commit to developing this area of your intimacy. Or perhaps, like many couples, you used to be more intimate in the past, but life has become so busy that you no longer make the time you need. Maybe issues between you in the practical day-to-day living stuff (see the following section) have got in the way of closeness. Whatever the reason, you can use the relationship health check-up questionnaire to mark how you feel (see the later section 'Taking a Good Look at Your Relationship').

Appreciating the significance of the practical day-to-day living stuff

Many couples don't appreciate the importance of being able to work together collaboratively on the practicalities of life. When daily life goes well, you take living together for granted, but if it doesn't, it can cause enormous stress and heartache.

Ironically, precisely because people think that differences in how they do things shouldn't matter, they find that in fact they matter hugely. People expect that if they love one another, have compatible values and share lots of intimacy, running a home and family is going to come easily. Or if things don't run smoothly, they can easily work around the problems. But often, these little irritations are what can be exhausting and draining and leave you with little energy to enjoy the bits of the relationship that do work well.

The good news is that you can overcome these practical differences relatively easily. But to do so, you need to establish where you want to make changes. Here's a list of the common day-to-day stuff that can cause problems:

- **Friends:** How often you see them and how much influence they should have.

- **Hobbies/activities:** Whether you should do things together or apart, and how much of a priority leisure should be in your lives.

- **Home:** Who should do what and how it should be done, from doing the dishes and the laundry, emptying the bins and mowing the lawn, to who should pay the bills and fix the boiler.

- **In-laws:** How often you should see them and how involved they should be in your lives. For some people, this is a particularly emotive issue.

- **Money:** How much you should spend and how much you should save. And what you should spend it on and save it for.

- **Parenting:** Like home, who should do what and how it should be done. But this time, I'm talking about things like what food kids should eat, what time they go to bed, which university they should attend, who should read the bedtime story and who should dish out the discipline.

- **Work:** How to get that ever-elusive work–life balance right and ensure that you still have time and energy for each other.

You may have noticed that this list contains a lot of 'shoulds'. That's because the decisions you make about the way you run your life often feel like imperatives. How you bring up children and the way you manage your finances and your home often feel like things that you can't compromise on. But in reality, many different ways exist of doing things right and only a few ways exist of doing things wrong.

Recognising the centrality of communication

Communication's the essential backbone of a relationship. It's how people keep in touch with each other at every level. People use communication to share essential information, pass the time of day, share personal thoughts and feelings, build intimacy and resolve differences.

In relationships, five different types of communication exist, starting with the basic banter that's generally easy to achieve to the negotiating skills that can take years to perfect:

- ✔ **Information updates:** This is the day-to-day sharing of facts and essential information that keeps the home running.

- ✔ **Small talk:** You talk about the weather and the news headlines and ask cliché questions like 'How are you?' knowing that the answer's always 'fine'.

- ✔ **Companionable chat:** This level of conversation is getting more risky because you share more personal thoughts and feelings about your life and about yourself.

- ✔ **Intimate sharing:** You talk on a deeply personal level, sharing difficult emotions and trusting the other person to handle them with care.

- ✔ **Conflict resolution:** This is the communication style that couples adopt to overcome problems in their relationships.

Some couples are good at all five types of communication; some may never bother trying more than one or two.

The easier you find talking, the easier you will find building intimacy within your relationship and also overcoming differences.

Taking a Good Look at Your Relationship

This section helps you explore what's good in your relationship and what's not. Using a relationship questionnaire, you can begin to see the strengths in your partnership, and those areas that are weaker. Then you can determine which areas you need or want to improve.

Completing the relationship health check-up questionnaire

Use the template shown in Table 2-1 to give your relationship a health check-up. For best results, make two copies of this table, one for you and one for your partner. Take time alone to complete it and then arrange a time when you can talk through what you've written. Work through the list individually, marking a tick in the relevant box, and then compare your answers.

Table 2-1　The Relationship Health Check-Up Questionnaire

How satisfied do you feel about each of the following areas of your relationship?	Very Satisfied: We work well together in this and feel close	Reasonably Satisfied: Only very occasional, mild niggles	Neutral: Can cause issues, but nothing major	Quite Dissatisfied: Regularly causes problems between us	Very Dissatisfied: This is a major source of conflict and unhappiness
Essential Compatibility					
Moral values					
Life goals					
Attitudes to commitment and fidelity					
Intimacy					
Emotional					
Physical					
Intellectual					
Spiritual					
Recreational					
Practical Day-to-Day Living					
Parenting					
Home maintenance and management					
In laws and other close family members					
Friends – mutual and individual					
Money management and decision making					
Work and life–work balance					
Hobbies and interests, shared and individual					
Communication					
Information updates					
Small talk					
Companionable chat					
Intimate sharing					
Conflict resolution					

If your partner answers the questions differently from you, then see whether you can compromise on an answer that's in the middle. So if you've ticked 'quite dissatisfied' and your partner's ticked 'reasonably satisfied', see whether you can agree on 'neutral'. This helps you to work together when you come to prioritising the areas you want to improve. However, if one of you ticks 'dissatisfied' and doesn't want to upgrade the tick, this indicates that this area is definitely a problem for that partner and therefore a problem for the relationship that you need to improve if you want to stay together.

If your partner isn't able to answer the questionnaire with you, don't worry, because you can still make plenty of improvements on your own. Many people find that when they start working on their relationships, their partners begin to change. When you behave differently, you get a different reaction from your partner and consequently the relationship can improve, even if only one person is consciously making the changes.

When you've completed the questionnaire, the following sections help you analyse and use your responses.

Assessing your relationship strengths

When a relationship's going through difficult times, you can easily forget the things that are going well and making you happy. You can become so blinded by the bad stuff that you no longer see the good. Or you may be so anxious about the relationship breaking up that you don't let yourself enjoy the good times, in an attempt to protect yourself from the pain of loss if it all crashes to the ground. Anger and resentment can also get in the way. If you feel let down by your partner, you may deny any pleasure in the relationship as a way of punishing her for the pain she's caused.

I've worked with hundreds of couples going through relationship difficulties, but I haven't found a single relationship that hasn't had some very real and significant strengths – strengths that many couples do not want to live without and strengths that they can use to turn the rest of the relationship around.

Establishing what works well

Once you've completed your relationship check-up questionnaire, look at the left-hand columns at the areas of your relationship that are already working well and making you happy:

- ✔ **Compatibility:** If you're either 'very' or 'reasonably' satisfied in the essential areas of compatibility, then you have good reason to be optimistic about your relationship's future. With shared moral values and life goals and the same attitudes to commitment and fidelity, your relationship's in a very strong position indeed. These fundamental similarities mean that both of you are heading in the same direction.

✔ **Intimacy:** If you ticked the satisfaction boxes in any of the intimacy facets, these are important areas where you can enjoy welcome rest and respite from the more difficult areas of your relationship. They are also areas where you can focus your energy and on which you can build.

If you've identified one of the facets of intimacy as an area of satisfaction in your relationship, make a commitment today to ensure that you spend more time enjoying this part of your relationship on a regular basis.

✔ **Day-to-day living:** You may have ticked a lot of positive boxes in the practical day-to-day living sections of the questionnaire. These may be strengths in your relationship that you really value, or you may be tempted to think they're not important compared with the other areas of a relationship. But remember, no matter how much a couple may love each other and enjoy being together, if they can't live under the same roof, their future's in jeopardy. A harmonious home is an important asset to any relationship.

✔ **Communication:** If you've ticked 'very satisfied' in all of the communication boxes, then I'm very, very surprised. Most relationship difficulties have their root in communication problems, so inevitably this is an area you want to improve. But if some areas are already strengths for you, this is a really positive start, as the job of improving your relationship is then much easier.

Valuing your strengths

Unfortunately, many people are guilty of taking the good things in relationships for granted – at least some of the time. People often forget the good things when a relationship's struggling, but this is the time when you most need to value those strengths. You can also be tempted to assume that if you were in a different relationship, you'd automatically get those good things too. But in reality, when people go into a new relationship, they often lose a lot of the good things they used to have and discover that they have to face problems that they've never experienced before.

If you're struggling to recognise the importance and value of some of your relationship strengths, imagine living without them. When you think of separating or perhaps of being with someone else, you tend only to consider the problems that go away, rather than the assets that you lose. Imagine being with someone who doesn't share your love of classical music, or take care of her health, or share your views on parenting or friendship. What if you can't talk on the same wavelength, or enjoy sex together, or if the person can't do commitment? Which of the current strengths in your relationship would you miss most?

Building on your strengths

When you know where the two of you click best, you can also make sure that you build on that area. If you both love the same leisure activities, do more of them. If you both work well together around the home, consider starting a new project. Or if your strength is in the bedroom, make time to be there more often.

Whatever your strengths, make sure that you maximise them. Not only does this make you feel closer together as a couple, but doing so also gives you the incentive to work on the other areas of your relationship so that you don't risk losing what you have.

Recognising transferable assets

Another great thing about relationship strengths is that often they represent skills that are transferable. You may be able to look back over your questionnaire and instantly see areas where this is true. For example, you may have ticked hobbies and interests as a strength for you in the practical day-to-day living section, but you didn't tick recreational intimacy. In this case, you can use your shared interest in hobbies to find something you can do together to bring you more recreational intimacy.

Some strengths aren't obviously transferable, at least not on the surface, but if you look at why you work so well in that area, often you can transfer that knowledge to something else. For example, if you're strong in intellectual intimacy, you can use your shared logical or creative way of thinking to develop solutions to your housework and money problems. Or if you have shared life goals, you can use these to help you get perspective on other issues and prioritise how to work through them.

Working on your relationship weaknesses

Are you like many people who feel so overwhelmed with problems that you feel as if everything needs to change? If that describes you, please don't despair: things are almost certainly not as bad as they seem. Difficulties in one area of a relationship often spread like a nasty virus and affect everything else, but once you can identify the source of the problem, you can tackle it head on and stop the infection.

No relationship's perfect. The picture-perfect big-screen romances of Hollywood are a fantasy, created for our entertainment, not for our guidance. Mr Right and Mrs Right are also fictitious. They are characters you may dream of as a child, but when you grow up, you have to accept that being human means living with imperfections – in ourselves, our partners and our relationships.

Undoubtedly, you can and should try to resolve many problems and difficulties, but some you may have to learn to live with. The challenge is knowing which is which.

CASE STUDY

Using what's working to work on what isn't

Colin and Terry had been together for eight years and had always collaborated well on most of the practical areas of their relationship. When managing their money, home, friends and family, they communicated well. They also had good intellectual and physical intimacy and were compatible in their outlook on life. Their problem areas were emotional intimacy and work–life balance. Whenever either of these areas came up, Colin flew into a rage and Terry became tearful and withdrawn. By exploring how they worked together in other areas, they discovered that differences in views don't inevitably mean conflict, and they began to respond to each other in less provocative ways.

REMEMBER

Recognising your strengths helps you to face your weaknesses with perspective and optimism. The previous section 'Assessing your relationship strengths', helps you value what's going well.

Confirming what needs to change

Upon completing your relationship check-up questionnaire, you'll have identified the areas in your relationship that you're not satisfied with and/or that cause problems and conflict. In order to confirm which areas you want to work on, you need to answer the following questions.

Is change possible?

You can address most problems, but unfortunately a few you can't – or at least not without paying an unbearable price. For example, if you ticked the life goals box on the check-up as a problem area because one of you wants children and one of you doesn't, then you have a significant problem on your hands. You can't possibly compromise on having children. You can't have a child for the weekends or just for a couple of years and then give the child back. If you've both made up your minds, then change isn't possible.

Another situation where change isn't possible is where you don't agree that you have a problem: for example, if one of you is very happy with the level of physical or emotional intimacy in the relationship but the other one feels it's seriously lacking. You may be able to compromise in these situations, but if one of you feels getting any closer will be suffocating and oppressive, or that you have to lose too much of your sense of self and identity to be more intimate, any change may be short-lived.

TIP

If while reading these paragraphs you've suddenly been hit between the eyes with a problem that you think may be irresolvable, you may find some professional help useful. You can find more information on this in the later section 'Considering professional help'.

Is change essential?

If change isn't possible, you need to ask yourself if that matters. Being forced into parenting or not having a child may be an absolute no-no for you, but you may not mind too much if your partner never shares your passion for gardening or if you have to see less of your mother than you ideally want. Some changes are essential, especially if they touch your moral values or seriously affect your quality of life. But others may be preferable changes that you know you can live without.

Go back through your list of areas where you're unhappy in your relationship, and put a red circle around those where no change probably means the end of the relationship. These are your priorities when you come to create your 'to fix' list (see the later section on this).

Prioritising what needs to change

Everyone knows that Rome wasn't built in a day, though I suspect very few people know how long it did take! But that's irrelevant; the point is that good things take time. The same is definitely true of building a successful relationship. You're very unlikely to be able to fix your relationship overnight. Indeed, some problems may take many months to resolve, especially those that have been bothering you for many years.

Once you've highlighted your areas for change in the relationship check-up questionnaire, you need to decide which areas you want to work on first. Areas that you've ticked as ones with which you're very dissatisfied need to be high on your priority list – assuming, of course, that you've confirmed they are things that can change – but those areas shouldn't all be at the top. Working on the big stuff is often simpler when you've developed a proven track record of improvements on the smaller, often easier, areas of your relationship. This can be particularly powerful if that small change can make a significant difference to your relationship. For example, finding some quick solutions to making housework or money stress free for both of you can minimise your arguments and leave you both with more energy and motivation to sort out any sexual difficulties.

Take a pen in a different colour than the red one you used to circle fatal areas of your relationship, and go through your check-up sheet and circle the areas that are easy to change and can make a big difference to your day-to-day happiness.

Couples often ignore the little changes they can make, because doing so feels irrelevant next to the bigger issues they feel confronted with. But whatever improvements you can make, no matter how small, can really boost your couple confidence.

Why small steps are best

When a couple are in crisis, the two people often become polarised. Like children on a seesaw, each is at the opposite end, staring at the other and clinging on for dear life. A mistake that couples often make is to try to move too quickly.

Here you can see John and Jane sitting on opposite ends of their seesaw. If Jane were to try to make too big a step, perhaps to resolve a big issue on her own, there's a danger of them toppling over.

But when they can make small steps together to get closer, they can maintain the balance until they're back to where they should be.

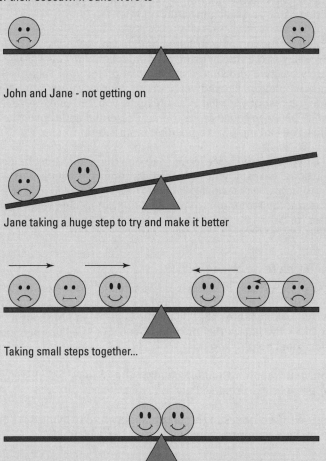

John and Jane - not getting on

Jane taking a huge step to try and make it better

Taking small steps together...

To get back to where they want to be

Creating a 'to fix' list

By now you hopefully have a completed relationship health check-up questionnaire with some scribbled pen circles on it. The red circles indicate your essential areas for change, and the other circles indicate the areas that are easier to change. You probably still have a few unmarked areas, which are your preferable areas for change.

Ideally, you and your partner can sit down together to create your 'to fix' list, but if your partner won't (too stubborn, perhaps) or can't (feels daunted by the task) do this, then make one on your own. As you begin to make the changes, you'll soon find out if your partner is pleased with the changes you're making and will jump fully on board to help.

The item at the top of your list should be something you think you can change fairly easily and that can bring maximum benefit. This change will help to create a positive and successful foundation for your relationship improvements to build on. Second you can put your most essential item. How you create the rest of your list is really up to you, but make sure that you find a balance between those areas that are essential and those that are easy to fix, so that you can maintain a positive momentum.

You can of course tackle more than one thing at a time. In fact, this is essential in some cases. If you've identified conflict resolution as something you want to improve (as most people do), then you need a conflict to practise on. This is another example where choosing something relatively straightforward is best for practising your skills, rather than jumping into the most contentious issue.

Finding more help

If you've ticked any of the boxes 'dissatisfied' in the essential compatibility section of the questionnaire, consider seeing a relationship therapist to see if you can establish how significant the issue is and find out if you can compromise in a way that works for both of you. See the later section 'Considering professional help'.

If you've ticked items under the intimacy heading, you can find help on how to improve these areas in Part II.

If you've ticked boxes in the practical day-to-day living section, you can find help on how to improve these areas in Parts III and IV.

If you've ticked anything under the communication heading, you can find help throughout this book, especially in Chapter 4 on prioritising your relationship and in Chapters 8, 9 and 10, which are dedicated to improving communication and resolving conflict.

Recognising Your Resources

When you're about to embark on a journey, you have to make sure that you've got everything you need for the trip. Have you got the time you need, the energy, the commitment? Do you need to make any preparations before you start? Do you need any additional professional resources (apart from this excellent book, of course)? In short, are you ready?

Checking your motivation and commitment

First and foremost, you need to check your motivation and commitment. You've bought this book and you're reading these pages, so I think it's fair to assume that you've made the decision that you want to improve your relationship and you're pretty serious about it. But other things can get in the way – stumbling blocks that trip you up, such as:

- External problems or emergencies
- Fear of failure
- Fear of making things worse
- Shortage of emotional and/or physical energy
- Shortage of time

To avoid any stumbling blocks, take a few minutes to ask yourself the key questions in the following sections.

Is now the right time?

For most people, 'now' is definitely the right time to improve their relationship. One of the most depressing things about being a relationship therapist is seeing people who've been struggling for years and years with a problem that they could have resolved in just a few months. Whatever you do, please don't leave things too late. If resentments are building and your communication and your love for each other are being damaged, 'now' is an excellent time to do something about it.

However, improving a relationship is hard work, and for some people, 'now' is not the right time. Perhaps you or your partner have started a new career or had a change in your family circumstances, or one of you is unwell or has recently been suffering with stress, anxiety or depression. If you know that your time and energy are very limited, then postponing this journey or at least making sure that you tackle only the more straightforward issues may make more sense.

You can only postpone working on your relationship for the short term. If you've been putting off improving your relationship for years, because you always have too many other things in your life, then the time has come to get professional help. You may have developed unconscious defences against change, which are keeping you permanently too busy.

What if things get worse?

An unfortunate reality is that relationships often get worse before they get better. Imagine stirring a muddy pond: all the muck that's settled at the bottom has to come to the surface so that you can sort it out once and for all. Working things out can be painful and difficult, and both of you need to persevere through this stage in order to get to the other side.

Many people don't embark on relationship improvements, because they're terrified of them not working. And if they can't improve the relationship, they have to make a decision about what to do next. Living in a difficult relationship may be hell, but for some people that's better than no relationship at all. If you discover that an essential component of your relationship's unfixable, what are you going to do? You don't have to answer that question right now, but you do need to be ready to face it if you're serious about improving your relationship.

If all of your relationship problems were resolved, would you still have doubts about the future of the relationship?

This is an important question, to which 99 per cent of you will have answered 'no'. Or probably 'no, of course not, what a stupid question'. If you're the 1 per cent who sighed and weren't sure, then the problem may not be the quality of your relationship, but rather that you don't want to be in a relationship with your partner at all. If this is true for you, then working on improving your relationship isn't the solution, because the problem lies within your heart, not the relationship. If this describes you, seek professional therapy to help you decide what you want for your future (see the following section).

Considering professional help

Some couples prefer to work through their relationship problems by themselves, but others find that outside professional help can be beneficial. For some, a few sessions with a trained therapist are all they need to get some guidance and advice on moving forward; others find that more in-depth therapy is best. What you choose depends on your individual circumstances and the kind of therapy you think works best for you.

The following sections give you the lowdown on relationship therapy, so that you can make an informed decision whether it's for you.

Knowing why people seek help

Couples choose relationship therapy for many reason. For some, this is a faster and easier way of addressing problems, because it ensures that they give the time and energy required by the process. For others, therapy's the only way of getting an objective third opinion to stop them arguing and help them to talk. For a few, it's an absolute last resort.

Here are some of the most common reasons people seek help:

- ✔ You have fundamental differences in your moral values, your life goals or your attitudes to fidelity and commitment.

- ✔ Conversations go round and round in circles and never get anywhere.

- ✔ Every conversation ends up in a bitter argument, with one or both of you feeling hurt.

- ✔ You can't possibly see each other's points of view.

- ✔ You face sensitive issues that both of you are worried about discussing.

- ✔ You feel like you really can't face trying to improve things, but you can't cope with your relationship as it is.

- ✔ You've tried improving issues within your relationship alone before, and doing so hasn't worked.

If any of these reasons is true for you, then you have nothing to lose by seeing a therapist. Therapy may feel awkward at first and a bit odd, but it gets easier very, very quickly.

For your own sake, don't leave therapy to the last resort – the sooner you get help, the sooner you can resolve your problems and the greater the chances of success.

Seeing how therapy works

How effective therapy is depends on both of you liking, or at least trusting, the therapist. If you don't like the therapist or you suspect she got her credentials from a Christmas cracker, the therapy's not going to work. A therapist's first job is to make you feel respected and valued as an individual and to provide you with a safe space where you can discuss your relationship difficulties.

Your therapist can give you both time to talk, to cry, to shout or just the time to think. You can discuss your thoughts, ask questions and explore your options. A therapist can't tell either of you what you should do, but she can help you to find the answers for yourselves.

Working through the big stuff hiding behind the small stuff

Jenny and Mark had been married for nine years when they came for couple counselling. They weren't having any major problems, just heaps and heaps of little ones. Jenny explained that she felt taken for granted. Mark frequently worked late without letting her know, was often grumpy when he got home and was reluctant to get into any conversation. Whenever they did talk, Mark seemed uninterested or critical. This had been going on for nearly two years, and Jenny described how she missed the old Mark she married.

Mark justified his behaviour, saying he was stressed at work and exhausted by the time he got home in the evenings. He expected Jenny to accept him just the way he was, and to make allowances for the fact that he wasn't as attentive as he used to be in the early days. Jenny tried to explain to him that she did understand

the pressure he was under and wanted their relationship to be a source of comfort and happiness for him. But she was tired of making all the effort on her own. 'I just can't live like this any more,' she exclaimed in one session. 'I love you, but I don't want to spend the rest of my life with you if this is how things are going to be.'

Mark was shocked. He knew Jenny was unhappy, but had no idea how depressed she was or how close she was to giving up. Suddenly he saw her and their relationship in a new light and began to make the changes that she wanted. Although it was difficult at first to break the habits he'd fallen into over the past two years, he was pleasantly surprised to see how quickly their relationship improved, not just for Jenny but for himself too.

Attending sessions

Ideally, both of you should attend couple therapy so that your therapist can hear both sides of the story and help you to communicate with each other and find collaborative solutions. But if your partner doesn't want to go, your therapist can help you to explore these things alone and encourage you to discuss them with your partner when you get home.

Some people prefer to see a counsellor alone to talk through their feelings about the relationship, and then go to a couple therapist later when they're clearer about what they want to achieve.

Choosing a therapist

Every therapist has her own individual style and preferred way of working. Some are very mumsy and caring, some are pragmatic and detached, some are bright and friendly, and some are frankly a bit odd. Some work with creative techniques, some set homework exercises, and some just listen and tell you what they see.

The best way to choose a therapist is either to chat to one for a while on the phone to find out what she's like, or arrange an initial appointment to meet her before agreeing to embark on therapy. Whoever you choose should be trained in relationship psychology and be accredited with a recognised professional body. A list of possible sources is in the Appendix.

Does therapy work?

Mmmmmm – that's a tough question, especially for couple therapy. The aim of therapy is always to help clients to discover and achieve their goals. Unfortunately, when you're working with couples, those goals are sometimes different. If you and your partner go for couple therapy with very, very different intentions, at least one of you is likely to feel that therapy's been unsuccessful. But if you go with a shared agenda and a common goal, therapy should help you achieve success more quickly and smoothly.

Maximising your change potential

Working on your relationship can be hard work and can take time. You need to make sure that you're not going to get knocked off course by someone else or by your own exhaustion. So here are some tips to maximise your chances of succeeding in the improvements you want to make:

✔ Tell your close friends that you're working through relationship problems at the moment, and ask them to be there to support you – they can listen and help you to switch off.

✔ If you have young children, ask family or friends to look after them so that you can have some additional time for you as a couple – to talk about your problems or just to let off steam together. If your children are old enough to understand, you may want to tell them that you need some extra space as a couple to work through some stuff. But do make sure to reassure them that relationship problems are a normal part of being a couple and it doesn't necessarily mean you're on the verge of splitting up.

✔ Don't allow yourself to become totally preoccupied by your relationship, so ensure that you've got a good novel to read or films to watch, or whatever helps you to relax.

✔ Book some holiday time or leisure activities into your diary so you can both have things to look forward to.

✔ While you're working through your relationship improvements, you're likely to feel more stressed than usual, so try not to take on anything new for the time being.

✔ Keep yourself in good physical condition by eating healthily and taking regular exercise.

✔ As well as talking about the problems in your relationship, make sure that you celebrate the progress you're making. Have regular 'aren't we doing well?' talks and enjoy good times together.

✔ Look after your self-esteem by spending time with friends who love and value you, doing activities you're good at or pampering yourself physically.

Chapter 3

Developing the Ground Rules for a Successful Relationship

In This Chapter

▶ Building positive self-esteem

▶ Liking and accepting your partner

▶ Dealing with change

▶ Connecting through communication

To improve your relationship, you need to know that you're building on a firm foundation – one of mutual trust, respect and love. In addition to this, you need to establish ground rules to ensure that your relationship grows strong and secure. This chapter explores the essential roles of positive self-esteem, friendship and communication, and the importance of accepting differences and change.

A successful relationship is built around two people who love themselves and consequently know that they are worthy of receiving love and have the resources to love in return. It's also built on people who like each other: people who can be friends as well as lovers and who can talk to each other. Good communication underpins every successful relationship. Intimacy grows when you can openly share how much you love and cherish each other, and you resolve issues when you can talk things through.

Myths that say the road to true love is smooth and problem free damage many relationships. But being human means that differences are inevitable and life changes, sometimes in ways you may prefer to avoid. As this chapter shows, accepting the reality of relationships and loving each other through-out life's twists and turns are essential if you're serious about improving your relationship.

Loving Yourself

Talking about 'loving yourself' in a book about relationships may seem a bit odd and self-centred, but the truth is, unless you love yourself, you're unlikely to believe that anyone else can love you.

Positive self-esteem is essential for building a successful relationship. When you feel good about yourself, in spite of your shortcomings, you can feel confident that your partner loves you as well. And when you know not being perfect is okay and you stop wasting your time beating yourself up for things you've done or haven't done, you become free to love your imperfect partner.

Realising the importance of positive self-esteem

Feeling good about yourself affects every area of your life. It makes the world seem brighter and more optimistic, and problems are easier to handle and overcome. This cheery disposition not only makes life more fun, but it also improves relationships.

Positive self-esteem leads to positive couple esteem, because partners feel worthy of love and have both the confidence to receive love from their partners and the resources to love in return.

How you feel has a direct and an indirect impact on your partner. Moods are very contagious, so if one person's feeling happy, the other's more likely to feel happy too. But if one person's feeling low and unable to cope with life, this can contaminate the relationship, leaving the partner feeling unhappy and struggling to cope as well. In a good relationship, a partner tries to lift the other's spirits, providing support and care as he goes through a difficult time. But if the root of the problem is low self-esteem, then this can leave your partner feeling helpless, because nothing he says or does seems to help.

Low self-esteem has its roots in the past (see the later section 'Assessing your self-esteem' for more on this). Negative messages from others and negative experiences damage who you think you are. When you have low self-esteem, you spend much of your time reflecting on those things rather than on the good things that are happening now. This means that even though life may be good in the present, someone with low self-esteem feels stuck in the past. And no relationship can move forwards when one partner's looking backwards all the time.

Finding low self-esteem at the root of a problem

Sara, 32, and Kam, 34, came for couple counselling eight years into their relationship. They both wanted to start a family, but felt they had to sort out some longstanding problems in their relationship first. Sara explained that they argued a lot because Kam complained that she was selfish. She felt that she had to reassure him continually by always putting him first in everything she did. Kam retaliated with a list of misdemeanours that supported his feelings. Then each told the other that they shouldn't be considering becoming a parent,

because they couldn't put other's needs first. They were both shocked by what they said and scared of what this meant for their relationship. But as we worked together over the following weeks, Kam realised that a lot of his problems were rooted in low self-esteem from his childhood and previous relationships. As he worked through those issues he found he was more able to trust Sara and be less demanding. And as his demands reduced, Sara felt her resentment subside, and they grew closer and more confident about their future.

A person with low self-esteem is also more likely to feel dependent on his partner. He relies on his partner to feel okay about himself. If the person feels unworthy of love, he can unwittingly make it his partner's job to continually prove that he's loved. He needs constant reassurance, but because the problem's within himself, not within the relationship, the partner can never make him feel better, so he can become increasingly resentful because his needs aren't being met. The partner with healthy esteem can feel drained and helpless and unable to voice his own needs.

A lot of problems within a relationship have their roots in low self-esteem for one or both partners. On the surface, the problem may seem to be something else entirely, like arguments about not spending enough time together, not sharing housework, differences in sexual desire, or jealousy. But underpinning these apparent difficulties is often a much deeper anxiety about not being loved, desired or respected.

Low self-esteem is often accompanied by low self-confidence, which can lead to bad relationship choices. When esteem is high, you make decisions based on what leads to pleasure rather than what alleviates the pain of low self-worth. So someone with positive self-esteem is more open to cherish and embrace the love of a committed partner, or to decide to improve an aspect of a relationship that isn't going well. Or the person may make a decision to leave a relationship that isn't working. Someone with low self-esteem may find himself stuck in a relationship that's unfulfilling, unhappy or even abusive, because he thinks either that he deserves this kind of relationship or that he can never find someone better.

The damaging effects of low self-esteem

Low self-esteem damages your relationship by:

✔ Affecting your capacity to feel loved and secure in your relationship

✔ Lowering the mood and esteem of your partner because he feels unable to resolve the problem

✔ Reducing your resources for giving support and love to your partner

✔ Affecting decision making

✔ Draining joy from your relationship by making you focus on the past rather than the present

When your self-esteem is high, you can be sure that you're with someone because you enjoy his company and he adds meaning to your life rather than because you're dependent on him for making you feel like a worthwhile person. In other words, you're together because you *want* the person, not because you *need* him.

Assessing your self-esteem

So what exactly is positive self-esteem? Where does it come from? And how do you know if you've got it?

First, you need to recognise that self-esteem isn't a fixed asset. How you feel about yourself changes over the course of your life. Various life events affect you, so sometimes you may feel great, confident, positive and self-assured, and other times you may feel down, insecure and generally a bit useless. Anyone who claims to have permanent high self-esteem is either deluded, in denial or very, very lucky. Low self-esteem is part of being human, and inevitably you have days when you're a bit down on yourself. But if you have more down days than up days, then trying to do something about it is worthwhile.

Use the questionnaire in Table 3-1 to check out how good your self-esteem is. Positive self-esteem builds positive couple esteem. The more confident you feel about yourself and your life, the more confident you feel about your relationship, and the more resources you have to improve it.

Table 3-1	The Self-Esteem Questionnaire			
How do you feel about the following questions and statements?	**Strongly Agree**	**Agree**	**Don't Agree**	**Strongly Disagree**
I am a warm and friendly person				
I am good at my job (paid or unpaid)				
On the whole I am a good parent				
I have friends that I feel close to				
I feel at ease with my body				
I look after my body and health				
I have ambitions for the future				
In spite of relationship difficulties, I know that my partner loves me				
I am able to recognise and express my emotions reasonably well				
People enjoy being with me				
I mostly cope with life's challenges				
I like being me				

If you discover that your self-esteem is low, you need to work out why so that you can challenge the underlying reasons. Take a look at these reasons for low self-esteem and see which ring a bell for you:

- **Messages from childhood:** If you were brought up being told you were a clever, beautiful, resourceful, kind, loving, friendly and generally wonderful little human being, you're likely to have positive self-esteem. But if you received negative messages from what people said, implied or didn't say, then you may have a very different view. Children get to know that they're lovable from their parents.

- **Previous relationships:** Even if you had positive messages in childhood, a negative experience in a previous relationship may have left your esteem damaged. If you had a partner who was abusive or unfaithful, you may be struggling to believe that this was his fault not yours.

- **Life experiences:** All sorts of things can damage your self-esteem in life. Money problems, career difficulties, redundancy, infertility, problems with children, family or friends: any situation that challenges your sense of being in control of your life or results in feelings of self-doubt or insecurity can leave a scar. Some of these problems are unavoidable and inevitably dent your confidence, but if your self-esteem is already low, they can be even harder to handle.

- **Personality:** Some people are born with higher self-esteem than others. You may have little choice over your character, but you can make sure that you operate to the best of your inherent ability.

Building a positive self-view

If you feel that your self-esteem's low (the questionnaire in the previous section helps you determine this), then you can take steps to improve it.

You are responsible for how you feel about yourself. That may be difficult to believe, but it's true. Even if you've had a terrible history of being told you're an unlovable person or being treated like you're unimportant, whether you believe that or not is ultimately up to you. How you feel is governed by how you think, so if you want to feel better, you can start by changing your thinking.

Low self-esteem is one of those things that can become a bad habit. But like every bad habit, it's one that you can break. You need time and determination to overcome what may have become a lifetime routine of negative thinking. Knowing that positive self-esteem improves not only your relationship but also your life hopefully gives you the motivation to change.

Here are some quick pointers for how you can start to build positive self-esteem:

- ✔ **Put your past into perspective:** There are people in the world who do bad, bad things. If you've experienced a lot of negativity in your child-hood or in past relationships that has left you feeling bad about your-self, try to leave this where it belongs – in the past. Those messages actually say a lot more about the people around you than they can pos-sibly say about you. They are their opinions and views; they aren't facts. Letting go of the past can be a challenge, especially if your past was very damaging, but where you are today is what really matters.

- ✔ **Don't globalise:** A common cause of low self-esteem is globalising a problem. For example, if you once had a boss who was critical of a task you undertook, you assume that all bosses are critical and you're not good at your job. Or if you didn't handle a situation with your child very well, you assume that you must be a bad parent. Or perhaps in a previ-ous relationship, you had difficulty being tactile, so you tell yourself you're unaffectionate. Your whole worth isn't based on individual inci-dents. If something doesn't go well, recognise that and move on – don't let it contaminate your whole self-view.

- ✔ **Practise positive self-talk:** Everyone has a little voice in their head. I'm not talking about crazy voices that tell you to wear your underpants over your jeans, I'm talking about the little voice that tells you who you are. If that voice is telling you that you're stupid, unlovable, useless, a failure, incompetent or anything else negative, then tell it to shut up. That voice is you and it's yours to control, so whenever you're tempted to say something bad about yourself, stop and replace that with some-thing positive. I know this is much easier said than done, especially if you've been playing the same record over and over for years, but with perseverance you can do it. This is how your positive voice sounds: 'You're lovable, you're special, you're important, you're competent, you're an all-round really, really wonderful human being who deserves to be happy and enjoy life.'

- ✔ **Forgive yourself:** Everyone makes mistakes. No one's perfect, and of course you've done things you wish you hadn't. But just because you've sometimes been inconsiderate or thoughtless, that doesn't make you a bad person. Forgiving yourself for the mistakes you make is essential for positive self-esteem and positive couple relationships.

If you're really struggling with low self-esteem, then do take a look at *Boosting Self-Esteem For Dummies* by Rhena Branch and Rob Willson (Wiley), which gives you a lot more information and advice on how to overcome the problem.

Letting your past mistakes go

John came for counselling when his second marriage was breaking down. His soon-to-be ex told him that she couldn't put up with his distant moodiness any more. John was heartbroken: he loved her very much. But he'd never forgiven himself for leaving his first wife and children to be with her, and as a result decided he was a bad person who didn't deserve happiness and definitely didn't deserve a happy relationship.

Unfortunately, this realisation was too late to save his relationship, but he made a commitment to forgive himself for the mistakes he'd made, so that he wouldn't push anyone away again. He also began to notice all the positive strengths he'd never lost, and whenever he heard the little voice telling him he was bad, he reassured himself it was a lie and began to look forward to a future he now knew he deserved.

Liking Your Partner

How often do you tell your partner those all-important three special words 'I like you'? In today's culture, people talk endlessly about the importance of loving someone, but because love's an emotion that comes and goes, what really matters is that you have a deeper foundation in your relationship that continues regardless of how you feel. A successful relationship needs like as well as love, so one of your ground rules needs to be liking your partner. When you like someone, you want to be with him. You enjoy his company and want to make sure that you can continue to do so for many years to come. Liking your partner gives you the motivation to overcome problems, large and small, because you don't want anything to get in the way of your friendship.

What's love got to do with it?

I'm not saying that love isn't important – of course it is – but I do believe that people give far too much credence to this fickle emotion. Philosophers, poets, musicians and artists have been trying to understand love for centuries as, more recently, have scientists. And in spite of countless explanations, some more eloquent than others, no one has a clear answer to the question 'What is love?'. But ignorance doesn't seem to stop people from using this love thing to make some of the most important decisions of their lives.

Don't believe everything you've heard about love, especially the stuff they print on Valentine's cards. The sentiments may sound nice, but remember that they're meant to give you a lovely fluffy sensation in your heart and tummy, not create a solid foundation for your relationship.

Here are a few common myths that you're wise to avoid:

- ✔ **Love is enough:** It's enough if all you want is to feel nice, but if you want to build a relationship together where you share a life, you need more than just love. You need to be able to share common interests and values and also have compatible goals for the future. You also need to be committed to working together through problems as they arise and continuing to communicate during good times and bad.

- ✔ **Love is the sweetest thing:** Sometimes it's sweet, but at other times love can be very bitter indeed. One of the most devastating experiences on the planet is feeling rejected by the one you love. Unfortunately, times occur in any relationship when you may feel this rejection, such as when a partner's preoccupied by ill health, stress, tiredness or an external crisis that takes his attention. The unpalatable truth is that love hurts.

- ✔ **Love conquers all:** Love doesn't conquer addictions, infidelity, domestic violence or abuse. It may also fail to conquer differences in core values and ambitions in life that feel crucial for an individual's happiness, such as wanting a child or giving money to charity. Everyone has their own list of minimum requirements, and if one of yours is missing, love can't fill the void.

- ✔ **Love is forever:** Unfortunately, divorce statistics prove otherwise. Although love may last forever, in many cases it's temporary because people change. Love can last forever, but only if it's accompanied by mutual commitment and effort by both partners within the relationship. If couples aren't able to negotiate the inevitable changes and challenges that come with life, love will fade and eventually die.

So what does love really mean? If you're expecting to get a definitive answer to that question, then I'm afraid you're going to be disappointed. I'm highly unlikely to succeed where centuries of philosophers and arty types have failed. What I can say, though, is that love is very complicated. It's something that you sometimes feel very strongly in your relationship, and at other times may barely feel at all.

Chapter 5 explains that when couples first get together, they feel passionate about each other, but inevitably that feeling seems to wear off. Recent research into biochemistry is providing a deeper understanding of this – an understanding that hopefully means that people can stop doubting their relationship just because they no longer feel 'in love'.

Love is an emotion that ebbs and flows in exactly the same way as any other emotion. No one can be ecstatically happy all of the time. In fact, if you were, you wouldn't know it because you'd have nothing to compare it with. Similarly, no one's always in the same state of anger or fear or surprise. Feelings change depending on the circumstances and the environment.

The history of love

Basing a relationship on love is a relatively modern phenomenon and one that's still considered daft in some cultures and societies. In the olden days, your choice of partner was either made entirely by your family or at least heavily influenced by them. The decision was based on practical matters such as what wealth, power or land your future spouse could bring to the family. People hoped that love would grow in these relationships, but it wasn't a prerequisite.

Romantic love first become popular in the early 18th century when couples courted and wooed each other. As time went on, people began to expect far more from their relationships than practical resources and security. Now they wanted personal satisfaction too. Perhaps that's one of the reasons why the divorce rates began to rise so sharply in the 1920s. So much for love, eh!

Many cultures around the world still believe that the old ways are best. They believe that as long as a couple are compatible and like each other, love will grow. These cultures tend to have much lower divorce rates, so maybe they're right not to base a relationship purely on love.

Some people say that love is a feeling, and it's also a verb. It's a 'doing' word – an active decision that you make. When you commit to someone, you make a decision to love him, no matter how you feel. By that I mean that you continue to be loving towards him, treating him with respect and care, regardless of your emotional state. Many people find this much more helpful than the traditional romantic ideals as a way of thinking about love. But whether love's an emotion or a verb, it's a lot easier to feel it and do it if you're with someone you like.

Understanding the essential role of friendship

Realising that feelings of love can change in a relationship can be scary. But knowing this can stop you being so dependent on your emotions and help you focus on creating something stronger: something that can truly stand the test of time and give you a firm foundation to build on.

Friends support each other through good times and bad, remaining loyal in times of need. Friends enjoy spending time together, and have fun together. A friendship is based on mutual respect and affection. Now, these ingredients of friendship are essential for a good couple relationship, especially when combined with a healthy dollop of physical affection and sex. The big difference between friendships and couple relationships is that the former don't rely on romantic love. Friendships rely on a mutual commitment to be there for each other, regardless of how you feel.

But what if friendship with your partner is a real struggle at the moment? Friendship's essential for a successful relationship, but unfortunately when a relationship's going through problems, remembering anything that you like about your partner can sometimes be difficult.

If you're struggling to remember what you like about your partner, imagine that you have to write an advert for him for a friendship website. If you need some extra incentive, imagine a huge cash prize is on offer for the person who writes the most encouraging and honest advertisement. Think about all the characteristics your partner offers a friend – loyalty, kindness, generosity, sense of humour. And if hurt, anger or resentment's getting in the way of you seeing anything you like about your partner, try stepping into someone else's shoes – someone who does like your partner – and look through his eyes. For example, pretend that you're his mum, a friend or a close colleague at work.

If your partner's done something that's crossed the line for you – if you've suffered a major breach of trust or abuse, or he's totally unwilling to cooperate in improving your relationship – then you may be feeling that you can't possibly ever like him again. If this is the case, you may find Chapter 15 helpful.

Friendship's an all-round wonderful thing. Research has shown that people who have good friends are physically, psychologically and emotionally healthier. One study even suggested that friendship can help you to earn more money! Being friends with your partner may not make you better off financially, but it does make your relationship a lot richer.

Accepting Your Differences

The realisation that they're not clones of each other can come as a shock to some star-struck lovers. When you first fall in love, you can feel as though you've found your perfect soul mate. You've found someone who thinks, feels, behaves and perhaps even breathes like you. In fact, some lovers seem so in tune with each other that they don't even have to speak. They can just gaze into each other's eyes and communicate in some weird, extraterrestrial kind of way.

At some stage, the bubble bursts and love's blindness wears off. And as the world slowly comes into focus, the inevitable differences between couples begin to show: differences that you can either walk away from, leave to blight your relationship forever, or discover how to respect and live with amicably.

Recognising the inevitability of having differences

Did you know that identical twins aren't actually identical? Although they come from the same genetic instruction, apparently their DNA's never exactly the same. In fact, nothing living on this planet can truly be called identical. Even rudimentary attempts at cloning have failed to reproduce another living organism perfectly. Every living thing's unique in some way or another.

Human beings are a particularly diverse group of individuals. The complexity of head, heart, body and soul means that even more room for differences exists. These differences spill over into our relationships and can either make them more interesting or more stressful.

Couples who can't accept their differences are building on a rocky foundation. Happy couples enjoy uniqueness and grow with each other. So don't waste your time and energy trying to make your partner more like you.

Here's a list of common areas of difference that sometimes cause problems in relationships:

- ✔ **Behaviours:** Everyone does things slightly differently, whether that's the way you cook or wash up, organise your diary, do the shopping, send text messages or assemble flat-pack furniture.

- ✔ **Emotions:** Couples can find things especially difficult when the way they express emotions is different. That may simply be not laughing at the same jokes or may mean getting angry or hurt by different things.

- ✔ **Friends and family:** Couples often differ in the way they relate to their own family and friends. Some talk more than others, share more secrets, invite people around more or are much louder or much quieter.

- ✔ **Opinion:** Differences of opinion can range from non-contentious issues such as whether blue looks good on you, to medium-weight issues like whether Liverpool's the best football team, to potentially mega stuff such as whether the UK should have gone to war with Iraq or not. (Apologies to any footy fans who would put point two on the list of mega, mega stuff.)

- ✔ **Taste:** Differences can appear in preferences for food, entertainment, home environment, hobbies, friends and sexual expression.

As you get to know someone, you discover more and more ways in which you differ. This isn't only because in the early days, love often blinds you to differences, but also because as you walk through life together, you have more and more experiences in which discrepancies are possible.

Challenging romantic idealisation

Hollywood has a lot to answer for. Much of people's anxiety about differences is rooted in the idealistic romantic view they have of compatibility. People think that if they're truly 'made for each other', all the creases will get ironed out and they'll think and feel the same.

Romantic films don't have couples arguing about the right or wrong way to do the washing up or pay the bills or deal with your moaning mother-in-law. They don't show couples falling out over what colour to paint the bedroom or what they'll do in it when it's done. In romance land, couples agree on pretty much everything.

The problem that many couples have with their differences is that they confuse them with incompatibilities. Being different doesn't mean you're incompatible. It simply means that you're human (and not a fictional character from a romantic film). You're only incompatible if you can't find ways to coexist happily in spite of your differences.

When you can accept that differences are an inevitable part of being in a loving relationship, you can discover how to cope with them healthily rather than fighting against them.

Living with differences

So as individuals you're different. As a couple, some of those differences are okay; in fact, they may be very beneficial. Maybe you always hated the thought of sushi until your partner's more adventurous tastes introduced you to it. Or perhaps you discovered that what you thought was a very unorthodox way of managing finances is actually much more efficient than your own method. Differences in relationships can give you great opportunities to grow.

You can overcome other differences with compromise or mutual accommodation. For example, if you think cream's the best colour for a living room, and your partner thinks it should be green, then you can either paint the room cream with a feature wall in green or go for a greeny-cream colour. Or if you want to be bold, go stripy. And if you're also disagreeing about the colour of the kitchen, you can accommodate each other by one of you having your way in the living room and the other one in the kitchen.

Some differences aren't so easily resolved, and in these cases you need to learn to live with them. By that I don't mean having a stiff upper lip and forced tolerance, but a healthy respect for your differences that can enrich your lives together.

In order to cope with differences, you need to:

- ✓ **Be confident in yourself:** Struggling with differences is sometimes a symptom of low self-esteem. If you often worry that you get things wrong or doubt your opinions, you may see differences between you and your partner as a matter of right and wrong, rather than simple variations. Each time you notice a difference, you may see this as evidence that you're wrong and feel even worse about yourself, or see it as a challenge that you're forced to defend. If this rings true, take a look at the earlier section 'Loving Yourself'.

- ✓ **Be curious, not challenging:** If your partner isn't making sense to you, be sure you clarify the disparity in a way that doesn't sound like you're telling him he's nuts. For example, if your partner rinses the dishes before putting them in the dishwasher, rather than saying 'What's the point in that?' say 'I've never loaded a dishwasher in that way, what do you find are the benefits?'

- ✓ **Highlight the similarities:** If you struggle with some difficulties, remind yourself of the many ways in which you're the same as your partner, and make sure you emphasise these things. So if you don't have the same taste in music but you do in films, go to the cinema more often. Or if you have very different political views, focus your conversations on topics you share an interest in.

- ✓ **Respect each other:** If someone thinks, feels or does something in a way that you don't, that means that person's different, not wrong. In your head I know you know this, but in practice it's often quite hard to grasp. For example, if as a child you always opened your Christmas presents after lunch on Christmas Day, discovering that your partner wants to open them on Christmas Eve may feel like sacrilege. But contrary to what your gut response may tell you, in 99 per cent of cases, doing something differently doesn't make either of you 'wrong'.

Unfortunately, some differences are almost impossible to live with. If you and your partner don't share the same moral values or ambitions for the future, then you may decide that you really are incompatible. You can find more on this in Chapter 2.

Discovering the many ways in which you and your partner are different can be a trigger for personal growth and it can stop your relationship slipping into boring mediocrity. When you can view differences as an opportunity rather than a threat, you're able to respect and embrace them as enriching your relationship and your life together.

Adapting to Change

Accepting and adapting to change is an essential ground rule for a successful relationship. Change can keep a relationship interesting and provide an opportunity for couple growth and intimacy. But, unfortunately, it can also be a painful experience, especially if you didn't want the change.

Because you can't keep life the same, adapting to change together is essential. You need to support each other through good times and bad, and build a solid relationship that can be a safe haven for both of you.

Not only does life change, so do individuals. You may change as a response to the events you experience in life, or you may make a positive decision to do things differently as a part of self-development. The fact that in 50 years your partner won't be the same person he is today is a huge relief to some. But for others, the prospect can be terrifying.

Understanding the impact of life stages

If you've been in a relationship for a long time or are planning to be, you've already been through or are going to go through a lot of change in your life during that time. Some of these changes are predictable: events that you want and expect to happen at some time, such as moving house and having a baby. Other changes are unexpected and unwanted, such as illness and redundancy.

Some relationships struggle with change more than others, and often you can't know how you may cope until something actually happens. Feeling able to talk about the effects of change and share the load can certainly make adapting easier, but even more important is simply acknowledging the fact that change creates at least some degree of stress.

All changes bring with them a degree of loss and a need to adapt to something new. In some cases your roles change, so you may find yourselves needing to find different ways to relate to each other. In most cases your routines are affected, so you need to find new ways of balancing the needs of your relationship with time for yourself and others.

 Change can be a real test, for you as individuals and for you as a couple. Faced with a major change, some couples instinctively pull together, while others find themselves falling apart. Some people find depths of resources within themselves, while their partners struggle to keep everything together. Some instinctively turn to others, including their partners, for support, while others prefer to manage alone. These differences in coping mechanisms can make feeling close during turbulent times particularly difficult, but if you can continue to communicate and respect your differences (see 'Accepting Your Differences' earlier in this chapter), you can come through stronger than ever before.

TIP

If a change is currently having a significant impact on your relationship, take a look at Chapter 13 on managing major life changes.

Growing together

Albert Einstein once said: 'Men marry women with the hope they will never change. Women marry men with the hope they will change. Invariably both are disappointed.'

That may have brought a whimsical smile of knowing recognition to your lips or perhaps a big fat sigh. Either way, you know that people do change, even if they don't always do so in the way you want or at the speed you prefer.

Personal growth, or personal development, is another of those inescapable facts of being human. Your brain's continually changing as you take in more information from your environment and your life experiences. You grow in your skills, your knowledge and your potential. Development's an endless task, which for most people's a good thing.

However, personal growth can put a pressure on relationships. If you loved the person you married just the way he was, you may experience difficulty in sitting by and watching as he morphs into something else. For some, this can create confusion and anxiety, provoking fears that the partner may turn into someone they can no longer love or who may no longer want to stay in the relationship.

CASE STUDY

Dealing with fear of change

Fran and Bo had been together for 27 years. Their children had left home and Bo was approaching retirement. They had always talked about moving to the coast when he retired, but Fran, who had recently trained as an acupuncturist, didn't want to leave her budding practice. This frustrated Bo. As they tried to resolve their differences over the course of therapy, Bo shared other concerns. Fran had a new group of friends, had radically changed their diet to healthy eating and had even changed her physical appearance by cutting her hair short and wearing a different style of clothes. Bo was openly critical of all these changes, which upset Fran. She had enjoyed focusing on herself since the children had left home. But Fran's personal growth felt threatening to Bo, and he worried that she didn't feel the same now about their relationship and its future. In therapy Bo was able to talk about his fears, and Fran reassured him that she still wanted to share the rest of her life with him. They had to renegotiate the timings, but the agenda was just the same.

Sometimes, change can drive a wedge between people. As life changes and people grow, some relationships drift apart. Some no longer feel as though they're in the same book, let alone on the same page. But this doesn't have to be the case. The relationship journey twists and turns. Sometimes you see a bend approaching; at other times it's on top of you before you know. Either way, you can work together to make sure you're travelling side by side.

Here are some tips that can help you ensure that you're growing together, not growing apart:

- **Embrace individuality:** You and your partner are unique individuals (see 'Accepting Your Differences', earlier in this chapter), and that means you cope with the events of life differently and develop in different ways. Whenever you're tempted to see individuality as a problem in your relationship, remind yourself that variety really is the spice of life!

- **Learn:** As you go through life's changes, you'll find that sometimes you have better coping mechanisms than your partner, and sometimes he has better ones than you. Rather than focusing on your inadequacies or resenting your partner's abilities, take the opportunity to gain from each other so that you can be better equipped next time.

- **Lean on each other:** Everyone has strengths to face different problems, so on some occasions your partner's the stronger one who's able to support you, and other times it's the other way around. Allow yourselves to be a source of strength to each other when one person's resources feel depleted.

- **Encourage each other's growth:** In their heart of hearts, most people do want their partners to reach their full potential, whether that's in a career or a hobby or anything else they want to achieve. If you feel threatened by your partner's growth, ask yourself why. Are you envious of his success? Are you anxious that it may highlight problems in your relationship? Are you fearful of him meeting someone else? Whatever the issue is, make sure that you confront this, rather than stunt your partner's growth.

- **Support each other's experience:** Make sure your partner knows that you're 100 per cent behind him, even if you feel that he's in a very different place to you – whether that's because he's coping with a bereavement in a different way from you or is struggling with his own personal crisis. Let him know you love, respect and value him.

- **Maintain points of connection:** If you feel as though you're drifting apart, focus your attention on the places where you still connect. Invest more time on mutual interests and focus conversations around the things you have in common, especially dreams for the future.

The key to adapting to change is flexibility – being able to bend with the flow of life and living. Being flexible isn't always easy, but it does keep relationships interesting and alive. And one thing's absolutely certain: adapting to any kind of change, welcome or not, is definitely easier when you're sharing the process with someone you love.

Talking to Each Other

The bedrock of any successful relationship is the ability to talk to each other. Communication's essential for a successful relationship. Communication's the way in which we build intimacy and work through differences. Many different ways of communicating exist – such as through behaviours, physical gestures and affection – but by far the fastest and clearest way is by opening your mouth and your ears.

Flick to Part III for lots more on communication.

Breaking barriers to intimacy

Talking to your partner is the only way you can find out who each of you is, what each of you wants and why you behave the way you do. Without talking, you are two individuals living in the same space; with talking, you become a couple who share a space.

You've heard the expression 'no man is an island'. That's not necessarily true. People who don't talk about their inner world leave themselves marooned in that world alone. But when you can talk to your partner and find out about his inner world, you break down the barriers of space and create a new continent together.

Some couples are really good at talking to each other in the early days. In their eagerness to get to know each other, they ask lots of questions and listen eagerly to the answers. But as time goes by, this level of communication can slip. You can horribly easily become complacent, thinking that you know your partner inside out and you have nothing new to discover. But people do change and grow, and your possible topics of conversation are endless.

If communication between you and your partner has deteriorated, the first thing you need to do is talk about it. Say that you miss the conversations you used to have and that you want to make more time for keeping in touch with each other.

Chapter 4 has a lot more about how you can build intimacy in your relationship, not just through talking but also through creating and spending quality time together. And in Chapter 8 you can find more information on improving general communication skills.

Building bridges across differences

Differences of opinion are a normal and common part of relationship life, so for a relationship to be successful, you need to find ways of managing those differences. Communication provides the bridge that couples need in order to build their understanding of each other and to find ways to work together when differences are getting in the way of their happiness.

Some couples work hard at avoiding conflict. But becoming good at arguing (in the sense of a calm, adult debate, not a screaming barney) is the best way of ensuring that minor skirmishes don't turn into full-scale warfare.

Couples who can debate an issue well don't have to worry about not always agreeing. In fact, a good disagreement can bring a couple closer, because they can feel confident about their relationship and their love for each other. Check out Chapters 9 and 10 for more on healthy disagreeing.

Part II
Boosting Your Relationship

'Do you ever think back and remember
that wonderful day we met?'

In this part . . .

Improving a relationship doesn't just mean getting rid of the bad stuff, it also means boosting the good. This part is all about building positives. Creating and making intimate connections with your partner through word, touch and behaviours that will build your bond and put funds in your relationship bank account.

I start by talking about how to prioritise your relationship and how to discover ways of being close through companionship. Next I focus on the touchy–feely mushy stuff with a healthy dollop of pop science to explain why both men and women really do need romance. The final two chapters are dedicated to the whats, whys, wheres and hows of sex – I'm assuming you've already decided on the who.

Chapter 4

Prioritising Your Relationship

*I*mproving your relationship means making time for it. Like people, relationships can quickly deteriorate if they don't get enough TLC. They need tender loving care to keep them growing and getting stronger.

The degree of intimacy a couple share is often indicative of how healthy their relationship is. Couples who are able to enjoy each other's company and talk openly about their thoughts and feelings report feeling close and connected to each other. They feel that their relationship's something special and rewarding to them – something they value and want to cherish and protect. Couples who don't do much together tend to drift apart. Not only do they have little to hold them together, but they have little incentive to be closer.

Prioritising your relationship and building good times together puts your relationship on a positive upward spiral. Not only do your love and affection grow, but so does your commitment to face difficulties together.

Making Time for Each Other

How come you seem to have so much more time when you first get into a relationship? You never seem to face the same pressures from work or family or friends. Are the days actually longer? Or do you automatically prioritise your new-found love?

Of course you do. And of course, as the years roll by, life gets busier for most couples. If children arrive, they bring with them additional financial responsibilities that you have to pay for through longer working hours. Ageing parents often need more care, and friends inevitably go through times when they need you more. Perhaps you do have fewer hours today than you had when you and your partner first got together, but if that's the case, deciding how you spend that precious spare time is even more important.

The best investment you can make in your relationship is to give it more time. When you spend time with someone, not only are you showing that you enjoy being with that person, but you're also demonstrating that she plays an important role in your life.

Separating the urgent from the important

I know that your relationship must be important to you. If it wasn't, you wouldn't be reading this book. But unfortunately, everyone can find that the urgent things in life squeeze out the important things.

Urgent things are those events and incidents that are very visible in your life and have either a risk or a time limit attached to them. Getting your child to the doctor is obviously urgent, and so's getting your VAT return completed. Urgent things also include crises that you can't plan for. If the boiler breaks down in the middle of winter, getting it fixed is a matter of urgency.

Urgent matters also tend to be out of your control. They're events that you react to and get an instant result, rather than making a conscious choice to spend your time on them.

But urgent things often aren't important. Your mobile phone ringing probably makes you stop whatever you're doing to answer it, but 99 per cent of the time you can wait. An invitation to a distant friend's celebration may seem urgent when it drops through your letterbox, but attending may not be important.

Important things are those that affect your values in life. Some are urgent as well as important: for example, looking after your children and managing any emergencies that affect your health or your home. Many others aren't urgent, like finding time for yourself and your relationship.

Unfortunately, you often completely forget these important but non-urgent things. Because they don't force you to respond instantly, you put these things on the back burner. You waste your time on the things that are urgent regardless of the fact that they make little difference to your life, and you forget to do the things that really matter to you.

Important matters don't give you the instant results that urgent matters do, but the long-term rewards are frequently much greater.

In relationships, people often prioritise urgent things and lose sight of the important stuff. So you answer the phone or check your emails rather than sit and talk to your partner. Or you visit your mother or a friend whenever she asks, but don't ever have time to go out as a couple. Or your children always seem to have needs that are greater than yours. The reality of committed couple relationships is that time together gradually slips lower and lower down the list until it drops off the bottom altogether.

If you're serious about improving your relationship, you may need to reprioritise your time. You need to discard the non-important stuff and focus your time and energy on your partner.

Write a list of all the activities you do in an average week. Then look at each activity and decide whether it's urgent and important, important but not urgent, urgent but not important or not urgent and not important. Table 4-1 gives you an example to work from.

Bumping your relationship up the 'to do' list

Ron and Moira had been married for 19 years and had spent most of it building their home and business. They had two children who were their pride and joy, a seven-bedroom luxury home and a business that was about to go international. They had little time for their relationship, but both were committed to getting around to that once they'd dealt with the urgent matter of establishing the life they wanted. They arrived for couple counselling two months after Moira's diagnosis with breast cancer. Thankfully, they caught the disease in the early stages and the prognosis was good, but the discovery had shaken them to the core. As they tried desperately to reconnect and support each other through the treatment, the distance between them became shockingly apparent. Fortunately, after Ron and Moira spent several months committed to reprioritising their marriage, like Moira, it made a full recovery.

Table 4-1	Prioritising Activities		
Urgent and Important	*Important but Not Urgent*	*Urgent but Not Important*	*Not Urgent and Not Important*
Paying bills	Eating meals together	Opening the mail	Washing up
Eating health-ily	Watching TV or enjoying a hobby	Answering the phone	Doing laundry
Looking after children	Food shopping	Replying to emails	Gardening
Responding to a crisis such as burst water pipes	Keeping in touch with friends and family	Running errands such as collecting dry cleaning	Darning socks

Ask your partner or a close friend to go through your list of activities and to challenge you on anything she doesn't agree with. People often get so used to operating in a certain way that they can no longer distinguish the urgent from the important.

After you've separated the urgent from the important, you can begin to make some decisions about how you want to spend your time. Time management's an essential skill for today's busy couples who want to create more intimacy and companionship in their relationships (see the sidebar 'Top time management tips' for more).

Choosing quality over quantity

I know that saying quality counts over quantity is a bit of a cliché, but when you're making time in a relationship, it's so, so true. No point sacrificing a whole load of other things to spend an extra evening with your partner if all you're going to do is veg out in front of the box. If time's scarce, make sure that every second counts.

A lot of the time couples spend together they're doing something else as well: going shopping, doing the chores, spending time with the kids or sitting side by side reading the paper or watching television. All of these things are important and valuable as they build a sense of companionship, but you also need to have time when you're eyeball to eyeball, relating to each other with no other distractions around.

Top time management tips

If time management's an issue for you, get yourself a copy of *Time Management For Dummies* by Clare Evans (Wiley), which is full of helpful advice and ideas. Here are a few quick tips to get you started:

✔ **Plan ahead:** Use a diary, write lists, bundle chores together, check the weather forecast, communicate with others and do anything else that streamlines your life. Ten minutes spent thinking about how you can maximise your time over the coming day can save you hours.

✔ **Delegate:** Do you really have to do everything? If someone else can do something for you to help you create time for your relationship, let them. That may mean getting the kids to wash up after dinner or asking someone to take them to school. Or

you may be able to distribute your workload more widely so that you can get home on time more often.

✔ **Say no:** This is probably one of most powerful time management strategies. Before you automatically open your mouth and say yes to every request, think about whether it's urgent or important. Then decide whether it should take priority over spending time with your partner. If the answer's no, then say no.

✔ **Cut back:** If life's ridiculously busy at the moment, you seriously need to consider not doing something. Giving things up can be difficult, especially if you enjoy them, but ask yourself whether doing a particular activity is worth risking your relationship.

Quality time is time that you spend exclusively with and dedicated to your partner, with the intention of increasing understanding and knowledge of each other or feeling closer.

The actual amount of time you spend together in hours and minutes is irrelevant. If all you can manage is 30 minutes here and there, grab it and enjoy it. But also try to slot in a few good chunks of time together when you can let conversation build and intimacy develop.

Scheduling couple routines

Making time for each other means changing habits and developing new routines. Many couples with relationship difficulties find that their time for each other has become more and more limited. When couple time stops being fun and starts feeling tense, individuals find other things to do rather than spend time together. In fact, they can consciously, and even desperately, avoid couple time.

You know you're spending quality time with your partner when . . .

✔ You're not thinking about work or the kids or what you're going to have for breakfast tomorrow.

✔ You're not trying to do something else at the same time.

✔ You're listening to what your partner's saying.

✔ You have a satisfactory feeling that you've spent the time well.

✔ You feel closer to your partner afterwards.

✔ The next day you can remember what happened.

✔ Your partner feels the same.

Changing these negative routines can be difficult unless both of you commit to creating more time in your diaries and finding new things to do. The following section, 'Finding Fun Stuff to Do', explores what you can do with your new-found time, but first you need to wring some extra time out of your diary.

The key to setting up routines is to be creative. That may sound like a contradiction, as routines can be the most boring things in the world, but it does depend on what you're going to be doing and how flexible you're willing to be. If you're worried that scheduling time's going to be rigid and unromantic, remember that the results may be quite the opposite.

Get your diaries out together and, using an average month as an example, see how you can schedule in the following:

✔ **Daily time:** Find bite-sized chunks of time that you can grab over the course of the day. That may be 15 minutes in the morning to share a cuppa in bed, 5 minutes at lunchtime to talk on the phone, and a chunk of time in the evening to walk the dog, eat dinner, watch the news or talk.

✔ **Weekly time:** Set aside bigger chunks of time when you can connect more intimately. Hopefully that's more than once a week, but remember that quality's more important than quantity (see the previous section), so if your choice is one full evening alone or two half ones with children around, choose the one alone. You may decide you need a babysitter to do this or that you have to get away from the distractions of home. You should also try to schedule time together each week to relax in front of a film and/or share a hobby together.

✔ **Monthly time:** At least once a month, try to book an away-day: one full day that the two of you can spend together with no interruptions or distractions. If this is genuinely impossible for you because of work commitments or children, take a mid-week day from your holiday allowance every other month. That's six days a year dedicated to your relationship.

If you're scheduling couple routines that you've never had before, you're bound to hit a few hiccups. If something isn't working as you hoped, sit down together and work out what you can do about it. If you have to drop something, then so be it. You're much better off succeeding at building a few quality times together that really work than stressing about the few that don't.

Finding Fun Stuff to Do

You may think only children say, 'I'm bored, I've got nothing to do,' but couples say it too – just not often as openly or honestly.

Relationships can get boring if you've got nothing to do or if you always do the same things. You may find yourself complaining that you never have any time to spend together, but when you do, you wonder what on earth to do with it. And I'm sure you've seen those couples sitting in awkward silence in a restaurant. They've finally found the time to get out for the night and do something together, but when they get there they're bewildered, wondering what to talk about.

Finding fun stuff to do in your relationship can do much more than keep boredom at bay. Couples who can laugh and play together also enjoy stronger feelings of companionship and intimacy.

Remembering that couples who play together stay together

Have you ever wondered why babies laugh when they're so young? Long before they utter the first vaguely understandable word, babies discover how to laugh, usually at around 6–12 weeks of age. After crying, laughter's the earliest form of verbal communication between carer and baby. It's a two-way bonding activity that leaves both parties feeling happy and connected.

Not long after babies first laugh, they get to know how to play: another essential skill for survival. Through play, babies discover about their environment, practise ideas and build their social skills. Children connect to each other through play, and the bonds are closest between those who enjoy playing the same games.

The same's true for couples. A sense of humour's still cited as one of the most important characteristics people look for in a prospective partner. Why? Because laughter and playfulness make people feel good and build emotional connections.

By making a conscious effort to incorporate more fun in your relationship, you can improve the quality of your interactions. Not only does fun improve the bond between you, but it also gives your relationship more buzz and makes you want to spend time with each other. Lots of evidence also shows that play and laughter reduce stress, improve your health, increase your creativity and build your resilience to life's setbacks.

If your relationship's lost its sense of humour, trying thinking back to the good times and remembering the things that used to make you laugh. Perhaps you can rent out that comedy again, or go and see that comedian. Alternatively, why not dig out the photo album and laugh your way down memory lane.

Creating companionship

'So what are we going to do tonight?'

'I don't mind; it's up to you.'

'Well, I don't mind either; what do you want to do?'

'I really don't mind; why don't you decide . . .?'

Does this sound horribly familiar to you? After you've managed to schedule some couple time, your next problem's deciding what to do with it.

Ideally, try to create a balance between the following:

- ✓ **Fun hobbies:** These activities that you can enjoy together evoke your playful side. You can try dancing, sports, games or creative activities. Sex is an excellent activity to add to this list – much more about that in Chapters 6 and 7.

- ✓ **Group activities:** Spending time with other people can help to strengthen the bond between a couple because it creates an 'us' that's separate from 'them'. You may want to increase your time with mutual friends or you can join a club or social group.

- ✓ **Intimate pastimes:** These are the planned times when you're alone and you have the space and time to talk. You can go for a walk, share a meal or just sit in the garden or the pub. What you do really doesn't matter as long as it doesn't distract you from each other.

- ✓ **Productive home-building activities:** These activities require team work and help you have a shared sense of purpose and roots. Examples are shopping, cooking a meal, gardening, decorating or clearing out the garage. I know some of these things sound horribly like chores that you prefer to avoid, but doing them together not only builds intimacy, but it also means you get them done in half the time.

> ✔ **Relaxing leisure time:** Unwind together and switch off. For active relaxers, that may mean going to the gym, listening to pumping music or going to the theatre. Passive relaxers may prefer to go for a walk, watch a film or read a book. Make sure that you respect the different ways you relax and share them when possible.

What you choose to do as a couple depends on your personalities and on the time available. Some people are naturally more active than others and prefer doing things that are physically or mentally engaging; others prefer gentler ways to unwind. Some people like creative hobbies or intellectual hobbies that they can do alone; others opt for team activities or sports. What you choose to do together doesn't matter, as long as it's something you can both enjoy and it enriches your relationship.

If you can't find anything in the relaxation and hobbies categories that you both want to do together, please don't worry. Your relationship benefits more if the two of you enjoy these separately and then come together during intimate times to talk about them, than if you force one or both of you into something that you don't want to do.

Avoiding boredom

Some couples do lots of things together, but they still describe their lives as boring and lacking in intimacy. This often happens when familiarity's firmly set in. Although you dance together, you've been doing it for so long that you know each other's moves off by heart. Or you've become closer to some of the members of your social club than you have to each other.

The secret for avoiding boredom is growth. When you engage in activities that include personal growth, you discover more about yourself and, consequently, more about each other. In this way, your activities broaden and deepen your relationship.

Personal growth can come in a number of different ways. You can choose activities that grow your skills, your knowledge or your awareness. For example, you can start an evening class at college on wine tasting, painting, creative writing or researching your family tree. Or you may decide to study psychology, philosophy or theology. If study isn't your thing, you can join a book club or your local environmental group, or expand your socio-political involvement by volunteering or campaigning.

The possibilities are endless. And as you open new doors as individuals, you discover whole new vistas for discovery as a couple.

Showing Your Whole Self

To be loved and accepted for who you are, warts and all, is one of a human's deepest needs, but you're likely to experience this kind of unconditional regard in few relationships. Aside from your parents, who may or may not have done a good job of loving you, your next hope lies with your partner.

Your ability to give and receive this kind of total love and acceptance is influenced by your experiences in the past. If you've felt rejection, you may struggle to open yourself up enough to feel this level of intimacy and may have little experience of how to demonstrate your acceptance of your partner. And if you've been having problems in your relationship, you may both be feeling more defensive and guarded against the level of vulnerability you require.

Sharing yourself is an essential component of improving a relationship. When you're able to talk about yourself openly, you can build trust and respect in a relationship as well as love. When you take the risk of laying your thoughts and feelings at the feet of your partner, you're offering her the gift of your self, sharing the very essence of who you are.

Appreciating the importance of opening your heart

Chapter 2 explains the different types of communication that happen between a couple – from the information updates that keep you in touch on a day-to-day basis to the deep and meaningful chats where you share your thoughts and feelings. All these levels of communication are important, but the one that separates a couple relationship from most other relationships is the intimate sharing of your deeper personal needs – open heart surgery, you may like to call it.

Making time for intimate sharing must be one of your priorities for your relationship. These are the times when you open up your hearts to each other, knowing that they are taken into careful, loving hands.

Becoming this vulnerable with a partner can feel very scary, but it offers huge benefits not just to the relationship, but also to yourself as an individual. The following are just a few reasons why letting your partner into your private world is beneficial:

- ✔ **Allows old wounds to heal:** Telling your painful or traumatic stories can be healing. You know the saying, 'a problem shared is a problem halved' – it's definitely true. Just being listened to is profoundly powerful.

- ✔ **Avoids misunderstandings:** This is perhaps the most important reason for intimate sharing. When you don't speak, you leave your partner with no choice but to work out for herself what she thinks is going on in your head. This is fine if your partner happens to be telepathic, but if she's a mere mortal, you run into problems. The vast majority of misunderstandings are caused by lack of communication.

- ✔ **Creates opportunities to be affirmed:** When you talk about your feelings, thoughts or experiences, you're providing your partner with an opportunity to praise you, whether that's for handling a difficult situation at work, overcoming a destructive habit or managing an emotion.

- ✔ **Helps you overcome negative messages:** Many people receive negative messages about life or themselves in childhood or in other relationships. By sharing such a message, you provide the space for someone else to say that it was wrong and reframe the message to something positive.

- ✔ **Provides a vehicle for overcoming shame:** Some people don't talk about private stuff because they 'don't want to wash their dirty laundry in public'. What this well-known saying assumes is that the laundry's dirty, but in reality this simply isn't true. By talking about your 'laundry', you can overcome the notion that you have anything dirty or shameful in your past that you should keep private.

Opening your heart takes courage, especially if you've been hurt in the past. But it's the only way you can create true intimacy in your relationship and build the love, trust and acceptance that you deserve.

Sharing your expectations

An essential element of healthy relationships is sharing expectations. A lot of people in the media like to blame a high divorce rate on people having too high expectations for their relationships. I don't agree with that at all. In every other area of life, people with ambition are praised, so why not be ambitious about your relationship?

I see absolutely nothing wrong in having high expectations for your relationship. Why shouldn't you want the best for yourself, your partner and your family? Those expectations need to be realistic and you need to be willing to work for them and not expect them to be handed to you on a plate, but assuming you're ready to do that, then good for you.

However, a successful relationship depends on two people. So if your partner doesn't share the same expectations as you, you may handle situations in very different ways. For example, if you think relationships are a rollercoaster, you react very differently to difficulties than someone who expects relationships to be a safe harbour, protected from the storms of life.

Look at the following list of statements that you may use to describe a relationship, and identify which one (or two) best reflects your view. If you think of something else altogether, write it down. Now ask your partner to do the same, and talk about the impact any differences in views may be having on your relationship.

Relationships are an opportunity.

Relationships are a journey.

Relationships are a struggle.

Relationships are a puzzle.

Relationships are a challenge.

Relationships are a refuge.

Relationships are an adventure.

Relationships are a gift.

Relationships are a responsibility.

Relationships are a game.

Relationships are a commitment.

Relationships are a mystery.

Sharing your expectations of a relationship not only improves your understanding of your partner, but it also provides the opportunity to collaborate and create a new mutual expectation.

If you become aware of differences, talk about where your expectations of a relationship have come from. Do they stem from your parents or a previous relationship? Are they healthy expectations? Then agree on an alternative statement that both of you want to embrace, and discuss how you can create a relationship to achieve that goal.

Disclosing your hopes, dreams and fears

Your hopes, dreams and fears are perhaps the parts of yourself that you keep most hidden. If you share your hopes and dreams and someone belittles them or says they're never going to come true, you may feel forced to give up on them. If you share your fears and someone laughs at you, you may feel stupid, weak and alone, but no less afraid.

Another reason you may not like sharing your hopes and fears is because they may say a lot more about you than you want other people to know. The accountant who says she's always hoped that one day she'll give up her job, sell her home and travel around the world on a motorbike is saying something about her desire for independence, freedom and adventure – perhaps qualities that she doesn't currently experience in her life. Someone who confesses to a deep fear of going grey may be demonstrating how important her appearance is for her self-esteem, and how negatively she views ageing.

Your hopes and fears can be deeply revealing of your inner self, which may make you more inhibited about sharing them. But this inhibition can also provide you with an extra incentive. By talking about these things with your partner, you're providing an excellent opportunity to let her into your inner world.

Some couples worry that their hopes for the future are different, but although they may look so on the surface, underneath they're often very similar.

Sharing their dreams, hopes and fears allows couples to work together – to plan how to meet a partner's needs without damaging the relationship. And by getting to the root of fears, couples can support each other in ensuring that those fears don't ever become a reality. That may be by challenging a negative belief that's causing the fear or by providing reassurance and security.

Some couples or individuals who've experienced particularly traumatic events can find sharing their experiences with their partners difficult. This is a very natural and common response to trauma, and you shouldn't feel compelled to speak about an event if that causes discomfort. If you want to work through the issue as a couple, see a trained professional.

Finding common ground

Rhona and Meena feared that their dreams for the future would drive them apart, and came for counselling to decide whether they should end their relationship now, before either of them got too hurt. Rhona wanted to earn enough money to give up her job and buy a smallholding where she would live a self-sufficient life. She'd always assumed this was a dream she would share with a partner. But Meena loved her job as a teacher and planned on writing children's novels when she eventually retired. As they discussed their dreams in the therapy room, they were able to see the similarities. Both wanted to work in an environment where they could care, nurture and grow things. They were both very creative people who had a desire to work hard and produce something of value. As they recognised the common themes, they began to explore how they could both achieve their goals through a mutual endeavour.

Becoming bestest, bestest friends

Intimacy's something that grows over time. You can't force or rush intimacy: it happens when it happens. But you can do a couple of things to encourage your intimacy to grow and your relationship to get deeper and deeper.

Steering clear of assumptions

One of the biggest blocks to communication is making assumptions. That may be the speaker making the assumption that the listener knows what she means or the other way around. Or it can be sharing an experience in silence while you both assume that you know what the other one's feeling.

Imagine this. You and your partner are taking a routine journey home from work when a deer runs out in front of your car. You manage to avoid it very easily and you both look at each other in surprise and let out a sigh. As you continue driving home, one of you is remembering the event fondly, thinking of the pleasure of living in the country and in a world where the unexpected can still happen. The other's feeling badly shaken, remembering a friend who was seriously hurt in a road accident and wondering why life can't be more predictable.

Couples often assume that they see life through the same lens, but everyone's experience is unique. When couples think that they think the same, they lose valuable opportunities to connect and discover more about each other.

Assumptions are dangerous things because they lead to misunderstandings and miscommunication. When information's missing, you fill in the gaps from your own experience and knowledge. Unfortunately, people regularly get things wrong. So the conclusion you reach in your head – the one that you think is blindingly obvious from your perspective – turns out to be something completely different from your partner's understanding.

Make sure that whenever you're speaking, you give the full story: your thoughts, feelings and a context for what you're saying. And if you're listening and any of that information's missing, ask for it.

Maintaining curiosity

Curiosity may have killed the cat, but it's improved many couple relationships. Boredom creeps in when curiosity's leaked out. When couples first get together they want to know everything about each other. They ask endless questions: How come you did that? Who were you with? What were you feeling? Would you want to do it again? What would have made it better? What would you have done if . . . ?

New couples want to get into each other's minds and see the world through their eyes. Unfortunately, this curiosity wears off with time and a dubious knowledge replaces it. Undoubtedly, you do get to know your partner better and predicting her thoughts and feelings becomes easier. But no one ever knows the full story.

If you're ever tempted to think you know everything about your partner, ask yourself honestly how much you really know about *yourself*. A lifetime in therapy isn't enough for anyone to know themselves fully. Humans are complex creatures living in an ever-changing world. No experience leaves you untouched and unchanged, so you're permanently evolving.

Recognising the Signs that You're Drifting Apart

Many people assume that conflict's the biggest killer of relationships, but in my experience, what does that is distance. Conflict may damage your harmony, but distance goes one step further and leaves couples not caring whether they're close or not.

You may already be very aware that you and your partner are drifting apart, or you may be like many couples who know that their relationship isn't as close as it once was, but aren't sure if that's a bad thing or just a natural progression.

No doubt, relationships do change over time. The initial urgency you felt when you first fell in love and couldn't bear to be apart matures into something much gentler and more restrained.

You may feel less close when life's busy and demands more of your attention. Most couples with a newborn baby find that they have less time and energy for each other for a while. This doesn't mean that they have problems in their relationship, it simply means that they're at a different life stage (more on life stages in Chapter 13).

When a relationship's going through a difficult patch, couples also commonly feel a growing sense of distance. Similarly, you may feel less close if one or both partners is struggling with stress or illness. When the distance is an obvious symptom of a temporary problem, the solution is to deal with the problem. But if the distance has been there for many months, with no obvious cause, then alarm bells should be ringing.

Becoming alert to early warning signals

Relationships don't drift apart overnight: it's a gradual process that builds up over a period of months and years. Unfortunately, many couples choose to ignore the symptoms because they don't want to face what the distance may mean.

Some couples fear that distance means a basic incompatibility or crisis within the relationship that may finish them off forever. But in my experience of counselling many hundreds of couples, the most common cause of growing apart is starvation. When a relationship's been starved of attention and affection and couples fail to prioritise their relationship and feed it, then, like a plant without water, it begins to wither and die.

When a relationship's drifting apart, you can identify some common warning signs. Take a look at Table 4-2 and see how many are true for you.

Table 4-2	The Early Warning Signs of Drifting Apart
Problem	*Examples*
Apathy	Having no energy or motivation to change anything in your relationship, even though you know some small changes may make a big difference
Indifference	Feeling little or nothing for your partner; not caring if you're together or not, if you're talking or not, or if you're close or not
Preoccupation	Staying at work late; going to bed at different times; taking up activities that avoid spending time together during evenings and weekends
Temptation	Finding yourself wondering what a relationship with someone else would be like; flirting with someone you're attracted to

The distance you feel between yourself and your partner will fluctuate throughout your relationship. Sometimes, distance is an inevitable side effect of life's hectic pace; at others, it's a symptom of a problem that you know you need to address. Either way, what you do about the gap between you is up to you.

Changing direction before you're too late

If your relationship's drifting apart but you know you're not ready to end it, now's the time to start prioritising time as a couple. If specific problems are causing the distance, look at how you can address these. If you're moving apart because of busyness, you can make a decision today to prioritise couple time and build intimacy.

Whatever you do, don't leave the growing distance between you until it's too late.

When you don't address the distance between you, other problems – or people – have a tendency to creep in. I've sat with many couples who are stunned that an affair has ripped their marriage apart. Both claim that nothing particular was wrong with their relationship and the guilty partner's adamant that she wasn't looking for someone else. But the further apart a couple are, the more space and opportunity exists for someone else to come between them. If this has happened to you, you can find more on coping with an affair in Chapter 14.

Chapter 5

Doing Oodles of Romantic Stuff

. . . .

In This Chapter

▶ Understanding the chemistry of love

▶ Harnessing the power of romance and affection

▶ Using fond memories to rebuild tenderness

▶ Showing love in ways that make a difference

. . . .

*R*omance and affection ain't what they used to be. No longer the domain of poets and artists, scientists now understand affection as a physical function that's necessary for the continuation of the human race. I hope that gives you an extra incentive, if you need it, to improve the romance in your relationship.

You may think those tender little moments just feel good, but new biochemical understanding means you can now see that they play a significant role in maintaining couple relationships. Unfortunately, when a relationship's under stress, romance is often the first thing to fly out of the window, and affection follows soon after. But thankfully, this situation's relatively easy to rectify.

Rebuilding romance and affection in your relationship can have a massive impact on how you and your partner feel towards each other. You can look forward to reviving those old feelings of tenderness and devotion, or perhaps even falling in love all over again. And those positive feelings give you extra impetus to collaborate on overcoming your problems and the resilience to face any difficult times ahead.

This chapter starts with a chemistry lesson (don't panic, I'm talking Year 7 stuff here, not PhD level). You discover what science has to say about maintaining loving relationships through romance and physical affection, and how you can cheat the system if you're not in the mood or your partner's playing hard to get. Then, moving on from the theory to the practical, you see how you can work some of this knowledge of love into your daily life.

Understanding the Chemistry of Love

Love may be in the air, but it's also very much in your brain. In fact, love floods every part of your body and makes all sorts of funny things go on. The fluttering in the stomach, the light-headedness, the weakness in the knees and the total inability to concentrate on anything other than your lover are all explained by the tide of chemicals that surges through your body. When you fall in love, you become biochemically addicted to your partner, quite literally. Scientists have discovered that the chemicals you produce in the early stages of a relationship are the same as those that addicts produce.

Falling in love and staying in love are both part of Mother Nature's plan. As a species, humans have particularly vulnerable newborns, so people have to develop a close attachment to their young and to their partners who help them raise children. The biochemistry changes over the course of the relationship in three distinct stages (lust, attraction and attachment; see the later section 'Differentiating between the three phases of love'), each designed to commit you further to your beloved and to your family group.

Love's biochemical response is essential for the survival of the species: the biochemical process of love ensures humans mate and look after their young. The triggers for that biochemical response are a number of factors that you know very well, such as physical appearance, smell and romantic actions, and a few that may surprise you, such as risk taking, fantasy, chocolate and diet yoghurt. And when you know what creates loving feelings, you can work to re-create them in your relationship.

Exploring the power of attraction

Scientists have been very busy looking at what love is, but they haven't been very good at explaining why people fall in love as they do. Many couples wonder why they were attracted to each other – especially when they hit difficult times. Some may begin to wonder if they made a mistake, if they unwittingly stumbled along the wrong path, propelled by a mystical chemical force.

Understanding why you found yourself magnetically drawn to your partner can help you to respect that force of nature and decide whether you want to fall in love again.

The chemistry of initial attraction is complicated. On the surface, it can seem totally mysterious, something that makes no sense at all – eyes across a crowded room or the waft of a scent as your beloved walks by. Some people talk about an almost tangible electrical current between them when they first spoke, while others remember being mesmerised by a smile.

But none of these events can truly explain the powerful surge of emotion that you feel. You can feel as though all reason has been biochemically hijacked, and the chemical high kicks into touch the niggling thought that this isn't the sort of guy or gal you normally go for. When a relationship's in difficulty, some people find themselves worrying about what they later see as an irrational choice of mate. But beneath all the superficial, fluffy, romanticised symptoms of falling in love lies a much deeper, and increasingly understood, biological drive.

Here's a look at what researchers have found out about attraction. They're all interesting theories, but as with a lot of scientific research, the results aren't conclusive. So although you may find these ideas interesting, don't assume that they're fact.

- ✔ **Appearance:** Looks really are important in the dating game, but they go far beyond pure aesthetics. One research study showed that you're attracted to people who look like you. In an experiment, subjects were shown a series of photos, including one that was a morphed version of themselves superimposed on a picture of someone of the opposite sex. In every case, this was the image they considered most attractive.

- ✔ **Smell:** Scientists have known for years about the power of smell in mate attraction – through pheromones (natural chemical signals you send out), you affect the behaviour of people around you. Animals are much better at picking up on these scents for themselves, whereas humans need the help of perfumers. For centuries, people have tried to manipulate these scents to their advantage, but they have a lot further to go before they can overcome natural instinct.

  In one experiment, a group of women were given the unenviable task of sniffing their way through a pile of men's sweaty t-shirts. The majority of the women were most attracted to the scent of a man who had a complementary immune system to their own (in other words, a mate who was most likely to provide healthy offspring). A similar experiment on men showed that they preferred the smell of women during ovulation, when the women were most fertile. Whether you're consciously aware of it or not, making healthy babies is very high on your list of favourable partner qualities.

- ✔ **Taste:** Once you're close enough to have a good old sniff, you're getting close enough for your lips to meet for that first, highly influential kiss. Research shows that, as well as finding out whether you're in sync with each other, you also pick up more essential information about your genetic compatibility through each other's saliva – another indicator that you're a suitable match for healthy babies.

  One piece of research in the USA found that 75 per cent of people had ended a relationship because of a bad first kiss. Of course, no one knows whether that was an unconscious decision to avoid the risk of an incompatible union or just because the other person had bad breath!

Not all couples feel powerful physical attraction. Some have a much gentler introduction that grows from friendship to a more intimate relationship. However your relationship started, keep reading, because everyone can recapture those euphoric feelings of being 'in love'.

Differentiating between the three phases of love

Most relationships go through three very distinct phases: lust, attraction and attachment. Lump them all together and you get what you generally define as 'love'. Not all relationships go through these stages, but if you're in a long-term relationship, chances are you've experienced all three.

When you get confused about your feelings, that's often because they've changed. But what you often don't realise is that those changes are natural and inevitable and are the result of your chemistry, not your emotions. If you don't feel the same about your partner now as you did years ago, don't assume that your relationship's in jeopardy – the feeling may be perfectly natural.

Lust

This first stage of love is the one you're most familiar with when you're in your teens. Dominated by the male sex hormone testosterone and the female sex hormone oestrogen, this is the powerful sensation that propels you towards the partner who's grabbed your attention. This is the pure animal attraction that forces you to sit up and take notice, also known as sex drive.

Lust is fairly indiscriminate. It doesn't really care who's the target, as long as he has good mating potential. Lust isn't meant to operate alone. It's the first ingredient in the love cocktail, but without the others it can do nothing more than satiate a physical urge.

Attraction

This is when you first realise you've 'fallen in love'. The sex chemicals of testosterone and oestrogen are still in full force, but now they're accompanied by dopamine, serotonin and phenylethylamine (PEA for short).

Dopamine is your pleasure-seeking hormone: like a high-octane sports car, it's excitement driven and destined for fun. *Serotonin* is your chilled-out chemical that keeps you calm and in control. Unfortunately, serotonin levels drop, so you're unable to keep dopamine's pleasure in perspective and you lose yourself in obsessive, excitable behaviour. *PEA* is romantically known as the molecule of love. It's like an amphetamine, which explains why so many people lose their appetite when they're in love, and seem to have boundless energy.

This amazing chemical cocktail blinds you to the rest of the world and leaves you focused on mating with your newfound love. This is an intense and amazing time in a relationship, but it's finite. Research findings vary, but most people agree that the attraction phase fades significantly after two or three years of a relationship. However, even more recent research has shown that you can boost your own levels when and if you want to (see the later section, 'Falling in love again').

Attachment

Fortunately, Mother Nature doesn't leave you in the lurch with a lost love and a broken heart. The lust phase has done its job of waking up your sexual desire, attraction has led you to your partner and encouraged you to mate, now attachment is going to bond you to each other to give the child you may want, to create the best prospects of reaching maturity.

Attachment is the phase when you bond to your partner. Dopamine and serotonin are now more settled and PEA is gradually waning. But in the path of this passionate cocktail come oxytocin and vasopressin. *Oxytocin* is nature's bonding chemical, which is most prominent in breastfeeding mothers, but is also produced by the bucketload when couples connect physically. *Vasopressin* is nature's monogamy molecule, which keeps your sexual extremes at bay and helps you to stay loyal to your partner in spite of external temptation.

The attachment chemicals don't come with a sell-by date. They're yours for as long as you want them, although at times you may have to work to keep them topped up.

When a relationship's in difficulty, many people find themselves wondering whether they're still 'in love' with their partners. Or they may say that they love their partners, but they don't fancy them any more. By understanding the phases of love and the biochemical influence, you can stop worrying that your changing feelings indicate an underlying fault in the relationship. Instead, you can focus your energies on doing something to influence your chemicals (see the following section).

Falling in love again

The previous section looked at the theory of love; this one moves on to the practical. So far, no one's found a way of replicating and manufacturing the essential hormones that give you that wonderful 'in love' feeling. Just imagine what life would be like if you could buy a bottle of the love molecule PEA (see the previous section) at the supermarket and slip a few drops into your partner's tea every morning? What a happy place the world would be. That is indeed the easy option, but thankfully Mother Nature left you with others. You can boost your own PEA levels and help yourself to fall in love again.

Love isn't just about chemistry. Tons of stuff also goes on psychologically and emotionally both within and outside our conscious awareness. Boosting your biochemical love box isn't going to be an instant solution, but it can help a lot.

Brewing your own love cocktail

The two chemicals you can most easily influence are:

- **Dopamine:** Increasing your dopamine makes you more motivated to recognise and seek pleasure in your relationship. It also increases your general energy levels and concentration and motivates you to be sponta-neous. And sexually, it increases your libido and makes orgasm easier.

- **PEA:** Boosting your PEA levels helps you to feel in love again. It inspires you to be romantic and to respond to romantic gestures from your part-ner. You can look forward to feeling light-headed and excited by your partner's presence and overlooking his faults more easily. PEA is also an excellent natural antidepressant and hunger suppressant.

You can change your biochemistry by what you eat and what you do. Certain foods are linked to both dopamine and PEA, and maintaining a good level of general health and fitness will ensure that ill health and stress don't over-shadow the chemical changes.

Table 5-1 lays out how you can increase your levels of these love chemicals.

Table 5-1	Boosting Your Love Chemicals
To Increase Dopamine	*To Increase PEA*
Eat a diet of protein-rich foods like meat and fish and tyrosine-rich foods such as almonds, avocados, bananas, dairy products, butter beans, pumpkin seeds and sesame seeds	Eat chocolate and eat diet yoghurt – yep, chocolate really is romantic, and apparently artificial sweetener increases PEA
Get plenty of sunlight	Watch romantic films, read books and lose yourself in fantasies of knights and dam-sels, Hollywood starlets and leading men, Heathcliff and Cathy, Antony and Cleopatra – anything that makes your heart flutter
Find a hobby that gets your heart racing, from sky diving or bungee jumping to rock climbing or even bingo; anything that gets your pulse racing and includes an element of risk will boost your natural dopamine levels	Allow old memories to trigger romantic feel-ings: look at photos, start wearing a forgot-ten perfume or aftershave again, go back to former romantic haunts
Take time to do the things that bring you pleasure, and focus on the positive sensa-tions they give you	Be romantic, even if you don't feel like it: romance is both the result and the cause of PEA

Commit as a couple to becoming better biochemical lovers. Change your diet together, find more pleasurable activities to share, and indulge yourselves in romance.

Vitamin T (touch) – the essential couple supplement

Love has one more essential ingredient, perhaps Mother Nature's most powerful chemical weapon against relationship breakdown. And it's the easiest one for you to influence.

Everyone knows how important daily vitamins are to keep bodies fit and healthy. But what people didn't know until fairly recently was that another essential vitamin exists, a chemical compound that keeps couple relationships fit and healthy.

Oxytocin is the chemical responsible for bonding in relationships, both between parent and child and also between couples. It peaks in your body when you touch someone, and inspires you to touch even more. It's addictive – the more you have the more you want.

Because of its link with touch, oxytocin is called vitamin T. When couples take their vitamin every day, when they make sure that they maintain physical proximity through shows of affection and their sexual relationship, oxytocin grows and bonds the couple ever closer and closer. But when couples literally lose touch with each other, their chemical bond weakens and they're more likely to drift apart.

Touch is essential for the survival of the species. Research has shown that without it, people can become ill and eventually die. Scientists also say that touch causes you to secrete *endorphins*, nature's feel-good chemicals, which elevate your mood and increase your pain threshold.

The fantastic thing about oxytocin is that you can directly influence it. The more you touch, the more oxytocin you produce and the more you want to touch and enjoy being touched. You get into a positive upward spiral. By ensuring that physical affection's a regular part of your relationship, you can help yourselves and your relationship to stay healthy.

You can get your daily vitamins in a number of different ways. You can either decide to build in regular time each day to lie in each other's arms, have a shoulder massage or a foot rub, or have a cuddle in bed (and whatever else that may lead to!). Or find ways you can touch on a more consistent basis, for example always kissing when you say hello or goodbye.

Developing a daily 'touch habit'

Scientists claim that the more you touch, the more oxytocin you produce and the closer you bond with your partner. To increase your level of Vitamin T, try taking five a day of any of the following:

✔ Peck on the cheek

✔ Kiss on the lips

✔ Caress of the arm or leg

✔ Holding hands

✔ Cuddle on the sofa

✔ Snuggle in bed

✔ Massage

✔ A hug

✔ Foot rub

✔ Sex

Remembering the Good Times

It's been said that nostalgia's not what it used to be. Perhaps that's true, but evoking memories of the good ol' days can be balm to the soul of a troubled relationship. When a relationship's in difficulty, current problems can easily overwhelm you and you can forget the days when you used to skip along the beach, hand in hand, into the sunset. Okay, maybe things were never quite that idyllic, but nonetheless, bringing back happy memories can not only lift your spirits but also remind you why you chose to be with your partner in the first place.

Considering why you fell in love

When you're angry and hurting and your partner seems to be doing everything in his power to make you feel worse, you can easily wonder why on earth you're with him. You recall all the reasons you don't like him, but the reasons you fell in love may seem like a dim and distant memory.

If your relationship's going through a particularly bad patch, then you may be wondering whether your choice of partner was a mistake. Perhaps you think you were so lost in the giddy chemical rush of being in love that you lost all rationality when you committed to being a couple for ever. Although love can be blind, it's not totally stupid as well. By looking back to those early days, you can rediscover why you made the decision to be with your partner, and perhaps you can make that same decision again today.

The 'I loved you because . . .' exercise helps you remember why you love your partner. Relate counsellors often use this exercise to help couples get back in touch with the positive traits in their partners' personalities. If possible, ask your partner to do this exercise as well. Follow these steps separately and agree a time to meet and swap papers and talk about what the exercise reveals:

1. **Take a sheet of paper and divide it into three columns.**

2. **In the first column, write down all the qualities that attracted you to your partner during the first few months of your relationship.**

   You may note down qualities such as confident in his appearance, easy going, spontaneous, good sense of humour, affectionate, kind and so on.

3. **In the second column, still thinking back to the early days, write down how those qualities made you feel.**

   For example, knowing your partner was confident in his appearance meant you didn't have to reassure him about his looks, and being spontaneous may have made your relationship more interesting and exciting. A good sense of humour hopefully made you laugh, and affection may have made you feel special and desired.

4. **In the third column, think about how those qualities make you feel today.**

   Do you still feel the same? Are these still positive traits that you value and appreciate? Or have those feelings become more negative? For example, does the fact that your partner doesn't make more effort with his appearance or that his spontaneity often means life is unpredictable now annoy you? Or perhaps his sense of humour now irritates you and his affection feels suffocating or demanding.

Hopefully, this exercise reminds you of the positive qualities you still enjoy about your partner. Those qualities may have been buried recently, but if you dig a little deeper, can you see that they're still there?

You may also have noticed that your feelings towards some of those traits have changed. This is very common for many couples, because unfortunately every positive character trait has a negative side. The laid-back person who helped you relax is also the person who sometimes can't make a decision. The organised person who created safety and stability can also be controlling. Or consider the fun-loving socialite who used to inspire you but may now seem incapable of chilling out. Or the calm, quiet, retiring personality who now often appears to be lifeless and depressed.

Flicking back to the start of the story

Emily and Sam had been married for 17 years and had two teenage children. Their relationship was struggling under the pressure of constant irritations and falling out. In therapy, they explored what may be beneath their problems and were relieved to conclude that no significant hidden issues existed. They were just exhausted: tired of work and bringing up children on a very limited budget. Both had begun to see the other as the source of the problem. Continually nit-picking and finding fault, each blamed the other for not making a difficult time easier.

When we began to explore how they met and what attracted them to each other, the atmosphere in the room changed. They started to talk about the same character traits that in previous sessions they said annoyed them, but this time with fondness and affection. They also began to talk about the times they enjoyed in the early days of their relationship when they were penniless students, and they resolved to find time to follow those pursuits again. Over the following weeks, they got closer and closer and love started to flourish again.

If you're identifying more with the negative side of your partner's character traits, make a conscious effort to remind yourself of all the ways those very same traits still bring pleasure to your relationship.

Your current circumstances influence how you view your partner now. But remember that beneath whatever's going on still beats the heart of the same person you fell in love with.

Another reason your feelings may change is that you no longer value the qualities in your partner that first drew you to him. If you've been together for more than ten years, you've grown as an individual. Perhaps you were attracted to your partner's strong decision-making skills because you didn't have much confidence in those days. But now you've changed, you don't value that quality so much any more. If that's the case for you, can you identify new qualities your partner's developed that you admire and respect?

Reminiscing about your early days

As well as remembering why you fell in love, reminiscing about your early days can help to revive your relationship. Evoking those memories not only has a direct impact on your PEA levels (the chemical responsible for the feeling of being 'in love' that we explored in the earlier section), but it also gives you some ideas for what you can, and perhaps should, be doing now.

When life gets busy or problems arise, couples often stop doing the things that are special to the relationship and bring them closer. They also lose the opportunity of demonstrating how much they still care for each other and value the relationship. But the solution's easy: bring back the good times and you bring back the love.

Think back to your early months and years together and think about the things that you enjoyed doing most. Was that going for walks, giving and receiving presents, exploring together on days out or spending a night alone together watching films? Make a list of your fondest memories and schedule time to relive the good times.

If you find remembering your early days difficult, dig out the photo albums and take a trip down memory lane. Even better, do this as a couple.

Keeping a record of love

Difficulties in a relationship seem to have a direct impact on memory. Or to be precise, they have a direct impact on your ability to recall the positives. You may remember the last row word for word and know the date, time and weather conditions when a partner did something thoughtless, but you forget the moments that are tender and thoughtful. Many couples find that keeping a diary of their partners' positive behaviours helps them to overcome this memory loss.

Over the next week, write down every positive thing your partner does that leaves you feeling loved and cared for. Table 5-2 gives you an example of how your Love Record may look.

Table 5-2	A Love Record
Day	*Positive Behaviours*
Monday	Asked me how my day was and was genuinely sympathetic when I said it was bad
Tuesday	Brought me a cup of tea in bed
Wednesday	Got the kids ready for bed quickly so we could enjoy the programme on TV together
Thursday	
Friday	Gave me a hug for no apparent reason at all!
Saturday	Left me to have a lie-in and complimented me on my appearance when we got ready to go out in the evening
Sunday	

You'll notice that Thursday and Sunday are blank. That's because some days you may not be able to find a positive comment about your partner. That's okay: everyone has bad days.

When you make a conscious effort to notice and write down your partner's positive behaviours, this helps to reinforce the good things in your relationship. Few relationships have no pleasure in them at all, but unfortunately, busyness and the inevitable differences often overshadow the good stuff. By increasing your awareness of the positives, you can value them more and feel more satisfied in your relationship.

Keeping Romance Alive

Being romantic seems to come instinctively when you first get into a relationship. You want to spend time with each other and do nice little things. You want to make each other smile and feel special. This is a time when you truly discover that giving is as good as receiving. Unfortunately, romance often wanes as relationships mature. You tend to take each other for granted and assume that your partner knows you love him, even if you don't show it very often.

But romance is essential for keeping couples in touch with each other as loving, tender, sensual human beings. It reminds couples that their relationship's something special, something they want to nurture and protect.

Knowing the real meaning of romance

Romance isn't just about buying flowers or chocolates. It's not only something you try to remember once a year on Valentine's Day. Romance is any thoughtful, kind or fun thing you do for each other or do together. For example, a romantic gesture can be helping your partner to clean the house, remembering to buy a favourite food at the supermarket, texting in the middle of the day to say 'How are you?', or sharing a tub of ice cream on the sofa. Romance is *any* activity that says 'I'm thinking about you and I care about you'.

When people talk about romance, they tend to think instantly of grand gestures. Don't get me wrong, I'm all for big romantic offerings, but outside of a Hollywood film set, people often don't have the time or the money to do them on a regular basis. To keep romance alive, you need to find ways of building thoughtful words, gestures and actions into your daily life. By all means throw in the occasional grand gesture as well (see the section 'Creating unforgettable memories', later in this chapter), but a regular daily dose of romance invigorates your relationship much faster than a one-off event.

Another misconception about romance is that women enjoy it more than men, which is blatantly untrue. The kinds of gestures men and women enjoy may sometimes be different, but both value equally the sentiment behind them.

True romance is never a tool for manipulation. Doing something nice for each other should always come from a genuine desire to demonstrate your love, not be a shrouded way of saying 'Sorry' or 'I want sex.'

Doing the little things that count

Finding the romantic gestures that mean most to your partner is often quite difficult to do. I've heard many people complain that their partners never do anything romantic, to the protestations of the partner, who sits and recites a list. Unfortunately, the partner's list doesn't count because his loved one didn't know he was trying to be romantic.

One of the biggest mistakes couples make when they're being romantic is following the commandment 'do unto others as you would have them do unto you'. This is a great guideline for almost every other human encounter, but not romance. The problem with this saying is that it assumes that everyone wants to be treated the same, but in relationships your needs are often very different from your partner's.

Romance is a demonstration of love, but love's a very complicated thing, so what each person interprets as loving is different. And at different times of our lives, different gestures take on different meanings. For example, if you've just experienced a bereavement, you probably don't want to be taken out for an extravagant meal or be bought a new pair of cufflinks. Those gestures may be very romantic when you're feeling in need of appreciation or attention, but not when you need comfort.

The following is a list of common love needs. Take a look through and put them in your personal order of priority. If possible, ask your partner to complete this exercise as well, and then share your answers with each other.

- ✔ **Affection:** Enjoying physical touch, both given and appreciatively received.

- ✔ **Affirmation:** Being positively praised verbally or through gifts for being the person you are.

- ✔ **Appreciation:** Being noticed and receiving thanks, verbally and/or through gifts.

- ✔ **Attention:** Spending time together and being able to share thoughts about your day and your inner world.

✔ **Comfort:** Showing physical tenderness, offering words of comfort and talking about difficult things.

✔ **Encouragement:** Being offered a helping hand, receiving motivating gifts and hearing positive words of encouragement.

✔ **Security:** Receiving anything – words, gifts or actions – that demonstrates commitment to the relationship.

✔ **Support:** Getting practical help and words of support.

More ways of being romantic probably exist than varieties of roses – and you can get loads of those! What you choose to do depends on your personality, the resources available and, crucially, the love needs of your partner.

Timing is everything when you're being romantic. When you can recognise your partner's love needs, you can time your romantic gestures to demonstrate your love when he needs it most.

Here are just a few ideas to inspire you:

✔ Give a traditional bouquet of flowers or a single well-chosen bloom.

✔ Say I love you, thank you, you're special, well done, you're beautiful, till death do us part, or whatever fits the bill. Say it face to face or send a text.

✔ Run the bath for your partner, sprinkle the water with rose petals, put lighted candles around the side and pour a glass of wine.

✔ Buy a favourite food or wine.

✔ Help with a chore or do a job that's normally your partner's responsibility.

✔ Go for a walk together.

✔ Be affectionate.

✔ Rent a favourite movie and snuggle up on the sofa.

✔ Put on some romantic tunes.

✔ Buy a little gift.

✔ Go somewhere special – an old haunt or a new discovery.

Making a few small romantic gestures on a regular basis keeps your relationship feeling special and alive. What you do doesn't matter as long as it's genuine and shows your partner you love him and care about his needs.

Creating unforgettable memories

Small, regular romantic gestures keep love vibrant and alive. But if you want the wow factor – something that's unforgettable and really kicks your relationship up a gear and makes your partner gasp with delight – you do need a grand gesture.

Grand gestures aren't measured by the cost or by the extravagant outcome, but by the amount of personal effort you make. Whatever you do, make sure that you put your whole heart into it and that it's something that fits your partner's personality. Richard Gere may have got away with carrying Debra Winger through her crowded workplace in *An Officer and a Gentleman*, but if you know your partner may cringe with embarrassment or get sacked, doing so isn't romantic.

Creativity and the personal touch are key, so take your time to think about what knocks your partner's socks off.

Here's a list of ideas to get you thinking:

- Write a poem from the heart, expressing how you feel.
- Make a music CD of romantic classics or songs that are special to you as a couple.
- Collate love quotes or snippets from love poems.
- Buy something extravagant (cost depends on your budget).
- Write a list of '101 things I love about you'.
- Frame a picture of a memorable event or place.
- Book a surprise day out or weekend away.
- Pack a picnic complete with soft rug and champagne.
- If you're the artistic type, paint or draw a picture.
- Arrange for your partner to do something he's always wanted to do – skydive, drive a racing car, go on a cookery weekend.
- Arrange for a bunch of flowers to be delivered to your partner's workplace or another public event.
- If you're musical, sing a serenade; if you're not musical, hire a string quartet or solo artist for your partner.

Falling in love all over again

Sue and Jerry had been married for nearly 50 years and had watched their three children grow up and get married themselves. Retirement hadn't been what either of them expected. Rather than enjoying the extra time together, they found themselves staring at each other with nothing to say. Somewhere over the past 50 years, they'd lost each other. But they weren't ready to say goodbye, so they entered therapy committed to rediscovering their lost love. They talked about when they met and how much fun they used to share. They'd both changed over the years, but they soon got back in touch with the core values they'd always shared. They began to revisit the places of their youth, hired out some of the old movies they enjoyed and replaced their old vinyl records with CDs. They became physically affectionate again and incorporated romance into their daily lives. Three months after they ended counselling, I received a card from Jerry thanking me for my help. He'd decided to surprise Sue with a weekend away to the village where they got married, and on the Sunday morning they renewed their vows in front of some of the same congregation. It was one of those cases that reminded me what a privilege doing my job is.

Chapter 6

Understanding the Essentials of Sex

In This Chapter

▶ Understanding why good sex is so important to relationships

▶ Establishing a basis for sexual improvement

▶ Refreshing your sex education

▶ Overcoming common sexual difficulties

Sex is an essential part of most couple relationships. When sex is good, not only do you feel good about yourself, but you also feel good about your relationship. A good sex life bonds couples together and helps them to withstand the trials and tribulations of life.

Most couples enjoy a good sex life in the early stages of their relationship. Mother Nature boosts both male and female desire to maximise the chances of reproduction and to build a strong mutual bond to help couples raise offspring together. But as a relationship matures, sex becomes less of an imperative drive and more of an optional, pleasurable extra. With trust, love and commitment, sex can continue to be a source of comfort, fun and intimacy throughout a couple's lifetime. But sex, like every other area of a relationship, requires work.

This chapter looks at the essential components of a happy and fulfilling sex life. You explore the role of sex in relationships, the way sexuality changes, and what you can do to maximise your pleasure. And you also look at how you can overcome some of the common sexual problems that many couples experience.

Getting Started: How's Your Sex Life?

Sex is the element that differentiates a couple from any other kind of relationship. You may have friends you share an emotional connection with, family members who know you really well and work colleagues you share common interests with. But your partner's the only person you're having sex with . . . well, probably!

Picture your relationship as a bicycle wheel, with sex as both the hub and the tyre. Sex is the core of your intimacy from which all other aspects of your relationship extend and the tyre that holds them all together. As the hub of your wheel, sex gives you strength and stability, and as the tyre it provides an easier and more comfortable ride through the bumps and troughs of life.

Sex is the glue that bonds couples together. So working on this area of your relationship makes for a closer, stronger partnership.

If sex really isn't important to you and your relationship, that's absolutely fine. As long as you and your partner have agreed and found other ways of keeping your relationship intimate and special, and neither of you feels that you're missing out, a sexless relationship can be as happy and fulfilling as any other kind.

Sex: Keeping you and your relationship healthy

You can probably think of plenty of reasons why sex is important. Apart from the obvious reason for sex – that it sustains the human race – most people also consider it to be jolly good fun. But researchers have also found that a good sex life provides a number of health benefits for both individuals and couples:

✔ **Physical health:** An active sex life makes your body produce a variety of chemicals that help you to feel happy and more resistant to emotional and physical pain. People who regularly enjoy good sex report lower levels of depression and anxiety and a general sense of wellbeing. Sex also boosts your immune system, making you more resistant to illness and disease. And if that's not incentive enough, apparently sex also increases lean body tissue and thickens skin tissue, which keeps you looking and feeling younger. One survey concluded

that regular sex can help you look between four and seven years younger and add an additional ten years to your life span.

✔ **Relationship health:** Sex plays an essential biochemical role in couple relationships. When you have sex, your body releases oxytocin, the chemical responsible for human bonding. When you orgasm, you release a sudden rush of the stuff. This sudden surge of hormones is responsible for the intense feelings of affection you experience after sex, feelings that make you closer to your partner and inspire you to have sex again and again. And a regular sex life also produces a chemical called vasopressin, especially in men. Vasopressin has been nicknamed the 'monogamy molecule', because it encourages you to stay faithful to your partner.

Evaluating the role of sex in a relationship

Sex means different things to different people at different stages of their lives. And the role sex plays in your relationship changes, depending on how long you've been with your partner and also what else is going on in your life.

In the first throes of love, you may experience sex as urgent and exciting, an activity that dominates your waking life. As a relationship matures, sex changes. A gentler desire replaces the urgency, and sex becomes less of a focal point. But that doesn't mean that it's any less important.

Sex isn't an inert product that you own or an unchanging personal quality. It's a complex combination of thoughts, emotions, behaviours and sensations that's intrinsically linked to how you feel about yourself, your changing circumstances and environment, and the relationship you have with your lover.

Sex plays a different role in your relationship over your lifetime together. At times it may feel essential. At other times it may be more of an optional extra. What role you feel sex plays for you really doesn't matter, as long as both you and your partner agree.

If you disagree about the role of sex in your relationship, you can have problems. You can also experience difficulties if you have different expectations of your sex life.

Some people expect sex always to be passionate and exciting. Others want it always to be romantic and affectionate. But the complexity of humankind, taking body, heart and soul into account, means that no two sexual experiences are ever the same. And the reality is that sex sometimes feels purely functional: a way to release physical tension.

Accepting that sex plays a different role in your relationship at different times and that your experience of sex often changes can help couples to adapt and grow together.

Making a mutual commitment to your sex life

Just because sex is natural doesn't mean that it happens naturally. Some couples are able to enjoy a good sex life without making much effort, but they're few and far between. The vast majority of people have to work at their sex lives, in the same way as they work at their relationships.

Working at your sex life means making a commitment to:

✔ Discovering the role sex plays for each of you

✔ Ensuring that sex is rewarding for both of you

✔ Talking about your sex life and finding out how you both feel about it

✔ Working through problems together when they arise (and at some stage in your life, they probably will)

Committing to your sex life also means understanding and accepting that sex changes as you age and as your life progresses together. But you agree that as your relationship continues to mature, you'll make more effort – not less.

Couples who still enjoy a great sex life after 10, 20 or even 50 years together aren't lucky – they're committed.

Creating a sexual growth plan

If your sex life is in the doldrums – if it's a bit dusty or rusty or getting close to becoming monotonous – then giving it a good polishing not only makes sex more enjoyable, but it also revitalises every other area of your relationship. Devoting time and energy to making your sex life something that's satisfying and rewarding to both of you is one of the most important investments you can make in improving your relationship. But doing so takes courage and trust.

To improve your sex life, you have to be able to talk about it. 'Opening up with pillow talk', later in this chapter, covers talking about sex. This section looks at how you can talk about the improvements you want to make.

Talking about improving your sex life is best done in the spirit of fun. Doing so is not about criticising each other or rubbishing your sex life, it's about sharing how you can make it even better than it is now.

The sexual growth plan is an exercise that you and your partner can do together to begin to talk about the changes you want to make. Working through a task like this together can be an excellent way of getting the conversation going. With your focus on the paper rather than each other, and prompts coming from the page rather than yourselves, you find cooperating and not feeling defensive much easier.

CASE STUDY

Seeing sex from a wider perspective

Craig and Beth had been married for nine years and had two children aged 5 and 3. They came for counselling because Craig was sick of waiting for their sex life to get better. He explained how their sex life had diminished to almost nothing since the kids were born and he was frustrated that Beth's sex drive hadn't returned. As we explored the role sex played in their relationship, Craig shared how, coming from a physically affectionate family, he associated sex with love, tenderness and acceptance, so when Beth turned down his advances he felt deeply rejected. Beth, an only child, had been brought up by her mother after her father left for another woman when Beth was 12. Although Beth always enjoyed sex, she thought Craig placed too much importance on it. As they continued to talk over the coming weeks, Craig began to recognise and appreciate the many other ways in which Beth showed her love for him. And Beth began to wonder if she was withholding sex as a way of testing his love for her and his fidelity. They both started to see sex from a wider perspective and made a commitment to increase the quantity and the quality of their sex life.

The sexual growth plan asks you both to consider whether you want improvements in the following areas:

- ✔ **Affection and intimacy:** Before you even get into the bedroom, affection can help you to get physically connected and close.

- ✔ **Sensuality:** One step on from affection, being sensual together can help to create the mood and the environment for luuurve.

- ✔ **Romance:** Not important for sex to everyone, but for some a little more romance can help to stoke the fire.

- ✔ **Playfulness:** If sex has become a bit serious between you, perhaps injecting more play can help to improve the mood and the outcome.

- ✔ **Eroticism:** This means different things to different people, but what I mean here are the types of raunchy things that get your juices flowing.

- ✔ **Adventure:** Focus your thoughts on whether you want to try new things.

- ✔ **Initiation:** Perhaps sex is great when you get around to it, but you want to improve the way you start your sexual activities.

- ✔ **Stimulation:** This is the nitty-gritty of love-making tricks and techniques and sexual positions.

> ✔ **Overcoming dysfunction:** Do you have particular sexual difficulties to solve, such as erection problems, premature or delayed ejaculation, painful intercourse, difficulty reaching orgasm or low desire? (The later section 'Overcoming Common Sexual Problems' may help.)
>
> ✔ **Talking about sex:** Look at how you communicate about sex, both inside and outside the bedroom.

Use Table 6-1 to think about the different areas in your sex life where you'd like to make improvements. If at all possible, do this together with your partner, so both of you can establish the areas you'd like to work on, but if your partner doesn't want to join in, you can still decide where you want improvements and begin to work on those areas on your own. To find out more about how you can improve in the areas you've identified, turn to the relevant chapters indicated in the last column.

Table 6-1	The Sexual Growth Plan			
	Partner 1 Would Like Improvement	*Partner 2 Would Like Improvement*	*Both Partners Would Like Improvement*	*Further Info*
Affection and intimacy				Chapters 4 and 5
Sensuality				Chapter 6
Romance				Chapter 5
Playfulness				Chapter 7
Eroticism				Chapter 7
Adventure				Chapter 7
Initiation				Chapter 7
Stimulation				Chapter 6
Overcoming dysfunctions				Chapter 6
Talking about sex				Chapter 6

Recognising Negative Sexual Thinking

Over the course of a lifetime, people pick up a whole host of information about sex – some of it positive and accurate, some a load of old tosh and, unfortunately, some downright destructive.

When you go into a relationship, you bring with you both conscious and unconscious messages about sex. Some come from your childhood and previous experiences, some from your culture and religious beliefs, and far more than are useful come from the media.

When you can recognise and understand the sexual messages you've picked up, you can make a decision about whether they're helpful. And if the messages aren't helpful, you can make a decision to ditch them.

Leaving history in the past

All people have a unique view of their sexual selves and a unique view of how sex should be. Those views start forming in early childhood and then grow and develop as you get older.

- **Childhood:** From the first moment you inquisitively put your hand down your pants or decided to take your pants off, your parents' response influenced how you view your sexuality. Was it okay to touch yourself? Or to run around the house in the buff? And as you got older, what happened if there was a sexy scene on television? Did the whole room go quiet or did your dad make a sudden lunge for the remote control? And how often did you see your parents kiss and giggle, or have an early night? Parents are hugely influential in what they say and in what they don't say. You discover whether sex is okay, natural, private, rude or even wrong, often before you even know what it is.

- **Puberty:** As your body begins to change during the puberty years, the voices of your peers join the parental messages. If your family celebrated your puberty, you're more likely to have positive body confidence, but if they made you feel embarrassed, you may have become more self-conscious. If you developed at the same time as your peers, the physical changes felt like a normal part of growing up. But if you were a particularly late or early developer, you may have developed more feelings of doubt and anxiety.

✔ **Early sexual experiences:** For some people, those early fumbles behind the bike sheds left fond memories, but for others they were awkward or even traumatic. Early sexual experiences should involve safe experimentation, but for some this is a time when they form fears and doubts about attractiveness and performance. Other people find that they form unrealistic expectations of permanent passion and buzz.

✔ **Religion and culture:** Those who were brought up within a strict religious or cultural environment are influenced by the sexual messages related to that doctrine. Of course you can have a strong religious faith or cultural heritage and still have great sex. You may choose not to engage in some sexual practices, but as long as you and your partner agree, then you have no reason why sex can't be great. But if those religious or cultural messages have had a negative impact, then you need to let them go and replace them with positive messages that fit the values you believe in today.

If the messages you received in the past about sex are getting in the way of you having the sex life you want, now's the time to ditch them. When you're aware of those messages, you can examine them with a critical and rational eye and tell yourself that they're either wrong or no longer relevant to your life. By doing this, you'll leave the past where it belongs and free yourself to rewrite positive messages for the future. 'Looking backwards so you can move forwards' offers more help for unravelling your sexual messages.

Unfortunately, traumatic sexual experiences are still commonplace in society. If you've had an experience in your past that's left you feeling uncomfortable in any way, then don't dismiss it. Please find someone to talk to. An experienced counsellor can help you to work through your feelings and reduce the impact the experience has on your future. You can find details of helping agencies in the Appendix.

Looking backwards so you can move forwards

Look at the list of words below and choose as many as you like to describe how you felt about sex when you were a child, a teenager, and at the time of your first sexual experience.

Exciting	Erotic	Intense	Animal	Gentle
Energetic	Thrilling	Ecstatic	Passionate	Sordid
Urgent	Primitive	Disgusting	Embarrassing	Loving
Rude	Immature	Alarming	Painful	Boring

Angry	Threatening	Frightening	Reassuring	Happy
Satisfying	Cosy	Intimate	Romantic	Fun
Mystical	Relaxing	Sensual	Friendly	Warm
Unifying	Memorable	Emotional	Magical	Silly
Tiring	Annoying	Pointless	Routine	Dirty
Mundane	Generous	Uncomfortable	Depressing	Sad

When you've identified the words that most represent the messages you learnt in the past, look at the list again and make a note of the words you want to represent your sex life now and in the future. And if you find those negative words creeping into your head again, kick them into touch with your new positive sex vocabulary.

If you can, make some time to share this exercise with your partner and discuss anything that you discover. By identifying your responses, you can use your new understanding of your background to enhance your sex life. Dispelling damaging myths

Myths picked up from society about sex affect everyone. Some of those myths you may reluctantly agree with; others you may wholeheartedly reject. Either way, myths have a big impact on you.

To improve your sex life, you need to establish whether any negative myths are hindering you from enjoying the sex you deserve. Here's a list of common myths – see how many of them ring true for you:

- ✔ **Wanting sex shows how much you love each other:** Some people use sex as a way of showing affection. This means that if their partner aren't up for sex, they feel unloved. Sex is a great way of getting close and showing how much you care for someone, but remember, it's only one way to express how you feel, not the only way.

- ✔ **Sex should be natural, spontaneous, frequent and always fantastic:** Couples who can't keep their hands off each other and grab every opportunity to have sex may make great television, and in the early days of your relationship you may have enjoyed this kind of sex too. But good sex takes communication and commitment, especially in long-term relationships. And even then, it isn't fantastic every single time. Hopefully, sex is always enjoyable, but if you expect earth-moving moments on every occasion, you're setting yourself up for disappointment.

- ✔ **Only young, fit, slim, beautiful and able-bodied people enjoy great sex:** TV screens and magazines hardly ever show anyone who's over 25 or doesn't have a perfect body enjoying sex. Anyone and everyone can enjoy sex if they have a positive sexual attitude. How old you are, how big you are, how fit you are or how symmetrical your body is doesn't matter.

✔ **Having sex means having intercourse:** Some people say that unless you're having intercourse, you're not really having sex, just 'foreplay'. Everything else, whether it's manual stimulation or oral or whatever, is just leading up to the main course – penetration. People who believe this myth are missing out on so much. Sex is about closeness, sensuality, pleasure and touch. Good sex starts when you *feel* sexy and stops when you don't.

✔ **Men always want sex, and are always ready for it:** A surprising number of men (and their partners) still expect the penis to respond like a well-oiled piece of machinery – completely detached from the brain, it's meant to be ready at all times and with minimal stimulation. Men generally do have a higher sex drive than women, but like women they also experience tiredness and stress. You can't separate your sexual functioning from your brain and your feelings. All men have times when they're just not interested or not up to sex.

✔ **Sexual liberation means that you enjoy everything:** The sex industry and the media have created a hierarchy. You start as a 'beginner' and learn the 'basics', and then move on to the 'advanced' techniques. But true sexual liberation means having the confidence to do what you want, when you want and if you want. It means accepting that sexual tastes vary from individual to individual, and that no right or wrong, or better or worse, way exists to enjoy sex.

Relaxing about sexual compatibility

'Sexual compatibility' is a term that's hit relationships over recent years, confusing many couples and leaving people doubting otherwise healthy relationships.

Sexual compatibility's a modern media creation. A few generations ago when our forefathers and foremothers got married, they had no chance to test the merchandise before purchasing. Sex before marriage was seriously frowned on, and with little efficient contraception, deciding to try before you buy could have devastating consequences. In the olden days, few people expected to click together instantly in perfect synchronicity. They expected to grow in knowledge together.

But today, in the so-called enlightened 21st century with its quick-fix, ready-made solutions, people have extended their expectation of instant gratification into their sex lives. Many modern couples expect their sex lives to be good from the start. And if it's not, they wonder whether perhaps they're not 'sexually compatible'.

The truth is that sexual compatibility is just one element of a relationship. If you happen to share an equal sexual attraction, the same sexual attitudes, the same tastes, the same sex drive and experience and equal levels of enjoyment, then congratulations. But if you don't, you're like the vast majority of people who get along well enough and work together to make up for any discrepancies.

As long as you share the same level of commitment to your sex life, you're compatible.

Getting to Grips with What You Need to Know about Sex

Sex is probably the only natural function that you have to be taught how to do. Admittedly, the basics almost certainly occur to you without any instruction, otherwise humans would have died out long before *The Lovers' Guide*, but the ins and outs of one another's bodies are things you have to discover.

The huge range and diversity of sex manuals and dvds, accompanied by varying degrees of spurious research, have made modern society very knowledgeable about sex. But in spite of all this information, many people still don't realise just how much they don't know. The following sections aim to fill in any gaps in your knowledge that you didn't know were there.

Understanding the difference between men and women

No one questions the physical differences between men and women, but do you really appreciate the impact those differences make on the way you think and feel about sex? Over recent years, a lot of noise has been made about bridging the gender gap, some of which has been really valuable. But unfortunately, some of the hoo-ha has drowned out the importance of accepting and respecting difference.

Here are some of the key differences that you ignore at your peril!

- ✔ **Women need safety:** On the whole, men are much stronger than women, and that puts women at a distinct disadvantage in anything physical. So while women may have earned the right to be as promiscuous as their male counterparts, safety's still of paramount importance. And only women get pregnant, so the unconscious primitive drive to ensure safety and security for prospective children is most pronounced. This means that women tend to be more cautious about sex than men are and need emotional and environmental security in order to relax.

✔ **Men want more sex:** Evidence continues to show that men want more sex than women. Not only is their desire for sex stronger, but also the way they pursue it. Men have up to 40 times more testosterone, the key hormone responsible for sexual desire, than women do. Testosterone is a competitive chemical that's proactive, assertive and even aggressive at times. This means that men actively seek out sex and are more demanding.

✔ **Women's sex drive is 'receptive':** Although women have some testosterone, their sex drive is most heavily influenced by oestrogen. Oestrogen's responsible for femininity and seeks intimacy. Not only does it give women their curves, but it also gives them their powers of seduction. Unlike the assertive drive of testosterone, oestrogen's more receptive. That doesn't mean that oestrogen's passive, more that it inspires women to be ready, willing and seductive. This means that men nearly always initiate sex more often than women – not just because their desire's greater, but because the nature of female sexuality's receptive rather than proactive.

✔ **Men are more visually stimulated:** On the whole, visual stimuli arouse men more than women. Evolutionary psychology suggests that this may be because of man's innate hunter nature, which makes him more alert to visual cues. And as female sexuality is more receptive, women are more likely to demonstrate their availability by showing off their wares.

✔ **Women's sexual desire decreases:** In the early stages of a relationship, male and female sexual desire's very similar, but as the relationship matures, female desire decreases much faster than men's. This may be Mother Nature's way of controlling the population or may simply be because the needs of looking after a family distract women more.

✔ **Men enjoy variety:** Scientists think that men's higher levels of testosterone are responsible for their greater interest in sexual variety. Most research has supported the idea that men generally enjoy more sexual partners and a greater range of sexual activities. But their choice tends to be fixed over their life span, whereas female tastes and desires change and adapt over the course of life.

✔ **Women's desire changes:** Perhaps the biggest difference between men and women is that women's hormones change over the course of a menstrual month. While a man's sexual needs tend to remain fairly constant, a woman's needs change continually. Not only does a woman's desire wax and wane based on her hormone levels, but evidence suggests that the type of sex she enjoys does also. No wonder men get confused!

Sexual desire and sex drive are not the same. Men generally have a stronger and more persistent desire for sex, but once a woman's sexually aroused, her drive for satiation can be just as powerful as a man's.

So if the sex drives are so different, does that mean that men enjoy sex more than women? Absolutely not! Physically speaking, women can enjoy sex more than men since they are capable of multiple orgasms. But great sex isn't just about orgasms, it's also about intimacy and eroticism.

Your personality and emotions play the major role in deciding whether you want sex. And regardless of what your hormones are doing, your mind has the final say.

Discovering what they didn't teach you in sex ed

Sex education teaches you how to make babies not how to make love, leaving you to work out for yourself how to become a confident, sensitive and caring lover. This chapter isn't long enough to go through all the tricks and techniques of love making, so instead here are just a few of the topics you may want to explore further together:

- ✔ **Exotic and erotic stuff:** Another common feature of sex that never comes up in any formal sex education setting is the huge variety of other things couples get up to in bed. Many couples enjoy the added excitement of sexy lingerie or dressing-up games, experimenting with sex toys and bondage, watching erotica together, acting out fantasies, or exploring the mysteries of tantric sex. Flip to Chapter 7 for more detail on this.

- ✔ **Manual techniques:** Your hands are definitely the best tools for giving and receiving sexual pleasure. You can start with a sensual massage to get you both in the mood and then move on to exploring the many non-genital erogenous zones, before homing in on the main attraction.

- ✔ **Oral techniques:** The mouth's a wonderful tool for both giving and receiving intimate sensations. Kissing, licking, nibbling, sucking and blowing can provide exquisite pleasure all over the body.

- ✔ **Penetration:** For many couples, penetration is the best bit of making love. It's the one act where both partners can give and receive pleasure at exactly the same time, with one single movement. But like everything else in sex, if you do the same thing every time, the passion can wane.

- ✔ **Play:** Of course, don't forget fun. Couples who play together stay together. Someone once said that fun is to intimacy what orgasm is to sex. It's not essential, but it makes it all seem so much more worthwhile.

- ✔ **Positions:** According to one recent women's magazine, you can try a thousand different sex positions, but in reality these are only variations on six basic ones: man on top, woman on top, from behind, side by side, kneeling or standing. Different positions can provide very different types of stimulation, so experimenting can significantly improve your sex life. Exploring different positions can also be hugely beneficial for couples with physical limitations caused by illness or ageing.

Many couples get stuck in a rut, using the same routines with varying degrees of success. By experimenting with something new, you can experience different sensations and heighten each other's pleasure.

The range and diversity of human sexual experience and adventure are limitless. Couples who are committed to improving their sex lives and maintaining them need also to commit to continuing to discover and experiment. Sex education's something that everyone can carry on enjoying for a lifetime.

You can find loads and loads more info, tips and advice in *Sex For Dummies* by Dr Ruth K. Westheimer and Pierre A. Lehu (Wiley).

Opening up with pillow talk

Body language just isn't enough if you're serious about improving your sex life. Neither you nor your partner's a mind reader, so you need to talk honestly about your needs.

For many people, talking openly about their sexual needs is awkward or even embarrassing, but like all skills, it's something that gets easier with practice. Talking about your sex life takes courage and commitment, but however difficult it may seem, it's well worth the effort.

Sex talk falls into two distinct categories: talking about sex and talking during sex.

Talking about sex

Discussing sex gives you the opportunity to share your thoughts and feelings and talk about things you want to experiment with or change.

Before you start, be sure that both of you are in a relaxed and settled frame of mind and are ready to talk about improving your sex life. Think through what you want to say. Make sure that you're open to having a discussion and you're willing to offer your partner something as well as asking for things for yourself.

Whether you want to suggest something new or talk about stimulation techniques, tact and timing are essential:

> ✔ **Tact:** People can be rather sensitive when talking about sexpertise, so any conversation about sex mustn't come across as criticism. If you want to change things, you need to make sure that you don't sound as if you're unhappy with how things are now. So rather than saying 'I want to make our sex life exciting,' say 'I want to make our sex life *even more* exciting.' This is particularly important if you want to talk about different stimulation techniques. Your partner may interpret 'I want you to do blah blah' as 'I don't like what you're doing' or 'What you're doing isn't good enough.' If you keep the conversation mutual – for example, 'I want *us* to discover some *more* ways of pleasing *each other*' – then the conversation remains about the two of you.

You may be wondering how to respond if your partner says 'What's wrong with things as they are?' or 'I'm happy with things as they are.' In this situation, remember to continue to be encouraging. So say something like 'Yes, things are good now, but I want to make them even better' or 'Yes, things are good now, but I want to make sure we don't get into a rut.' You can add that the reason you're raising the subject isn't that you're unhappy, but that you've recently read about it (like in an excellent new book you've bought: this one!).

✔ **Timing:** The best time to talk about trying new things is when you have no chance of trying them right now. If something weird or wonderful pops into your mind in the middle of a love-making session, you're generally safer to leave it there. Many a night of passion's been wrecked by a carelessly timed whisper of 'Do you mind if I try this?' Unless you're 100 per cent sure your partner's going to be as enthusiastic as you are about doing something new, always discuss it first.

Finding time to talk intimately about sex can be tricky. Obviously, you need to be alone and away from distractions, but over the dinner table can seem a bit out of place. Some couples have found the best time is when they're both relaxing together – perhaps a Sunday morning lie-in or relaxing on the sofa in the evening.

Try this simple technique for exploring new things to do with your partner. Get two sheets of paper and on one sheet write three headings: 'okay', 'not okay' and 'give it a try'. With your partner, brainstorm all the sexual practices you can think of and write them on your blank sheet of paper. Include absolutely everything, from the everyday activities to the exotic and erotic and even the dark and dangerous. Then mark down each practice under one of those headings. Anything that's under the 'not okay' heading for either of you is a no-no. Those under the 'give it a try' heading are open for experimentation and for those that are 'okay', if you're not doing them already, try them tonight!

Saying no

Whenever you're talking about making changes to your sex life, both of you must feel comfortable saying no. You need to be free to say no to a new idea, and also mid-sex if you don't like something when you try it. Lots of couples avoid trying anything new because they don't want to hurt their partners by stopping if it doesn't feel good. But this approach means that new experiences that both may love remain undiscovered.

Whenever you have any conversation with your partner about sex, confirm and reconfirm that if either of you is uncomfortable with anything you're doing, at any time in the process, then both of you are okay about stopping.

Talking during sex

Talking during sex allows you to fine tune your techniques and maximise each other's pleasure. Some good and some very bad ways exist of talking about technique. The best way to improve your technique is to ask for feedback while you're actually touching your partner.

A lover who's impatient or gives the impression that your arousal or orgasm's a chore is a total turnoff. Therefore, show your partner that pleasing her also pleases you. The reason you ask for feedback is because you want to enjoy each other even more.

Asking for feedback may sound very simple, but here are some essential guidelines to follow to ensure that your questions are effective and not intrusive:

- ✔ **Ask specific questions:** Think about the information you really want to get and frame your questions accordingly. For example, do you really want to know whether what you're doing's nice? Or do you want to know whether your actions are more arousing for your partner? General questions give you general answers, whereas specific questions can give you the information you need to fine tune your skills.

- ✔ **Ask closed questions:** By this I mean questions that require just a one-word answer. While you're stimulating your partner, you want her to stay relaxed and focused on her sensation, not to disappear into her head to provide you with a thoroughly thought-through response (during which time she's gone off the boil). Therefore questions like 'Do you want me to be firmer or gentler?' are much better than 'What pressure do you want me to use?' Similarly, 'Do you prefer this, or this?' is much simpler to answer than 'What do you want me to do?'

- ✔ **Use scaling questions:** Ultimately, the feedback you want is going to tell you whether what you're doing is getting your partner more or less aroused, closer or further from orgasm. An effective way to achieve this is to agree on a scaling system. For example, you can agree that on a scale of 1–10, 1 is pleasant and 10 is orgasmic. Then, if your partner's on 5, you can ask 'When I touch you like this, where are you?' If she responds with a 6, you know you're heading in the right direction. If she says 4, then you need to change what you're doing.

When you first start seeking feedback, you can feel as though you're asking a barrage of questions. But you'll quickly discover the types of touch your partner prefers, and from that point on you'll be asking for clarification of what she wants today.

Don't ever think that when you've got the hang of something once, you know it for life. Bodies are incredibly complex, and what sends you off the orgasm scale on Saturday may only get you to level 3 the next day. So if you want to enjoy great sex on a regular basis, make asking for feedback an ongoing part of your love making.

Accepting differences in taste and style

Sex has many different styles and flavours, and few right or wrong ways exist of experiencing and enjoying sexual pleasure. Differences in the type of sex you enjoy are unique to every individual. As a couple, the challenge is to find the mutual activities that both of you find fulfilling.

If your partner wants to experience a particular type of technique or activity and you feel neutral about it, then you may be happy to compromise and please your partner in that way. For example, some people don't mind giving oral sex but don't want to receive, and as a couple, that can work fine. But if one of you wants to do something that the other feels strongly against or really doesn't like, then a compromise may feel more like a violation. For example, if one of you positively dislikes anal sex, you need to agree that's a no-go area.

Appetite for sex is often compared to appetite for food. But having sex together is much more intimate and mutual than sharing a meal. You're unlikely to feel offended if your partner eats a curry in front of you, no matter how much you hate it, but if you're force-fed that curry too, you've every right to feel that your civil liberties have been infringed.

If you enjoy a particular sexual activity that your partner objects to, rather than focusing on what you're missing out on and risking feeling resentful, focus on all the things that you can share and enjoy together.

Overcoming Common Sexual Problems

Most couples can take the occasional sexual hiccup in their stride. Tiredness, stress, illness and the normal ups and downs of life affect how you feel and perform sexually. Your body isn't a machine that can operate in isolation: your heart and mind affect your body and its responses.

But if sexual problems continue for a long time, they can begin to put a strain on an otherwise happy relationship. Whether your problem is low desire or difficulty getting aroused or reaching orgasm, the longer it goes on for, the bigger the problem can seem to become.

Overcoming sexual difficulties can be very straightforward, but to do so you have to accept them as a normal part of being human and commit as a couple to working through them.

A problem shared is a problem halved

When one partner in a couple isn't able to enjoy sexual pleasure as much as the other, each sexual encounter can leave that person feeling unequal. If you're the partner without a problem, you may feel guilty and sad that you're still able to have a good time. And if you're the person with the problem, you feel guilty because you can't prevent your partner from being affected by what you perceive as your problem.

The reality, of course, is that sexual problems never belong to just one person. If your sex life's being affected, then both of you have a problem. When couples are able to grasp this fully, working together to overcome the problem becomes much easier.

When you don't share and discuss problems, resentment can grow. If you're the person with the problem, you can feel guilty and ashamed that you can't overcome it by yourself, and if you're that person's partner, then you can begin to wonder whether the cause is something you've done or not done. As anxiety grows in both partners, distance can develop and the problem can feel insurmountable.

Admitting that your relationship has a sexual problem that isn't going to go away on its own is the first step to resolving it. Once you acknowledge that the problem exists, you can research your treatment options and get on with overcoming it.

The most common cause of sexual difficulties is relationship problems. If either of you is feeling angry or upset with the other, that can affect your sexual relationship. Even if you think you're able to keep your feelings under control, you may still act them out in the bedroom, or they may cause you to avoid sex altogether.

If you think that your sexual problems are the result of unresolved issues within your relationship, you need to address these first. Once your relationship's back on an even keel, you may find that the sexual problems disappear, but if not, you can focus your energies as a couple on resolving them.

Whatever the cause of sexual difficulties, most couples can overcome them. If you can be open and honest with each other, patient and understanding and share a sense of humour, you can both look forward to enjoying a great sex life again.

Looking at female problems

Sexual problems seem to be more common in women; in fact, one survey found that 43 per cent of women experienced a problem over the previous two years. Women may experience more difficulties for a number of reasons. First, women's sexuality fluctuates with the menstrual cycle and hormonal changes that occur over the course of a lifetime. Second, external factors such as stress, tiredness and distractions often influence women more. And because women's sexual desire tends to be lower than men's, women don't have the same biological motivation to overcome external influences.

The good news is, no problem in the bedroom's insurmountable. The following sections explain some of the most common sexual problems women experience and offer some self-help techniques to overcome them.

Having difficulty experiencing orgasm

The most frequent sexual problem affecting women is difficulty experiencing orgasm. This problem's usually due to a lack of adequate stimulation. Some women find that although they can experience an orgasm alone through masturbation, they struggle with a partner. Some are able to orgasm with some types of stimulation, for example oral, but never through intercourse or manual stimulation. Others are unable to have an orgasm at any time, so never experience orgasm at all.

Research suggests that only a third of women are able to orgasm through penetrative sex. For most women, intercourse doesn't provide adequate stimulation of the clitoris unless they're in exactly the right position (woman on top generally works best) or use additional stimulation (for example, fingers or a sex toy).

Occasionally, underlying physical reasons exist that make experiencing orgasm difficult (these are similar to those that men with erection problems have – see 'Examining male issues', later in this chapter). But assuming that a woman's fully aroused, the problem's more likely to be psychological. Psychological reasons include feeling self-conscious or having low self-esteem, fear of losing control, shame or guilt about sexuality, and being distracted, perhaps by children or others in the house.

Being able to feel fully relaxed is the most important thing you can do to make experiencing orgasm easier, although being told to relax generally makes people feel more stressed, not less! Taking time to build the right environment and sensuality before you get into the bedroom can help significantly, as can increasing communication with your partner to maximise adequate stimulation.

You may also find the following orgasm triggers helpful:

✔ Breathe deeply or pant to pump extra oxygen to tensing muscles.

✔ Arch your back or try a different position to maximise clitoral stimulation.

✔ Rhythmically squeeze your pelvic floor muscles (see the later sidebar 'Tightening up your sex life' for more).

✔ Escape into a fantasy to block out any distractions or negative thoughts.

✔ Try a vibrator or sensual massager – the extra stimulation strengthens the reflex required to trigger an orgasm.

Finding intercourse painful

Painful intercourse is common to many women at some stage in their lives. Sometimes an underlying physical problem such as endometriosis or fibroids causes the pain, or it occurs after childbirth. But for the majority of women, painful intercourse is due to not being sufficiently sexually aroused. As a woman becomes aroused, her vagina becomes wider and more lubricated, ready to accept a penis, so lack of arousal means that entry's more likely to be painful.

Many women find themselves caught in a negative pain cycle. Because intercourse hurts, they fear more pain and become anxious. And because they're anxious, they don't get aroused. When they're not aroused, they experience pain again, and so the cycle continues. Breaking this cycle means knowing how to relax fully, and having a supportive partner who's willing to do everything he can to maximise your arousal.

If you still experience pain on intercourse when you know you're fully aroused, then you should check with your GP to rule out any underlying gynaecological problem.

For some women, intercourse is blocked completely because their vaginal muscles go into involuntary spasm, a condition that professionals know as *vaginismus*. Even though she feels fully aroused, as soon as penetration is attempted, the woman feels as though the door's been locked and firmly bolted.

You can overcome vaginismus by very slowly and gradually stretching the vaginal muscles. When you're feeling fully relaxed, use some lubricant and start by trying to insert just the tip of your little finger. As that becomes comfortable, see if you can insert your forefinger. Take as much time as you need and gradually build until you can comfortably insert a finger, and then perhaps two. When you're ready, practise with your partner's finger. Reconditioning the muscles of the pelvic floor can take quite some time, but it can and does happen, so don't lose heart.

Examining male issues

Admitting to sexual problems can be particularly difficult for men, because the myth of male sexuality says that 'real' men are ready for sex 24/7. But like women, men do experience sexual problems, especially during stressful periods of their lives. One study found that 35 per cent of men regularly have problems with sexual functioning.

The following sections take you through some of the most common problems and how you can get past them.

A number of medical conditions can cause erection problems, the most common being diabetes, vascular or heart problems and neurological disorders. So if your problem's not improving, and especially if you have additional health concerns, ask your GP for a check-up.

Encountering erection difficulties

Most men experience erection problems at some stage in their lives. In fact, estimates are that up to 40 per cent of men experience problems before they're 40, and 70 per cent by the age of 70.

In most cases, psychological factors play a role. The most common psychological cause is anxiety. Most men don't have a problem shrugging off the occasional flop, but for others the experience can be deeply humiliating. Unfortunately, this creates anxiety, and anxiety is likely to cause more flops. So many men find themselves in a Catch 22.

The best way to cure erection problems is to develop a sense of humour and have a supportive, understanding partner. Other things to remember are:

- **Check your conditions:** Make sure that you're really in the mood for sex, emotionally as well as physically.
- **Do some pelvic floor exercises:** The sidebar 'Tightening up your sex life' has the lowdown.
- **Get sensual:** Make sure that you take time to enjoy and stimulate all of your body.
- **Relax:** It's an obvious suggestion, but essential.
- **Use fantasy:** Block out anxious thoughts by slipping into a favourite fantasy.

Chapter 7 explores these get-you-in-the-mood ideas in more depth. If these self-help techniques don't work, then consider seeing your GP to investigate one of the increasing number of medical options.

Experiencing ejaculation problems

The most common ejaculation problems are climaxing too quickly, too late or not at all.

Premature ejaculation

Researchers believe that this frustrating condition affects between 30 and 40 per cent of males. Most men climax more quickly at times of stress or after a long time without sex, but having little or no control most of the time can cause distress for both partners. Like erection problems, anxiety contributes to quick ejaculation. Researchers have also discovered that some men are born with a highly responsive central nervous system, which makes them quick reactors – excellent if you want to be a Formula One racing driver, but not so good in the bedroom.

Getting rid of anxiety is essential, so your first line of attack is stress relief and relaxation. The other thing you must do is make sure that you focus fully on your sensations. Contrary to what common sense may tell you, the last thing you should do is think about something else. Conjuring up images of the mother-in-law, or counting backwards, gives you less awareness of your sensations and consequently less control.

Your goal is to train your body to recognise and tolerate ever higher levels of sensation and for you to be able to adjust your stroke accordingly. To do this, you can try:

- **Exercising your pelvic floor:** Many men say they are able to delay ejaculation by 'squeezing' or 'pushing' their pelvic floor muscles (see the sidebar 'Tightening up your sex life' for the technique).

- **Stopping and starting:** This exercise helps you to recognise the point of inevitability. Start by stimulating yourself to the point just before ejaculation, then stop. Start again when the sensations have subsided. Repeat this three times. Gradually, you should find that the length of time before each stop is getting longer.

- **Changing strokes:** When you've gained more control with the stop-and-start technique, try changing your stroke to something less stimulating rather than stopping altogether. If you're having intercourse, also try changing position.

Delayed or absent ejaculation

This is a much less common problem but one that can be particularly difficult to understand. Sufferers of this condition do not conform to the myth that men struggle to control their urges. On the contrary, they find reaching orgasm very difficult, if not impossible. Partners often feel inadequate and blame themselves, which can put even more pressure on the man to perform, and just makes matters worse.

Usually, delayed or missing ejaculation is a psychological problem. Although your body may be ready to have sex, and you may think you're in the mood, something's blocking you. For some men, it's fear of losing control; for others, it's stress and anxiety; for others, it may be too much concern for their partners.

As with all sexual problems, your first line of attack is stress management and relaxation. Make sure that your relationship isn't harbouring any lingering problems and that you really do want to make love to this person. You can also try:

- ✔ **Changing strokes:** Practise with a variety of sensual and sexual strokes to ensure that you're getting maximum stimulation.

- ✔ **Being present:** Make sure that you're focusing on your sensations and not just waiting for orgasm.

- ✔ **Fantasising:** Slip into a favourite fantasy to block out negative thoughts and anxieties (Chapter 7 has more on fantasy).

- ✔ **Changing masturbation routines:** Penises can be creatures of habit, and if you've got into the pattern of always masturbating in a certain way, you may be struggling to emulate the sensations with your partner. Expand your masturbatory repertoire and gradually your body will discover how to respond to a wider variety of touch.

Tightening up your sex life

Guess what? Pelvic floor exercises aren't just for pregnant women, they're for everyone. Exercising your pelvic floor helps to increase blood flow to the genital area, making arousal quicker and strengthening muscles that make orgasm stronger.

To start off with, you need to be sure you have located your pelvic floor muscles. You can do this by stopping your flow of urine next time you go to the bathroom. The muscles you use to do this are your pelvic floor muscles.

Now, start by squeezing and releasing these muscles 15 times. Don't hold the contraction, just squeeze and release. Begin by doing one set of 15, twice a day. Try to concentrate on squeezing *only* your pelvic floor muscles, not your stomach and thighs. It will become easier

with practice. Do the exercises every day, gradually increasing the number until you can do 40 or 50 at a time. Build up slowly. When you are comfortable doing 40 or 50, you can vary the exercise by holding each contraction to the count of three before releasing. Again, build up slowly until you can achieve 40 or 50.

You can do these exercises anywhere, any time. No one needs to know you are doing them. Practise doing them sitting, standing and lying down. Most importantly, find a time when you remember to do them *every day*. This is an exercise for life! It may take up to six weeks for you to notice the benefits in your sex life, but you will feel them.

You can find out more about these muscles in *Sex For Dummies*.

Dealing with diminished desire

Psychosexual therapists say that the fastest-growing problem they see is reduced desire, or *libido* as it's also called. A growing number of people struggle with low desire, and many couples find that their desires are mismatched.

Sexual desire varies from person to person. And that desire changes over a person's lifetime, depending on her relationship and other circumstances in her life. But if you have a persistent problem with low libido or mismatched sex drives, this can cause issues in a relationship.

Boosting low libido

Going off sex for a few weeks during times of illness or stress, or after a significant life change such as a bereavement or job change, is perfectly normal. Similarly most women, and quite a few men, find that their desire changes when they've just had a baby.

All couples go through times when one partner (or both) experiences lower desire, and accepting these changes as part of the normal ebb and flow of a sexual relationship is important.

But if desire doesn't return when the original cause is long gone, this can put a strain on even the healthiest of relationships. Many couples experience feelings of guilt and rejection, and both partners can begin to doubt their sexuality and attractiveness. And going off sex can be particularly disturbing for men. The message from the media is that men always want sex, so when his doesn't happen, both partners can feel anxious and confused.

To overcome low desire, you first need to establish what's causing it:

- **Psychological:** Your mood affects your libido. Relationship problems, poor self-esteem and negative previous experiences are the most common culprits. Resolving your relationship difficulties and working on your self-esteem really help. You may feel able to do this alone, or you can consider seeing a counsellor or therapist for professional help. The Appendix contains details of organisations who can help you find a suitably trained therapist.

- **Physical reasons:** These include illness, stress or the side effects of medication. For these, time is the best healer. You may also find that boosting your arousal helps. In Chapter 7 you can find lots of advice and suggestions for turning up your sexual thermostat.

- **Sexual functioning problems:** For example, you may be having problems with erections or reaching orgasm, which cause you to lose desire as well. By addressing the other sexual problems within your relationship, you should find that your libido naturally returns.

Going on amber

When I'm working with couples with low desire, one common feature is that both partners fear making any sexual advance unless they have a 100 per cent guarantee of success. This means that they avoid any kind of physical or sensual connection for fear of giving out the wrong signals or being disappointed, but without this connection, sex is unlikely to occur in the first place.

An analogy that works for many couples is the traffic light system. When you're on red, you definitely don't want sex and therefore don't want to do anything sexual. When you're on green, you definitely do want sex and probably have no problem enjoying sex. But the vast majority of the time, your desire's on amber. In other words, the answer's not no or yes, it's maybe. Going on amber means agreeing that if the lights go red, you stop. But experience shows that in the vast majority of cases, the light goes green.

Adjusting mismatched sexual desire

Each couple has to work out between them how much sex is okay in their relationship. Few couples think they're having too much, but some occasions certainly occur when at least one partner feels that the amount is not enough.

No 'right' number of times exists to have sex. If you want sex every day and your partner wants it once a month, you're both perfectly normal. But you need to work together to find a compromise that both of you feel happy with.

Negotiating different sexual needs can be tricky, because emotions often run high when one person feels that the other's withholding and rejecting, and the other partner feels that her partner's demands are unreasonable. The first step to resolving the dispute is to accept that neither of you is in the wrong and that your differing needs don't reflect any kind of personality defect. When both of you can accept each other as different rather than wrong, you can cooperate with each other to find a solution.

Both partners need to take equal responsibility for creating a relaxed and sensual environment within the home, where sex is more likely to occur. To avoid any miscommunication, some couples agree sex-free days where they can feel free to get close with no expectations. Focusing on intimacy and sensuality can significantly increase the desire of the lower-desire partner. Going on amber (see the sidebar on this) can also significantly improve your chances.

Table 6-2 outlines a few more ideas for you to consider.

Table 6-2	Tips for Mismatched Couples
Low-Desire Partners Can	*High-Desire Partners Can*
Take responsibility for boosting your desire (Chapter 7 has lots of ideas)	Ensure that you maintain an intimate emotional and physical connection with your partner, regardless of whether it leads to sex
Talk to your partner about building intimacy and sensuality	Recognise when you need affection or attention rather than sex, and ask your partner to meet those needs
Don't avoid physical contact, but be clear that you're not necessarily saying you want sex	Find space for yourself to meet your sexual needs through masturbation
Minimise stress and tiredness (more in Chapter 7)	Share your feelings of frustration, but be sure not to sulk or become a bully
Consider providing sexual favours for your partner without wanting anything in return	Continue to work on any issues within the relationship that may be hindering your partner's desire for sex

Getting help for sexual addiction

Contrary to popular belief, sexual addiction actually has nothing to do with sexual desire. Men and women who are struggling with sexual addiction don't necessarily have high sex drives. Their libido may be the same as anyone else's, but their sexual behaviour feels compulsive.

Sexual addiction can be defined as any sexual activity that feels out of control. That activity may be compulsive masturbation, looking at porn, sex with a partner, sex with strangers and so on. The thing that makes it an addiction is the fact that the person feels compelled to seek out and engage in her chosen sexual behaviour, in spite of the problems it may cause in her personal, social and work life.

If either you or your partner is engaging in sexual activities that are causing you a problem, but you feel unable to stop, then the first step is to acknowledge that this is a real problem. Most addicts need the support of professional help in order to overcome their problem and begin to enjoy a healthy sexual lifestyle that they feel good about. You can find help from ATSAC (the Association for the Treatment of Sex Addiction and Compulsivity) at www. sexaddictionandcompulsivity.co.uk.

Chapter 7

Turning Up the Sexual Thermostat

- -

In This Chapter

▶ Increasing your desire

▶ Optimising your opportunities for sex

▶ Discovering ways to add interest and excitement

- -

*T*his chapter's for those of you who want to revitalise your sexual relationship and get a bit more oomph behind your engine. That may be because you're struggling with low libido, because your sex life has got into a rut or just because you want to rev up the passion. The chapter offers a wealth of tips on creating the mood, breaking out of tired, boring habits and injecting more spice into your sex life.

A good sex life can only happen when you take responsibility for it and commit as a couple to creating and maintaining an environment where sex is a natural extension of a loving relationship. To enjoy good sex, you need to feel good about yourself, and relaxed and comfortable with your partner, and you need to make time to get in touch with your sensuality.

Creating a Positive Sexual Environment

The first step towards improving your sex life is to ensure that you're living in an environment that encourages your sexual feelings to blossom and flow. That environment includes not only your physical surroundings, but your emotional and psychological space as well.

A positive sexual environment's a place where you feel confident to be the sexual person you are and to express your needs and desires with your partner. It's also a place that provides the safety and security you require to stretch gently beyond your comfort zones and experiment.

Identifying your conditions for good sex

Making sex sexier often means taking a few risks. And before you can take risks, you have to make sure that the conditions are right. Everyone has different sexual needs. And when you're getting those needs met, you can look forward to a sex life that's satisfying, fulfilling and exciting. Sexual needs fall into three categories:

- ✓ **Emotional needs:** For sex to be good, you have to feel good. Anxiety, depression, sadness, anger or any negative emotion can get in the way of you getting in the mood and enjoying a sexual experience. Most people also need their heads to be in the right place. If you're preoccupied with work or with other responsibilities around the home or to children, sex can either be the last thing on your mind or feel like another chore to get through.

- ✓ **Relationship needs:** Your greatest sexual needs are usually to do with your partner. Feeling safe with your sexual partner means knowing that he accepts you, that he's not judging your body or your performance. And you need to know that your partner's enjoying the sexual experience as much as you are. If your relationship has tensions or unresolved issues, you need to sort these out before you get into the bedroom. Or at least you need to know that the two of you are equally committed to working through your problems.

- ✓ **Physical needs:** Your general physical wellbeing's an important consideration. For example, most people need to feel reasonably relaxed and awake in order to enjoy sex, and they need to feel in good health. The environment must also meet your physical needs. For example, you may need to be in a warm, comfortable room, or to have soft lighting and quiet. Some couples have to know that they can't be disturbed or overheard. And people's physical needs often change over the vyears. The back of the car might have been okay in the early days, or even added extra excitement, but if your back's playing up or you're less confident about your body than you used to be, you may want a more sensitive and salubrious environment.

Think back to two occasions when you had really great sex. Now think back to the last two sexual experiences that were disappointing. Comparing those positive and negative sexual experiences, what was different? Think about the emotional factors, how relaxed were you? Were any other things going on in your life at that time? Think also about physical things that were different, for example the place or the time of day. Finally, think about whether you felt differently towards your partner on those occasions. Now use that information to begin to build your personal list of sexual needs.

Before you start any sexual experience, ask yourself the following questions:

✔ Am I feeling basically relaxed and happy with myself?

✔ Am I confident that my partner's happy and relaxed?

✔ Do I feel our relationship's in a good enough place?

✔ Am I physically comfortable?

Maintaining a sexual connection

Moving from being partners to lovers can sometimes seem like a big step. You've worked all day, you're raising a family and you're running a home. Together you may be a great team, but at the end of the day, connecting as lovers feels a bit out of place. Some couples describe themselves as being really good friends, but they don't seem to see each other sexually any more. This is often because they've lost their sexual connection and their relationship's become more functional.

Creating and maintaining a sexual connection can help you to shift into lover mode quickly and seamlessly. Rather than leaving your sexuality in the bedroom, you make it something that's open and shared between you. When both of you can communicate comfortably about your sexual and erotic feelings at any time of day, your whole life together becomes a form of foreplay.

Keeping a sexual connection is in part about the romance and intimacy I discuss in Chapter 5, but it's also about the words, looks and caresses that reinforce the sexual relationship that you share. Here are a few examples of how you can make a sexual connection within your relationship:

✔ Play footsie under the dinner table or when you're out at the pub or a restaurant.

✔ Send saucy text messages during the day.

✔ Say 'I fancy you,' especially when it's unexpected, or pay a compliment that's sexually loaded, such as 'Your bum looks great in that.'

✔ Be bolder with affection, for example a pat on the bottom or a caress of the breast, or slip your hand in your partner's trouser pocket and see what you can find.

✔ Speak with your eyes – a lingering look at breasts or bottom or a good old-fashioned wink – still profoundly intimate and meaningful.

Couples who maintain a sexual connection are keeping the pilot light of passion alight, ready to turn up at the slightest touch. How you choose to maintain a sexual connection depends on your personality and on your circumstances. But whatever you choose to do, it should be something that lets your partner know you love him and desire him.

Creating sensual space

The physical space you inhabit can have a huge impact on how you feel. The colour of the walls, the lighting, the amount of clutter and the size of the pile of ironing all affect how relaxed and sensual you feel.

Ensuring your home is a sensual space is another great and simple way of improving your sex life. Your goal is to create a sensual space that allows you to enjoy all your senses. When creating your sensual space, consider how it appeals to each sense in turn:

- ✔ **Sight:** Think about the lighting you have. Soft lighting's more flattering if you've got a less than perfect body (who hasn't?), and it also helps to create a relaxing and calming mood. Candlelight can be particularly romantic and can throw some interesting and absorbing shadows across a room. Think about colour as well. What colours excite and inspire you? Change your bed linen or invest in a big red or leopard-print throw to get your pulse racing.

- ✔ **Sound:** Music can often help couples to get in the mood for intimacy. Discover what kinds of beats get you into what kinds of emotional states. For example, do some tunes make you more chatty and playful with your partner, or do some melodies soothe and relax you? Perhaps particular beats make you feel sexy or bring back fond memories of the past.

- ✔ **Smell:** The sense of smell is powerfully evocative and one that you can easily stimulate. Get into the habit of wearing your partner's favourite scent or spray it around the room. Or invest in an aromatherapy burner and add the essential oil to suit your mood. Choose lavender for relaxation, ylang ylang for sensuality, bergamot if you want to be uplifted and enlivened, chamomile to relieve stress and sandalwood to boost your sexual energy.

- ✔ **Taste:** The link between food and sex has been around for centuries. Your tongue's packed with nerve endings. As well as tasting food, your tongue also enjoys the sensual texture and feel of it in your mouth. A few well-chosen nibbles to tantalise the taste buds on a quiet night in can lead to all sorts of shared sensual pleasures.

✔ **Touch:** Your skin's the biggest sensory organ you have, yet many people are guilty of ignoring the intricate pleasures of the flesh. Some well-placed textures around the home can help you to get back in touch with touch. Try fur, silk, feathers, satin, rubber, sheepskin, lace – whatever tickles your fancy. Don't save nice lingerie for special occasions, wear it every day and enjoy the sensual feel against your skin.

Next time you have a bath, spend time really focusing on the physical sensations of your skin. Feel the warmth and the texture of the water, and notice how different it feels on different parts of your body. When you take time to really, really focus on your senses, your sensory awareness increases. So the lightest touch that may previously have left you cold can send shivers of delight down your spine.

Putting Sex on Your 'To Do' List

Sex is a great idea and something that lots of couples really enjoy. The problem's getting around to doing 'it'. People have so much to fit in to the average day that often they're too exhausted by the time they fall into bed at night. In fact, many people say they're in the mood for sex all day and looking forward to it, but as soon as the big hand hits ten o'clock, their libido flies out the window.

If you want to improve your sex life, you have to make it a priority in your busy schedule – your individual schedule and your couple schedule. You need to find ways of keeping sex at the forefront of your mind (not a problem for some, I know) and also keeping it high on your list of things to do as a couple.

Taking responsibility for sex

One of the biggest mistakes that people, especially women, make is thinking that their partner's responsible for their sexual desire. When you first got together, the mere sight of each other may have been enough to drive you into a frenzy of passionate yearning, but unfortunately this wonderful response inevitably wears off. Regardless of how drop-dead gorgeous the two of you may be, attraction alone is never enough to sustain libido. When the lust diminishes, some people worry that they don't fancy their partners any more. But this is rarely true.

Changes in the strength of desire, especially female desire, happen in all long-term relationships. So when desire wanes, you have to take responsibility for making yourself sexually aware, sexually alert and sexually responsive. Creating intimacy takes two of you. Your partner can help to create the environment, but particularly in long-term relationships, you have to be responsible for your own desire.

One of the best ways of stoking your fire is by getting into sensuality (see 'Creating sensual space', earlier in this chapter). Assuming that you're feeling reasonably relaxed both physically and mentally, and your mind isn't stressed and preoccupied with urgent stuff, next you can turn your thinking towards sex.

Here are some ways to get your brain into gear:

- **Get in the mood by conjuring up sexual memories:** Reflect back to your top three sexual encounters. That may be a long, lingering evening when you made love into the early hours, a particularly saucy session when you were on holiday, or maybe an impromptu grope in the office stationery cupboard. Whatever the occasion, allow your memory to recreate the scene in as much detail as possible. Remember the physical sensations of arousal and yearning, the scent in the air, how you felt being touched and touching. And finally, remember the feelings of release and relief as the passion ebbed from your body. Now put those memories in a jar and put them on a shelf in your mind where you can find them whenever you need them. Next time you're in the bath or you're waiting for your lover to come to bed, take the jar from the shelf, open it and enjoy the encounters all over again. You can even write down your memories, creating your very own erotic true story.

- **Inspire erotic thoughts:** The information you put into your brain directly affects your thoughts. So if you spend all your free time reading about fishing and surround yourself with pictures of trout, fishing is likely to occupy a lot of your grey matter. But if you spend time reading about sex and looking at sensual images, you find your thoughts drifting to sex on a much more regular basis. Try reading a sexy book at bedtime, investing in a nude (or rude) sculpture, photo or painting for the house, or drinking your tea from a raunchy mug – whatever takes your fancy. 'Discovering erotica', later in this chapter, contains other ideas.

The more you bring sex to the forefront of your mind, the easier you find slipping from the practicalities of being a couple to the pleasures of being lovers. Changing your thinking habits takes time and effort, but it's more than worth the trouble.

Negotiating the rituals of initiation

Once you have a good sexual connection and you're feeling sensual and in the mood for luuurve, you've got to make it happen.

Many couples slip into the habit of leaving sex to happen by chance. Or they hope that the other partner takes the initiative when his drive's high enough. But all too often, this approach means that although both of you may be in the mood, neither of you makes an approach, because you're left trying to guess the other's feelings. You need to find a way to gauge your partner's willingness for sex. Check out the traffic light system in Chapter 6.

The style of approach varies from couple to couple and depends on the mood you're in and the type of sex you're hoping to enjoy. Sometimes you may choose a subtle approach, while on other occasions you may opt to be more daring. Changing your approach can keep your sex life interesting.

Here are some different styles of initiation that you can try:

- ✔ **Romantic and tender:** This advance may start with a candlelit dinner, or massage, or foot rub, or anything that says 'I love you'. That can just mean doing the washing up and accompanying a romantic kiss with 'Let's have an early night.'

- ✔ **Brazen and bold:** No messing around, just straight to the point. You say something like 'Fancy a shag, darling?' or if that's too abrupt, perhaps simply 'You're sexy, I want you.' If you want to avoid words, just slip your hand straight to your partner's sexual hot button.

- ✔ **Urgent and frenzied:** Start with the usual hug and kiss, but then quickly increase the tempo to a snog and wandering hands.

- ✔ **Daring and erotic:** This takes guts, but if the timing's right it can be fantastic. Let your partner find you sexily dressed or naked and ready for action. Or if you're brave enough, perform a seductive strip.

Dealing with 'Not tonight, dear'

Even the best approaches sometimes get no for an answer. If you say no respectfully and lovingly, then apart from disappointment, both of you should be okay with this.

If you're the one saying no, try to give an explanation as well, and perhaps suggest another time. Sexual rejection can be painful if you don't offer a reason, and some partners can take it much more personally than necessary. Explain that you love your partner and still find him sexually attractive, but because of 'xyz' you're not in the mood today. Your partner may not be able to turn off his sexual desire instantly, so you may need to give him some personal space to relieve himself or, if you wish, lend him a helping hand.

If you're the one who's turned down, try not to sulk, get angry or whinge about it. In spite of how rejected or frustrated you may feel, remember that your reaction's going have a direct impact on future initiations. If you feel you're being rejected on a regular basis and this is becoming a problem for you, arrange a time to sit down and talk to your partner about how you can increase your sexual frequency.

Making time for sex

Making time for sex takes a bit of planning, especially if you have busy schedules or you have children. Some people hate the idea of putting sex in their diaries because they believe in the myth that sex should always be spontaneous. This is a particularly dangerous myth for busy couples, who soon find that they never have time to be spontaneous.

Planning sex doesn't make that sex less enjoyable – in fact, it can do the very opposite. When you plan something in advance, you build anticipation. And anticipation can increase arousal. Holidays are no less fun because you plan ahead and look forward to them.

If you've booked a sex date in your diary, you can make sure you feel at your sexiest. Decide what to wear, take a relaxing bath or shower first or slip into some erotica. You can also spend days teasing each other with what you've got planned when the time comes.

A particular problem for many couples is children. Whether you have a newborn baby in the house, toddlers, teenagers or all three, maintaining a regular sex life can seem impossible. But if you and your partner can agree to become more creative and even more determined, then you can manage it. Here are some ideas that can help:

  ✔ **Babies:** Sex after childbirth is tough. As wonderful as your bundle of joy may be, avoiding the exhaustion that goes with caring for the needs of a newborn 24/7 is difficult. In fact, 80 per cent of new mothers report lowered desire in the first months. Chapter 13 has more advice to help new parents.

✔ **Toddlers:** Toddlers are pretty demanding, so finding time for sex may be hard. You need to develop a balance between planned sexual marathons and passionate quickies. If at all possible, try to ship your toddler off to Granny or another responsible adult so that you can have a whole afternoon, evening or even night of love making. When that's not possible, snuggle up after your toddler goes to bed (but before you do chores or watch TV and discover that bedtime's arrived and you're too tired). And become experts at recognising and grabbing opportunities for a quickie. This may include nap times or when your little angel is transfixed by a new DVD. Whenever you can safely slip away for 15 minutes or so, grab your chance.

✔ **Teenagers:** The good thing about growing teenagers is that they begin to go out more regularly. If you've got more than one child, try to get their out-of-school activities coordinated. The hour when they're at youth club is your hour to jump into bed. Sleepovers are also an excellent opportunity for a whole night of uninterrupted passion, so grab every chance you can to ship them out to their friends. And if you struggle to feel comfortable having sex now that your kids are staying up later, try to maintain your sexual privacy, for example by putting a lock on your bedroom door. Set a good model for children, adopting an attitude that says sex is natural, healthy, enjoyable and private.

Minimising stress and tiredness

In spite of a growing range of labour-saving devices and leisure activities, people's lives are becoming busier and busier. And for many people, all that business leads to stress. Your mind may be constantly full of all the things you need to do and the people you've got to please.

When you're stressed, you may find enjoying any sex difficult, let alone feel enthusiastic about turning up the thermostat. Not only does stress leave you feeling physically drained and exhausted, but it can also distract your mind with bothersome thoughts and worries.

Some people use sex as a positive activity to reduce stress. They find that losing themselves in sex helps them to unwind and switch off from a busy day. But for others, stress is a passion wrecker. If you and your partner have different views of stress and sex, you may struggle when life gets busy. Recognising that nothing's right or wrong can help you to respect your differences and support each other in finding ways to minimise stress for both of you.

If you're tired and struggling with stress but you still want to have an active and fulfilling sex life, start saying no to other tasks more often. Making sex a priority in your life means putting boundaries around your time and deciding that other things have to wait. If you want to increase both the quality and quantity of your sexual experiences, you need to make a mutual commitment that sex is important to you as a couple and therefore deserves to be high on your list of things to do.

Beating Bedroom Boredom

Sex can become boring if you do the same things all the time. No matter how erotic or fantastic your activities may be, familiarity and routine can soon make them seem rather dull.

The great news is that probably thousands of different ways exist of having sex, so you need never run out of new things to do. And if you do manage to work your way through the complete A–Z, you can go back to the beginning and start all over again, secure in the knowledge that you've probably forgotten most of it.

Beating bedroom boredom starts by identifying that sex is becoming routine and then making a mutual decision to spice things up.

Identifying the boredom traps

Many couples slip into boring old habits that take the excitement out of sex. If you recognise any of the following potential problem areas, make time to talk to your partner about how you can break away from boredom:

- **The same come-on:** This is when your partner says the same old phrase such as 'Fancy an early night?' or gives you that wink and a smile. When you feel the hand wandering over to your side of the bed, do you think 'Great' or 'Here we go again'? If the latter, the time's come to talk about changing your initiation moves.

- **The same time:** Sex has become a routine that happens at the same time. No one says anything, but at bedtime on Friday night, sex is inevitable. Many couples fall into this pattern, and knowing that you have a scheduled slot for sex can be nice, but make sure you change the time occasionally. Don't forget the power of the quickie: when you're getting ready to go out in the evening, in the bathroom in the morning, while the baby's having a snooze.

✔ **The same place:** Sex doesn't always have to happen in bed, but unfortunately this is another one of those routines that many couples slip into. Even when you've mastered a range of come-ons and regularly enjoy a quickie, you still head up the wooden hill to the bedroom. A great way to spice up your sex life is to change the scenery. Doing so probably also makes you more adventurous with sexual positions. Remember the shower, the bath, the sofa, in front of the fire, up against a door, over the kitchen table, on a chair. Or al fresco – in your own back garden, or go for a walk, take the travel rug and see where your passion takes you (note – this is illegal if you get caught!).

✔ **The same technique:** Using the same stimulation technique may be functional, in as much as it works, but this can become less and less erotic. Even if your tried-and-tested techniques always result in orgasm, do remember that you can have great orgasms and mundane ones. To stop sex becoming functional, change and adapt your touching techniques and your sexual positions.

Discovering erotica

Whether something's erotic or pornographic is purely a matter of taste. Say 'erotica' to most people and they automatically think of top-shelf magazines and videos with subtle titles like *Busty Blonde Blowjobs*. But the range of erotica nowadays is much, much wider. Anything you read or see that turns you on is erotic. Erotic doesn't even have to include naked bodies; in fact, many people find the allure of suggestion far more arousing than blatant genitals.

Many people enjoy reading or looking at images during masturbation, and others like to read things alone to get them in the mood for their partners. But many couples also enjoy sharing erotica together.

If you're new to erotica, start with something light that both of you are comfortable with and then build up as, when and if you want to.

Here are some ideas of erotica that can add some zing to your sex life:

✔ **Erotic literature:** A huge range of erotic literature is on the market. Your local bookshop almost certainly has plenty of copies on the shelves, or shop online if you want more time to browse. Reading erotica tends to appeal to people who prefer to use their imagination to conjure up the images or who find that prescribed images get in the way of them focusing on their own arousal.

- ✔ **Magazines:** Magazines are still one of the most easily accessible forms of erotic material, and the range is vast and ever growing – starting with magazines aimed at women and men like *Scarlet* or *Loaded*, to the mags you find on the top shelf of most supermarkets. If you want something more risqué, you can almost certainly find titles at a good-sized newsagent or shop, or you can subscribe online.

- ✔ **Art:** Erotic art has been around for centuries. Ever since man (or woman) began drawing, they've been drawing the naked form in compromising positions! Some art is subtle and discreet, some is funny and humorous, some is set in a historic context, and some is simply beautiful to look at. You can choose from black-and-white or colour illustrations, photography, comic-book styles and sculpture. Probably the best place to begin to explore what's available is on the net.

- ✔ **Film:** Many couples enjoy watching an erotic film together. Again, the choice is vast. Just going down to your local rental shop can provide you with a huge range to choose from. You may fancy a comedy romp or something more romantic, erotic thrillers and dramas, or movies specifically made to tease. If you find yourselves enjoying adult-only movies and running out of choices at your local store, the Internet provides opportunities to rent or buy online.

Exploring fantasies

Erotic fantasies seem to be a universal part of the human sexual experience. They've been around for centuries; young or old, rich or poor, male or female, everyone seems to fantasise about the same sorts of things. For some people, fantasies are simply perfected memories of previous experiences, while for others they're bold leaps of the imagination.

A rich fantasy life can have many benefits for a sexual relationship. Fantasy can add novelty to a sex life that's beginning to lose its sparkle, it can provide an arena to practise things alone before trying them with a partner and it can be a helpful way of blocking out anxious thoughts.

Understanding fantasies

Some people feel uncomfortable with their fantasies, especially those they know they may never enjoy in reality. Understanding why you find the things you fantasise about exciting can help you to feel more comfortable.

Some people are very aware of the source of their fantasies. A fantasy may relate to something a person has seen on TV, in a magazine or in a book. For others, the fantasies that they enjoy indulging in are based on particular memories of erotic encounters. But some fantasies seem to come from nowhere, perhaps from deep within the unconscious mind.

Although some fantasies are hard to understand, many follow common themes:

- ✔ **Domination during sex:** These fantasies are often about enjoying the freedom of not having to take any responsibility or give anything in return.

- ✔ **Sex with a stranger:** You have the opportunity to enjoy the physical encounter with no emotional constraints.

- ✔ **Adventurous sex:** Sex with an added element of adventure, such as being outside or with props, allows you to enjoy risk with no potential consequences.

How you feel about your sexual fantasies depends largely on your sexual attitudes, and also your sexual tastes. If you feel worried about the content of your fantasies, invest some time in researching the psychology of fantasies (you can find info online or in books) so that you can put your mind at rest.

Talking about your fantasies

Sharing a sexual fantasy involves a great degree of trust, particularly because once you've told the fantasy, you can't untell it. If you and your partner have similar fantasies, then sharing them is likely to be a rewarding and enriching experience. Both of you are likely to feel more comfortable with your fantasy lives and consequently you may expand your repertoire to include even more fantasies.

Fantasies are extremely personal, and disclosing them, especially to someone you care for, involves risks. Sharing fantasies can be liberating, but only if your partner accepts them. If you think you want to share your fantasies, talk to your partner first about the general theme before proceeding with caution.

Acting out fantasies

Some people want to act out their fantasies, while others prefer to keep them to themselves, knowing that they may not enjoy the reality. Some may never have the opportunity to experience their fantasies in real life. This may be because of their own inhibitions or their partners', or simply because they're not physically able to or their celebrity idol isn't available. And many fantasies, like making love on a Caribbean beach or on the deck of your own private yacht, aren't going to happen, because you simply can't afford them.

Deciding whether to act out a fantasy is a very personal thing with no rights or wrongs. If you do want to act out a fantasy, then obviously your partner needs to be into the idea as well.

Consider how you may feel if the fantasy doesn't live up to your expectations. The reason fantasies are so sexually arousing is because they're always perfect. Unfortunately, reality rarely is. Some people regret trying to act out their fantasies, because that spoils them. The dream isn't as good as they hope and the fantasy loses its sparkle.

Whatever you choose to do with your fantasies, remember that ultimately, great sex is also about intimacy. The only good reason for sharing or acting out your fantasies is to enrich your relationship.

Trying adult toys

The sex toy market is growing rapidly. In fact, it's one of the fastest-moving areas of the current economy. More and more couples enjoy adding a few accessories to their sex lives to give them added excitement and stimulation.

Here are just a few of the sex toys available:

- ✔ **Novelty items:** There's a wide variety of novel sex items on the market that are bound to satisfy everyone's needs, from edible toys to various shapes of candles and 'I Love Sex' jewellery. Or invest in your very own erotic book, personalised for you as a couple (look online for more info).

- ✔ **Lubes and lotions:** Not only is good lubrication essential to avoid painful sex, it can also increase the sensual experience of touch. As well as the standard lubes, you can now buy warming or tingling varieties, which add an extra level of sensation. Many lubes also double up as massage lotion, so you don't have to reach for an extra bottle if things hot up. And often the products are designed to taste good as well as feel great. Most supermarkets and large chemists stock a good range or you can buy online.

- ✔ **Sensual massagers and vibrators:** Vibrating stimulators are by far the most popular and most common sex toy on the market. In fact, if you talk about sex toys, vibrators are probably the first thing that comes to mind. Whatever you choose, make sure it's good quality and from a reputable company. And generally speaking, the more money you're willing to invest, the better the quality and the quieter the motor.

The Internet is an excellent place to buy sex toys, especially if you feel awkward in a shop.

Playing grown-up games

A lot of adults have a serious problem with play. Their parents may have told them to grow up and may have frowned on them being silly, so they associate playfulness with something immature. Others feel that playing is about becoming more child-like and vulnerable, and they worry about letting their hair down.

Being playful together is a great way of injecting more oooomph into your sex life. As well as being fun, it can also increase feelings of trust and intimacy. Here are a few ideas for playful adult games:

- **Sex up your normal daily routines:** For example, do any chore in the nude. That could be your accounts, the housework or cooking the evening meal, although you may need to be extra vigilant with the last one!

- **Add sexy twists to old favourites**: For example, play saucy hide and seek. You hide an object somewhere around the house, and attached to it are details of a sexual favour that you perform if your partner finds the object. Or use strip poker rules when playing any board game.

- **Buy a blindfold:** Losing the sense of sight often heightens other senses, so blindfolding your partner and then teasing his body with different textures can be particularly exciting. Touch with items that give a range of sensations, or a few saucy objects with sexual connotations, and use parts of your body as well.

- **Play dice:** You can get hours of fun from a pair of dice. You can write a list of sexual activities that relate to certain throw combinations. For example, rolling a 3 may be a kiss, a 4 may be a fondle and a 9 may be sex. You may want to reserve a double 6 for something really special. Alternatively, you can assign 1 to 6 on one die with different body parts and 1 to 6 on the other with different types of touch. Roll the dice and follow the instructions.

- **Invest in a commercial sex game:** Many games on the market are specifically aimed at couples. Look online or visit your high street adult shop.

- **Play fights:** These aren't just for kids. Getting your adrenalin going with a friendly tussle not only gets your heart beating faster but also leaves your body more responsive and easily aroused.

✔ **Water fun:** People have been having fun with water in many different ways for many years. And that goes for lovers too. Lathering each other up in the bath or shower can give endless pleasure. The silky sensation of water and bath oils can make the skin feel beautifully sensual. Do spend some time rinsing each other down with the shower head. If your shower has a pulse function, you may find this particularly invigorating!

✔ **Dressing up:** Many men and women enjoy the sensual touch of satin, silk, lace or leather next to their skin, and a huge range of lingerie is available for both sexes to enjoy. Whether you prefer pretty, sophisticated or raunchy, you're bound to find something you can feel comfortable in.

✔ **Role play:** You may fancy a game of doctors and nurses, chambermaid, serving wench or stripper. The clothes may not stay on for long – or you can enjoy working your way around them.

An intimate and exciting sex life can keep a couple relationship alive and fulfilling. And although sex can sometimes begin to feel routine in a long-term relationship, you have endless ways of turning up your sexual thermostat. With commitment, communication and a little bit of inspiration, you can look forward to a lifetime of great sex together.

Part III
Improving Communication and Resolving Conflict

'Isn't it time we started to talk to each other again, Barbara?'

In this part . . .

The bedrock of any successful relationship is good communication. When you can express your thoughts and feelings with each other you not only build intimacy, but you also avoid misunderstandings and create bridges. Even the happiest of couples disagree with each other sometimes, though, and when that happens it's those with good conflict resolution skills who grow closer rather than farther apart.

The first chapter in this Part establishes the rules of effective communication, with strategies and advice on becoming a better talker and an even better listener. I then move on to how you can resolve the inevitable fall-outs in your relationship in ways that leave both of you feeling the winner. And if you're one of the many couples who find themselves trapped in a cycle of never-ending arguments, I help you to identify what's going on underneath – and to break the cycle for good.

Chapter 8

Establishing the Rules of Effective Communication

Effective communication's the backbone of any successful relationship. As well as easing day-to-day living, communication allows you to overcome differences and deepen intimacy.

When you can acknowledge your thoughts and feelings and share them with your partner, and when you are open to hear your partner's thoughts and feelings and ensure that she knows you've heard them, you can enter into each other's worlds and see life through each other's eyes. As you do this, you grow in understanding of one another, and your relationship improves.

This chapter looks at the basic rules of effective communication. I help you get honest about your communication style – looking at how you communicate and how you discover how to do so. And then I move on to explore how you can optimise your conversations to ensure that both you and your partner feel heard and valued.

Unpicking Your Communication Style

How you communicate with your partner today is based on the skills you've developed over your lifetime. You begin your education with parents and within a family home, and then practise those skills in the school playground with playmates. Over those years, you're likely to pick up some good habits but also some bad ones which are most often challenged when you enter your first couple relationship.

Unfortunately, you don't always know which habits are good and which ones are bad, and you may clumsily continue through life wondering why people misunderstand you so often. Understanding the origin of your individual style is the first step in improving your communication skills.

Realising what Mum and Dad taught you

Your lessons in communication start before you've even muttered a single word of your own. As a little baby in your mother's arms, you instinctively know how to communicate your needs, and you discover how your mother responds. As you grow into a toddler and begin to develop a language of your own, you practise many different ways of expressing yourself and start making unconscious decisions about what's most effective.

Beneath the cute exterior of any toddler is a little person who's determined to get her needs met. If using words doesn't work, she may deploy other less direct methods such as sulking, whining, throwing a tantrum, crying, becoming anxious, being ill or being charming. If she never gets her needs met, a child may give up and become silent and withdrawn, or find ways of meeting her needs independently.

Think back to an occasion in your childhood when you can remember not getting what you wanted. That may be a toy or food item you didn't get, not being allowed out to play or perhaps being forced to go somewhere you didn't want to go. Now see whether you can remember what techniques you used to get your own way and also how your parents responded. Now the really hard question: do you ever use these same methods now to persuade your partner around to your viewpoint?

Family dynamics also play a critical role in what you know about communication. Each family has its own individual style, one that works to a lesser or greater degree. You may have adopted the same style as your family or you may have made a deliberate attempt to do something opposite. Either way, your family style affects how you communicate today, and if it's very different from your partner's family style, you may find yourselves running into difficulties.

Look at the following list of common family styles and see whether any of them ring a bell for you. Perhaps you can find yourself in a combination of two or three. If your partner's willing, ask her to see whether she recognises any of the family styles for herself, and talk about the impact this may have on your couple conversation style.

✔ **The chatty family:** In these families, conversation's free and plentiful, but mostly focused around the practicalities of living and information updates. Everyone in the home is aware of what the others are doing, but they hide difficult feelings or gloss them over with practical solutions. They openly express differences of opinion and often diffuse them with superficial platitudes, but they avoid deeper needs.

✔ **The quiet family:** The quiet family don't talk very much at all. Home is a tranquil place that they keep free of conflict and difficulties, because no one really knows each other well enough to say anything. Members of this family may be very good communicators, but intimate conversation happens only with friends to ensure that the home remains safe and peaceful.

✔ **The reserved family:** Thoughts and feelings are shared on a 'need to know' basis only. They see open discussion of difficult or painful subjects as inappropriate unless they have a very clear reason for doing so. This family may be quite judgemental of people whom they perceive 'let it all out' and have no conversational boundaries.

✔ **The sensitive family:** This family lives by the motto 'If you can't say something nice, say nothing at all.' Although talking about personal views and emotions is okay, saying something that may be hurtful is never okay. On the surface, the home is calm and ordered, but resentments are often bubbling beneath the surface.

✔ **The upfront family:** What you see is what you get with this family. No topic's out of bounds, and if you're not happy about something or disagree with someone, you can voice your feelings openly and directly. Tact and diplomacy are often missing in this family, as members may speak out before thinking through the impact on others.

✔ **The hot-blooded family:** The hot-blooded family are the best at showing and sharing emotion, and no one ever has to doubt how the others feel. All members feel completely natural expressing anger, sadness, disappointment and anxiety openly. They relate to each other through emotion, and once the emotion subsides, the communication stops, leaving many differences unresolved.

✔ **The light-hearted family:** To the outsider, this is the most attractive family. They can talk about anything and express their feelings, but with one condition: everything must remain light hearted and optimistic. They hide hurtful comments and challenges behind humorous sarcasm and turn tragedies into a comical farce. Beneath the happy veneer of these families is often a huge amount of sadness and/or anger that no one dares acknowledge.

Whatever your childhood family dynamic, once you've recognised it, you can decide whether the habits you picked up are helpful to your current relationship or whether they get in the way. If the latter, you can begin to make some positive decisions to develop new habits to make your communication more effective.

Recognising the power of previous relationships

If your current relationship's the most significant one you've been in, then this section may not be relevant to you. But if you've been in another long-term relationship, consider whether you picked up some negative messages or habits that are affecting your current relationship.

When you enter into a couple relationship, you find that previous messages are either confirmed or disproved and you create a new communication dynamic that may be positive, negative or even totally destructive. When a relationship ends and you go into a new relationship, you have the opportunity to start all over again, but unfortunately some of the messages from your last relationship may be so deeply ingrained that you don't even know they exist.

When you enter a new relationship, don't assume that your current partner talks or listens in the same way as an ex did. All couple communications have both good and bad points, and as a couple you must commit to discovering each other's communication styles and developing a new dynamic of your own.

CASE STUDY

Seeing where you're both coming from

Simon and Nicole were both divorcees who'd been together for eight years. When they came for counselling, the fact that they hadn't yet developed a communication dynamic of their own quickly became apparent. They often argued about the assumptions they each made. Simon's ex came from a reserved family, and he knew not to expect communication on anything of a personal nature. He unconsciously assumed that Nicole was the same, so rarely raised difficult topics. Nicole was from a hot-blooded family and so was her ex, so she was used to talking openly and expressing emotions freely. When Simon didn't bring subjects up or responded coolly, she interpreted this as not caring. As they began to talk about their differences, they gained more insight into one another's perspectives and agreed new rules for communication.

Leaving baggage where it belongs

Leaving history in the past is often much simpler than it sounds. Negative messages from childhood about your own and others' communication skills are often reinforced in early relationships, because you may unconsciously choose a partner who fits your assumptions. You end up with unquestioned assumptions about other people's communication abilities but also labels about your own style.

Recognising these assumptions and labels gives you the power to rewrite them and to create a new dynamic for your relationship, rather than living within the prison of the past.

Take a look at the list of words below and tick those that you think best describe your conversation style. Then tick the words that best describe your partner's conversation style. When you've finished, ask your partner to do the same and compare answers.

quiet	reserved	aggressive	sarcastic	direct
assertive	nagging	energetic	charming	sensitive
open	intense	superficial	friendly	awkward
confrontational	demanding	attentive	distracted	hesitant
complaining	calming	disinterested	interested	manipulative
distant	dramatic	emotional	impatient	

Whatever your communication style was in the past, and whatever negative messages you may have received about yourself or others, you're not too late to change or to discover new, positive ways to communicate together.

Identifying common blocks to communication

You may not be aware of it but you have a list of techniques that you use to block conversation when you're tired, not in the mood, uncomfortable or desperately looking for a way to avoid an argument. Communication blocks are your way of stopping a conversation dead in its tracks or changing the direction. They're not necessarily confrontational, although they may cause an argument, but they're your subtle way of taking control. Some of these techniques you know very well and may use deliberately, others may be unconscious strategies that you employ – habits that are difficult to break.

Although communication blocks are natural, they're never healthy. If you don't want to talk, then you're always better to be open and ask for a rain check, rather than sabotaging the conversation (see 'Minimising distractions', later in this chapter).

Check out this list of common blocks to communication, and see which ring a bell for you:

- **Advising:** Rather than listening to the full story or showing empathy, you go straight to finding a solution to the problem so that you can get on with the rest of your evening.

- **Assuming:** Similar to expecting mind reading, but now you're the one who thinks you're gifted with telepathy. Rather than asking your partner to explain something, you assume that you know what she thinks and feel so you don't require any further conversation.

- **Belittling:** Often with body language rather than words, you find subtle ways of saying 'I think you're being stupid' – rolling your eyes, tutting, looking smug.

- **Changing the subject:** Easily the most common block, you just change the subject to something easier and perhaps quicker.

- **Competing:** You turn the focus of the conversation into a comparison between you and your partner. Competing doesn't necessarily mean saying you're better; it can equally be saying that your situation, experience, feeling or whatever is worse.

- **Expecting mind reading:** Everyone's guilty of doing this sometimes. You either feel that you've explained yourself enough or think that your partner really should know what you mean. But expecting telepathy is basically lazy and gives you an excuse not to bother explaining yourself.

- **Feeling that talking's futile:** If your communication's never really been good, you may be unconsciously ruining your chances of improving it by giving your partner the signs that you think it's pointless: sighing, arm folding, being distracted, saying 'whatever' and just generally demonstrating that you can't really see the point.

- **Generalising:** When listening or speaking, you avoid getting into the details of the conversation or becoming personal, by pointing out what a common issue this is for so many people.

- **'I don't know':** Pleading ignorance is one of the conversation blockers that teenagers use most. Saying 'I don't know' is the equivalent of saying 'I don't have anything to say.'

- **Interrupting:** A very irritating habit that many people fall into. Rather than listening and giving your partner the time she needs, you're impatient to move the conversation on.

- **Minimising:** You may think you're doing this in your partner's best interests, but rather than listening to how painful or difficult something is, you play the problem down and say that it's not that bad.

- **Monologues:** The opposite of the silent treatment, this is just as powerful. You hog the floor with your story, so that you leave absolutely no room to listen to your partner or get into a discussion.

- **Not listening:** You either literally don't listen or you make clear that you're not giving your partner your full attention, by getting on with chores, looking around the room or interrupting to talk about something else.

- **Placating:** 'There, there, there dear, it'll all be okay in the end' – you may think you're being kind, but if you say this too early or too often, you can sound intolerant and insincere.

- **Replaying the past:** Rather than sticking to the here and now, you bring back things that happened in the past, either to support your opinion or to rubbish your partner's.

- **Silence:** The silent treatment's perhaps one of the hardest for partners. You may look like you're listening, but all you're really doing is keeping your mouth shut, hoping your partner realises that you don't want to talk and gives up.

If you've recognised some of these blocks to communication for yourself, talk to your partner and ask her to point out to you if you're using them. This may feel like a painful reminder, but it's the quickest way of breaking the habit.

Creating the Right Environment

If you want your communication to improve, one the simplest things you can do is make sure that you create an environment in which talking is as easy as possible, and listening is even easier.

The right environment includes not only your physical surroundings but also the atmosphere between the two of you. With regard to physical surroundings, what's most important is that you can be physically comfortable, away from avoidable distractions (sometimes kids are unavoidable), and that you have the time you need to cover the topic. But as well as these practicalities, you also need to check your internal environment: your timing, your motivation and your objectives.

Choosing your timing wisely

Good and bad times exist to have almost any conversation. Even if you think your subject's the most non-contentious on the planet, time a chat badly and you can have World War Three on your hands. Many a couple have found themselves shocked and bewildered by an argument that seemed to spring from nowhere. In nearly all cases, the cause was bad timing.

External factors can significantly influence the effectiveness of your communication, whether that's a cosy chat or an in-depth exploration. Whatever the type of conversation, if either of you isn't in the right emotional or mental space for it, you have more chance of running into difficulties.

If you know that the topic you want to discuss is sensitive, choosing your timing wisely is particularly important. Talking about the difficulties with your in-laws is likely to run much more smoothly when you're relaxing in a restaurant at the end of your holiday than when both of you've been working 14 hours, the kids are clamouring for attention, dinner's burnt in the oven and you've just discovered that your MOT expired two weeks ago.

Here's a list of external factors to be aware of before you start talking:

- **Tiredness:** When you're tired, you're often more irritable and more sensitive, and consequently you're more likely to become defensive or take offence when none's intended.

- **Stress and anxiety:** If the kids are causing problems or you have difficulties in other relationships or at work, you can easily lose perspective and begin to see every issue through the lens of complication, hassle or threat.

- **Celebrations:** Although birthdays, holidays, Christmas and other festive occasions should be a time of joy, unfortunately they also bring with them unrealistically high expectations of peace and goodwill. This can result in you being over-sensitive to anything that may possibly damage your enjoyment of the occasion.

- **Hormones:** Both women and men can find themselves struggling to cope when their hormone levels fluctuate. For women, the monthly menstrual cycle, childbirth or the menopause can bring emotional upheaval that makes other things in life harder to cope with. And men whose testosterone levels are dented by a sudden loss of employment or demotion can be similarly affected.

- **Lack of time:** Some couples find that they argue more when they don't have enough time together to feel close, while others find that they argue more if they spend too much time together. When you feel disconnected from each other, you can lose touch with the important things you share and find yourselves bickering over trivia. But unless you balance this with sufficient 'me time', you can feel that conversation becomes another burden on your time.

✔ **Alcohol:** One of the most common culprits of miscommunication and overreaction is alcohol. Your vision can become blurred in every sense of the word and lowered inhibitions may make you say things that you later regret.

Unfortunately, you can't always avoid all these external factors. And indeed, some busy couples would never talk if they always waited for the perfect, serene environment. But when you're aware of these external pressures and the possible impact on your conversation, you can at least acknowledge them together and recognise their influence. And if a conversation does collapse or become tense, hopefully you can laugh it off together, knowing that the failure's your environment, not you.

Checking your motivation

As well as considering your external environment, you also need to check your motivation.

If you have something on your mind that you want to talk about, honestly ask yourself the following questions before you proceed:

✔ **Should I be having this conversation with my partner or should/could I be talking to someone else?** Although I believe that you should be able to talk to your partner about pretty much anything, some conversations are more effective with someone else. For example, if you're unhappy with your partner's current work hours but you know she can't do anything about this and she's unhappy as well, moaning is unlikely to help either of you. And if you're not sure how to manage the romantic advances of a colleague or you're struggling with feelings about an ex, talking to someone else may be more sensitive. Talking to a friend makes letting off steam easier, and then you can decide how much you want to share with your partner.

✔ **What else is going on for me right now that may be influencing why I want to talk about this?** Looking back at the list of external factors in the previous section, consider whether anything else is going on in your life that may affect your perspective. If external factors exist, you may still decide to have the conversation, but both you and your partner can be fully aware of the context.

✔ **Am I willing to listen, think and change my mind?** Have you already made up your mind about how your partner thinks and feels about this and how she's going to respond? Or are you genuinely open to having a two-way conversation and seeing things in a new way? If you've had similar conversations with your partner in the past that have always turned out the same way, start the conversation by voicing this anxiety and saying that you want both of you to be open to doing things differently.

✔ **Am I feeling emotional about something else or someone else?** Ask yourself whether what you're feeling is totally to do with your partner or whether someone or something else has triggered your emotions. For example, are you feeling more sensitive to criticism because of something at work, or more insecure because a friend's marriage has recently broken down?

✔ **Am I taking any baggage with me?** Are you making assumptions about this situation based on the conversational style of your family or experiences with a previous partner? Or do you need to let go of or forgive other issues within your relationship? Whenever possible, make sure that you always enter each conversation with a clean slate and no preconceived ideas.

✔ **Is this conversation the one I really want to have or am I hoping that it leads to something else?** Many people start talking about one topic hoping that this leads them on to the conversation they really want to have. Although this may seem like a sensitive approach, it can leave partners feeling ambushed, manipulated and defensive.

✔ **Do I have an end result already in my mind or am I open to any outcome?** You're not doing anything wrong if you start a conversation when you already have a potential outcome or solution in mind, but make sure that you're clear about this and that you're open to other suggestions.

✔ **Am I willing to own my thoughts and my feelings and share them in a non-blaming way?** If you want your partner to take your thoughts and feelings seriously, you have to take full responsibility for them. That means starting sentences with 'I' and making clear that the conversation's about you. Blaming your partner for your feelings or using generalisations such as 'many people feel like this' is confusing and opens debate, but clearly stating 'I feel... I think..' allows the focus to remain on you.

✔ **Am I just spoiling for a fight?** You can easily kid yourself that you want to talk to your partner when what you really want to do is talk *at* her. If you're angry or upset and you want the opportunity to share those feelings, that's fine, as long as you're honest about it and you're willing to be on the receiving end when your partner feels the same.

To get your conversation off to a good start, be 100 per cent real about your thoughts and your feelings, both good and bad. Even a successful conclusion can feel hollow and unrewarding if you don't allow yourself to be completely honest and, consequently, fully understood.

Agreeing objectives

Not all conversations need to have an objective. If you're just having a chat or catching up on some news, starting by stating an objective sounds totally daft. But if your conversation's of a slightly more sensitive nature, clarifying what you're hoping to achieve can be immensely helpful to the outcome.

Stating your objective clearly before the conversation starts allows your partner to get herself in the right frame of mind for talking and ensures that she knows what frame of mind you're in. Doing so can also help both of you to stay on track.

If at all possible, you should agree your objectives together. That may simply mean that having agreed your objective in your head, you check with your partner that it's okay with her as well. So you can say, 'I want to have a talk later tonight when the kids have gone to bed about your holiday plans, so I can book somewhere before the weekend – is that okay?'

Here are some possible outcomes (undoubtedly many, many more exist, but hopefully these can start you thinking):

✔ **Resolve an issue:** If you want to resolve a particular issue between you, make clear from the outset that your goal is to reach a mutually agreeable solution. Flick to Chapter 9 for more on this.

✔ **Understand each other better:** If you're unsure how your partner thinks or feels about something, or you think that perhaps she's not understanding you, explain that your desired outcome is understanding. This stops your partner from thinking that she's meant to find a resolution to a problem that doesn't exist. It can also help to prevent a partner feeling that you're challenging her when you ask questions, and it encourages her to ask you more questions to clarify her understanding.

✔ **Discuss ways to improve a situation:** Sometimes you don't have a particular problem to resolve but you want to think creatively together about making an improvement in some area of your life. Stating this clearly can help prevent defensiveness and ensure that you work as a team.

✔ **Make a complaint or share your feelings:** If the objective of your conversation's simply to let off steam and share your feelings, then say so. This can be difficult for partners to hear, but doing so is better than pretending to have a constructive conversation, if all you need is for your partner to hear you.

✔ **Understand what went wrong in a previous argument:** Some conversations simply aim to clear the air and help you understand what happened in a previous argument. The golden rule is to stay focused on gaining from your mistakes, not resurrecting the same argument again. Chapter 10 has more on moving on after arguments.

Talking So Your Partner Listens

Communication's a two-way process. Every transaction has a speaker and a listener, and those roles change constantly. When you get your turn to be the speaker in any dialogue, you need to focus on getting your message across clearly, including not only your thoughts and opinions but also your feelings.

Saying what you mean

As the speaker, you must say exactly what you mean. If you want your partner to really understand you, you have to be completely real and honest about who you are. That means sharing your thoughts and feelings authentically and being ready to clarify anything that comes across as unclear.

Communication can move through five stages. Not all conversations fit into this format, but using as many of these elements as possible helps you say what you mean.

1. **Make a factual statement.**

   Start with a brief statement of the facts that have led you to this conversation. For example, 'Last night, you were two hours late home.'

2. **Give a personal, tentative interpretation of the facts.**

   Keep to 'I' statements and ensure that you're tentative, as your interpretation may be wrong. So the conversation may continue, 'Last night, you were two hours late home and I wondered whether that was because I haven't let you know that I prefer advance warning when possible.'

3. **Explain how you feel about the interpretation that you made.**

   The example may continue ' . . . I feel frustrated that I haven't conveyed this message sufficiently well.'

4. Offer any additional information that may be contributing to your feelings or interpretation.

For example, ' . . . I feel angry that I haven't conveyed this message sufficiently well, although I may be crosser than usual about this because I made plans for yesterday evening.'

5. Say what you want to do next.

You can simply say 'I want to hear your views on this' or 'Can we please agree to do something differently?'

Meaning what you say

Meaning what you say is often trickier than it sounds, because other people may apply a different meaning to the one you intend.

Here's how you can clarify your message:

- ✔ **Think about your choice of language.** If you're not sure that your partner attaches the same meaning to a word as you do, add some more words for clarification. If you need to use three words to explain something clearly, do so. Speaking in shorthand's much more likely to lead to misunderstanding than explaining yourself more than you need to.

- ✔ **Ensure that your body language matches what you're saying.** If you're expressing sympathy, make sure that the expression on your face matches it. If you're open for a discussion or want feedback, keep your body posture open and receptive. If you're angry or trying to make a point, adopt a posture and expression that show you're serious about what you're saying. You can find out much more on this in *Body Language For Dummies* by Elizabeth Kuhnke (Wiley).

- ✔ **Express emotion as well as saying it with words.** As well as describing how you feel, try to emote what you're saying as well. The intonation of your voice can help to convey the depth of your emotion. Saying that you're angry or upset in a chirpy voice is confusing. Similarly, trying to express your concern or say how much you care about someone in short, curt tones comes across as contradictory.

Making the message even easier to understand

Everybody hears things in different ways, depending on their personality, their previous communication experiences and the mood of the moment.

If your message is important and you're not sure that your partner understands, add some of the following:

- **Examples:** Understanding someone's point of view is often easier if they can add at least one example. Saying 'I feel like sometimes you don't want to talk' but with no examples to back up your view can be very frustrating for the listener who wants to understand but is unable to relate what you say to her own experience. Whenever possible, have at least one concrete example to hand.

- **Similes:** If something feels particularly hard to explain, try to make a comparison to something else that may be within your partner's experience. For example, you can say, 'When you're distracted with your work, I think I feel the same way as you do when I spend all evening on the phone.'

- **Symbols:** Sometimes an abstract metaphor or symbol can be a useful way to convey a complicated emotion or thought process. You may say something like 'I feel wrung out like an old dish-cloth' or 'I feel as though we're children in a playground, fighting over an ice cream.'

Speaking in a way that's easy for your partner to understand is a lifetime's commitment. As the years pass and you get to know each other better, this becomes easier, but times always occur when you have to make more effort. Investing time and energy in becoming an eloquent speaker reaps huge benefits, not just for you, but also for your partner and your relationship.

Listening So Your Partner Feels Heard

The saying that God gave you two ears and only one mouth contains a lot of truth, because listening is twice as important as speaking. Listening to your loved one is how you demonstrate your care and consideration. It's how you demonstrate her importance to you and how much you value who she is and what she thinks and feels.

The two essential ingredients in being a good listener are presence and availability. Being present means not just being physically present, but giving someone 100 per cent of your focus and attention. Being available means demonstrating that listening and understanding are important to you. Think of communication as a telephone line. Being present means having a handset each; being available means making sure that the line's not busy.

Using active listening techniques that really work

A huge difference exists between hearing and listening. When you hear, noise goes in, and that's about that. But when you listen, the noise goes in and your brain interprets it into something that makes sense. Active listening goes one step further and means that not only does the noise go in and get interpreted, you also do something with it and demonstrate the whole process to the speaker.

To get in touch with your natural active listening skills, remember the last time you got lost and you stopped someone to ask for directions. In those few moments, you gave that person 100 per cent of your attention. You listened to the words and reflected them back to ensure you'd understood correctly. You also read the person's body language and tone to establish how she felt. If she was confident in what she said, you'd have headed off in the direction she gave you, but if she was hesitant, you'd probably have politely thanked her and started looking for someone else to listen to.

To improve your listening skills, try to incorporate as many of the following techniques as possible in your conversations:

- **Attending:** This means showing that you're paying attention. You can do that by ensuring that your body language is open and that you're facing your partner, and by giving good eye contact. Also nod your head to show you're listening, and provide minimal verbal cues such as uttering 'uh um' at key points.

- **Restating:** If your partner has said something particularly important, demonstrate your understanding by repeating it back – 'So you're saying you want me to pick up the kids on the way back from work tomorrow.'

- **Clarifying:** If you're not sure that you've understood something, ask for clarification – 'So are you saying you want me to pick up the kids on the way back from work tomorrow?'

✔ **Summarising:** When you've shared a lot of information, you can draw together the main threads to show that you've got the full story – 'So you're going to have a really stressful day tomorrow and you're worried about finishing on time, so you want me to pick up the kids on the way back from work.'

✔ **Encouraging:** To demonstrate that you want to listen and you want to hear more, use minimal encouragers to keep your partner flowing. For example, say something like 'And then what happened?' or 'In what way?' or simply 'Go on.'

✔ **Being quiet:** Make sure that you don't do all the talking. Give plenty of space for your partner to speak, and allow quiet times when she can think about what she wants to say next. While this is happening, make sure that you don't get distracted and start fidgeting or writing tomorrow's shopping list, but continue to attend physically.

Showing empathy

Showing empathy takes active listening skills a step deeper. As well as showing that you're listening to what your partner's saying, you demonstrate that you're also listening to what she's *not* saying. You're hearing not just the information but the feelings as well.

Hearing feelings is essential in building couple intimacy. Knowing that your partner understands how you feel is much more important than whether she remembers the intricate detail of what you said.

Most human beings are instinctively good at picking up on other people's emotions, but unfortunately people often aren't very good at showing that they have empathy. This can leave your partner feeling alone and isolated with her feelings, simply because you forgot to communicate your understanding.

Here are some ways to make clear that you understand the emotional message:

✔ **Reflecting:** Repeat a single word or phrase that expresses an emotion, or say out loud the emotion that you're picking up. For example, you can repeat 'You feel angry about this' or 'You look really hurt about this.'

✔ **Interpreting:** By saying how you interpret something, you're offering a tentative emotional explanation that your partner can clarify or correct. So you can say, 'It seems as though you felt really angry.'

✔ **Give feedback:** This is similar to interpreting, but what you're sharing now is the emotional impact that something's had on you. For example, if your partner describes nearly being hit by a car, you may say, 'I'd be really frightened if that happened to me.'

✔ **Mirroring:** This is a body language technique that demonstrates that you're hearing what the speaker is feeling. By adopting a similar body posture to the speaker or the same facial expression that shows sadness or frustration or disappointment, you show with your body that you're hearing what she's saying with hers.

✔ **Asking questions:** Asking a few well-timed and thought-through questions can help your partner know that you want to understand her experience fully. Use questions that start with 'how' or 'what' to help your partner expand and explore her emotions, but avoid asking 'why' questions as these can sound challenging.

✔ **Show gratitude:** Simply saying thank you when someone has shared something important with you can be incredibly powerful. Doing so shows that you value what they've said and you appreciate the time and effort they've put into talking to you.

Minimising distractions

Giving a partner your undivided attention isn't always easy. When life's busy and your head's full of clutter, listening to your partner can feel like yet another burden on your time. In these situations, remember that good communication's essential for your relationship.

Because good communication means being fully attentive as a listener, if you're not able to do that, then you're better to say so. If your partner says she wants to talk and you know that you're not going to be able to listen properly, ask for a rain check. Say that being able to listen properly and hear what she's saying is really important to you, and for that reason you want to postpone the conversation until another time. Whenever possible, agree that time immediately, so that your partner doesn't feel fobbed off.

On some occasions, it's not possible to wait until a better time. When that happens, take just a few minutes to write down onto a piece of paper the things that are in your head. Dumping your thoughts onto paper can be a powerful way of clearing your mind, and if you want to ensure they don't creep back, take a further psychological step and shut them in a drawer. You can just write a few words like stress at work, talking to Mum about Christmas, and what to have for tea. Or it can be a list of things you know you need to do and don't want to forget...

Chapter 9

Settling Disagreements

. . . .

In This Chapter

▶ Understanding how your argument style fuels disagreements

▶ Stopping an argument escalating

▶ Being an effective negotiator

. . . .

Differences of opinion are inevitable in every relationship, and consequently so are disagreements. When they handle disagreements with mutual care and respect, couples can discover more about each other and deepen their intimacy. But if disputes are painful and leave difficult feelings, couples can feel isolated and driven apart.

This chapter explores how you can improve your relationship by managing disagreements in a healthy way. I start by exploring the five individual argument styles that most often fuel the negative spiral of conflict, and then move on to see how you can break those patterns and stop the conflict developing. Finally, I explain some practical techniques that you can adopt to become a better negotiator and ensure that you reach a win–win conclusion whenever possible.

Note: The information in this chapter mostly relates to managing and avoiding the minor skirmishes of couple life. If the issues you're facing are much bigger or related to a specific issue or life stage, you can find more help and advice in Part IV.

Identifying Your Argument Style

Most couples find that their arguments tend to follow the same old pattern. One or both partners may start a conversation with every intention of avoiding an argument, only to find himself in the middle of a flare-up. Hoping to calm things down, the person ups the ante, only to find that the row escalates.

If your arguments are following the same familiar pattern, but neither of you seems able to stop it, chances are that each of you has developed a conflict style that negatively sets off the other. You may know that what you do doesn't work, but you both feel helpless to change.

Your individual argument style is something you pick up from your family. As a child, you discover how to argue from the way your family does it. You witness both the overt and covert disagreements between your parents and discover what methods are most likely to win. You also gain knowledge from the times you fight with your parents and fall out with your siblings. And early relationships have a significant impact on how you refine and use those discoveries.

If you come from a home where little or no disagreement occurred, this can be as big a handicap as coming from a home with permanent full-scale warfare. Because disputes are inevitable, everyone has to get to know from somewhere how to handle them. If home doesn't provide the classroom for you, arguments within a relationship can come as a massive shock.

Naming the arguers

The following sections look at the most common argument styles. You may identify very clearly with just one of the types, or you may find that you're a combination of two. Some people find that they flit between two different types depending on their mood or the intensity of the conflict. For example, you may start off as a peace-seeking missile, but if your attempts to cool things down fail, you may find yourself being unconsciously catapulted into being a high-level attacker.

The subtle subversive

On the surface, people who adopt this style seem to be avoiding confrontation, probably because arguments were such a negative experience in childhood. They don't like big bust-ups, so they subtly and persistently make their thoughts and feelings known through a variety of covert strategies. Rather than saying outright that he's not happy with something, the subtle subversive hints at a problem through silence, nagging or whinging, until his partner finally notices the signs and says or does something.

If you live with a subtle subversive, you may often feel frustrated and exhausted. You know that something's bubbling under the surface, but your partner answers early 'what's wrong?' questions with 'nothing'. With perseverance, you know you can eventually get to the bottom of what's up, but in the meantime you have to bide your time.

The problem with this conflict style isn't so much what happens during the actual argument, but the long, painful build-up that occurs. The subtle subversives may be good negotiators once communication's finally started, but a resentful and uncooperative partner who's sick of waiting is often what meets them.

The high-level attacker

This person's probably had to fight for his rights his whole life. He's discovered that the world's a tough place where you have to stand up for yourself and you either win or get beaten.

High-level attackers come in two distinct types:

- ✔ Those who come from volatile families where disputes were loud and frequent, but the storm always passed quickly. They see this level of conflict as normal and can often be surprised at the impact their conflict style has on their partners, whom they leave dazed, bewildered and emotionally battered for days to come.

- ✔ Those who, beneath the tough angry exterior, are vulnerable and fragile. They want to avoid conflict at all costs, but their way of doing that is to hit out first or hardest.

When their strategy fails, both types of high-level attacker can feel guilty about the impact their behaviour has on their partner.

Living with a high-level attacker is hard work unless you happen to be one yourself. Although you may be able to negotiate effectively and overcome your differences once the battle's died down, the experience may be so painful that it's not worth the process. To avoid confrontation, partners often find themselves suppressing their thoughts and feelings, either until they themselves erupt or they leave the relationship.

Violence, or threats of violence, are never okay in a relationship. If arguments are always aggressive or you avoid conflict because you're scared of things getting out of control, then you should seek help at once. Chapter 12 has more information on this, and you can find details of helplines in the Appendix.

The pre-emptive striker

If you're a pre-emptive striker, you're one step ahead of the rest. Or at least, that's what you hope. People with this conflict style really hate blow-ups, but unlike the high-level attacker who wants to nip an argument in the bud, the pre-emptive striker aims to dead-head it. Highly attuned to any possible disagreement, this person does anything in his power to prevent a full-scale battle – whether by being hurtful, issuing threats, laying down the law or claiming righteous indignation.

The pre-emptive striker is sensitive and defensive, and although he may be good at discussing issues, at any hint of tension he's off. If you're the partner of a pre-emptive striker, this tactic can be hugely frustrating, and you may either find yourself constantly having to suppress feelings of anger or uncharacteristically blowing up in exasperation.

The shock absorber

The shock absorber is afraid of arguments. He may come from an abusive background or have so little experience of conflict that even the slightest whiff of a dispute is terrifying. Unlike the other styles, the shock absorber refuses to engage in a row in any way at all. He sits and wait for the storm to pass, saying as little as possible and hoping that his silence makes the problem go away.

Shock absorbers may be used to playing this role in their families and be fearful that standing up for their rights or expressing their point of view would fuel the fire. Or they may be very judgemental of anyone who's unable to control his emotions and may rationalise their position by telling themselves that they're not going to stoop to the same level.

On the surface, people who use this conflict style can seem to be doormats, and partners may find themselves becoming more and more confrontational in an attempt to get a response. But beneath the silence of a shock absorber is a raging fury of resentment and bitterness that may leak out in destructive behaviours that distance him from his partner, such as spending hours on a hobby, drinking or having an affair.

The peace-seeking missile

If you're tempted to think that this is the best conflict style, think again. Peace seekers don't like conflict and see their personal responsibility as calming things down. They're rational and reasonable and do everything in their power to find a solution as swiftly as possible. But the solution they're seeking is how to stop the argument, not how to resolve the issue. Consequently, peace seekers can find their job a never-ending one.

Partners of peace seekers can often feel like the unreasonable, demanding one in the relationship: while they're stating their opinions and expressing their feelings, the peace seekers seem to have no thoughts or needs of their own. The partner of a peace seeker may get very frustrated, trying to draw the peace seeker into a mutual discussion, but the peace seeker's fear of conflict means that he hears everything as confrontation and either denies or suppresses his views.

Becoming comrades in arms

Although some of the styles that the previous sections outline seem very different, all of them are about avoiding conflict in some way. If you and your partner are the same, you may be sharing the same blind spots that stop you from moving on. But if you're different, you may be fuelling each other and inadvertently maintaining the status quo.

If you're in a loving, committed relationship, you can't avoid disagreements. That may sound like a contradiction or perhaps a bit sad, but nonetheless it's a reality. The only way in which two people can live together peacefully is by working through the difficult times and finding a resolution together.

The bottom line in managing arguments together is to recognise the issue as your joint enemy and to fight side by side to overcome it. The battle isn't with each other but with the differences that are temporarily dividing you.

Once you can identify your argument styles, you can make a conscious decision to beat these old habits and develop a new way of overcoming differences. The new style you should aim to develop is that of the negotiator. The negotiator recognises what's going on, makes an appraisal of the situation, cools emotions down and then discusses a mutually agreeable solution. Easy, eh? Unfortunately not, but the sections that follow can get you started with tips and ideas on how to become a successful negotiator.

When different styles collide

Jo had been a shock absorber all her life. Her dad was an angry and aggressive man who could never be reasoned with, so she knew to keep her mouth shut for the sake of an easy life. Her husband, Don, was a pre-emptive striker. He was brought up in a tough neighbourhood where he anticipated trouble as a way of avoiding it. They came for counselling because Jo was on the verge of leaving. Jo felt that she could no longer live with Don's temper tantrums whenever she asked for even the smallest thing. Their combined argument style meant that whenever Jo wanted to discuss something, Don became defensive and instantly blew up. Jo sat and listened to an increasingly abusive list of complaints from Don, saying nothing and hoping that the row would pass. But Don became increasingly frustrated at Jo's inability to stand up to him and finish what she'd started. Every disagreement ended painfully, with Don apologising and feeling guilty and Jo quietly building yet more resentment about another need unmet.

Knowing How to Stop a Storm

The best way to prevent an argument getting out of hand is to recognise what's going on before it even starts, and stop it. That doesn't mean slipping into silence or avoiding difficult conversations or differences of opinion, but recognising when your interactions are healthy and productive and when they start down the slippery slope towards a falling out.

You can avoid or stop a row at many different stages. If you can identify the warning signs that a storm's brewing and set up a reasonable, adult discussion (see 'Mastering the Lost Art of Negotiation', later in this chapter), you almost certainly continue in the right direction. But even the best-laid plans can go awry, so if you start going off course, the sooner you can do something about that the better.

Imagine that your relationship is like the weather. Hopefully you have sun a lot of the time, or perhaps you get a mixture of sunshine and showers. Occasionally you see storm clouds looming on the horizon. When you do, you can either face those clouds head on and blow them away, or you can wait until they're right overhead and the rain starts. And as the raindrops begin to fall, you can decide whether to put up with a light shower or hang around and get drenched.

Recognising when a row is looming

You can sometimes feel as though an argument suddenly erupts from nowhere. But in reality, this is rare. As tensions arise between couples, the partners begin to send and receive signals that they're not okay. When you can recognise these early warning signs, you can make a decision to stop an argument before it's even started.

Here are the most common early warning signs that conflict's brewing:

- ✔ You find that your thoughts are focused on your partner's negative qualities.
- ✔ You keep replaying something irritating that your partner's said or done over and over in your head.
- ✔ You keep contradicting or questioning your partner on everything.
- ✔ You avoid eye contact, physical affection and sex.
- ✔ You respond to any attempt at conversation with short, curt replies.
- ✔ You find yourself getting more irritated than usual with the children, friends, work or other family members.

✔ You find yourself irritated by your partner's small talk, and his sense of humour's driving you up the wall.

✔ You develop physical symptoms of tension such as muscle tightness, churning stomach, backache or teeth grinding.

✔ You struggle to have sympathy for or empathy with anything that's going on in your partner's life.

✔ You notice your partner showing any of the previous signs.

Think back to the last argument you had and see how many of the signs in the list you can identify in the days or hours leading up to the argument. Now use this knowledge to become more aware of the signs that you and your partner send out when you're not okay.

All these signs are telling you that something isn't okay between you and your partner. You may know exactly what the problem is or find you have one or two inklings of what may be going on. If your partner's displaying these signs, you may be mystified. Either way, this is the window of opportunity to face the tension head on and resolve your differences before the storm clouds break.

Cutting conflict dead before it starts

When you've recognised that a storm's brewing, you have to act fast to cut it dead before it takes a grip on your relationship. How you do this depends on whether your stuff or your partner's is in the boiling pot. Either way, your goal is to establish what's going on and find a healthy way of dealing with the problem.

Defusing the bomb when you're the one with the problem

If you recognise any of the early warning signs listed above in yourself, use the AID steps to calm things down:

1. **Acknowledge your feelings.**

   Start by establishing exactly what's going on inside you that's making you feel annoyed. For example, are you angry, hurt, frustrated, disappointed or confused? Try to pinpoint the exact emotion or combination of emotions that you're feeling.

2. **Identify the trigger.**

   Now think about what's happened or what's been said that's kicked off this emotion within you. The trigger may be a single event or perhaps a few things have been building up over time. Consider also whether external circumstances such as stress, tiredness or issues with other people are making you more sensitive.

3. Decide whether the issue really matters.

Finally ask yourself whether what's happened is something that's really important to you that you want to do or say something about, or whether it's a trivial thing that you prefer let go.

If the issue's something that's important to you or perhaps the last straw in a catalogue of issues, then arrange a time to sit down calmly with your partner and talk about it (see the section 'Mastering the Lost Art of Negotiation', below).

If the issue's something you really don't think is worth saying anything about, then use the three Rs to get yourself back on track again:

- ✔ **Relax:** Take some deep breaths, shake out your muscles, have a soak in the bath, go for a walk around the garden – do whatever helps you to relax.

- ✔ **Reassure yourself:** Repeat the reasons why the issue doesn't matter. Use positive self-talk to calm your anger (more on this in Chapter 12) and get your focus back on the good things that are happening right now.

- ✔ **Reconnect with your partner:** Either use physical touch or words. Talk about something positive, pay a compliment or simply ask how your partner is and perhaps gain more understanding of the trigger.

If the three Rs don't work and the issue isn't going away, then perhaps it means more to you than you're ready to acknowledge. If that's the case, take a look at Chapter 10 to see whether you can recognise what may be going on underneath that's causing you such strong emotions.

Avoiding a barney when your partner's showing signs of blowing

If you know you're feeling fine but you're noticing the early warning signs in your partner, you have two choices: you can just wait it out, hoping that the storm blows over or he starts the conversation, or you can approach him directly.

If you want to increase your chances of avoiding a blow-up, approaching your partner first is almost always the best option. Not only does this end the tension more quickly, it also demonstrates that you're aware of and care about his feelings.

You can use a slight variation of the AID steps to approach a simmering partner:

1. **Acknowledge his feelings:** No matter how confident you are that you know what's going on in your partner's head, ensure that you make a tentative enquiry that doesn't challenge his autonomy or sound antagonistic. For example, you're much better to say 'I feel as though you're angry or upset about something' than 'Why are you in a bad mood?'

2. **Investigate the cause:** Assuming your partner agrees that he's not okay, either ask what's upset him or, if you suspect that you've said or done something, ask for confirmation. For example, 'Are you angry with me because dinner's late?'

3. **Discuss the issue:** If the timing's appropriate and your partner's in agreement, talk about what's happened immediately. If that's not convenient or your partner wants more time to calm down, agree a time to talk the issue through.

Unfortunately, the best of intentions aren't always enough to stop a storm. If your partner either refuses to acknowledge the problem himself or refuses to talk about what's wrong, then you can do very little. You're generally best to back off. You can try again later to see if he's more open to discussion, or bide your time until the storm clouds either pass by or break. But even if you haven't managed to avoid a row altogether, you can still do things to make sure the problem doesn't escalate (see the following section, 'Stopping a row in its tracks').

Having a row always takes two people. You may not be able to stop your partner from being in a bad mood with you, and he may continue to spoil for a fight in spite of your best efforts to avoid one. But the choice is yours. If you don't want to argue, then don't.

Stopping a row in its tracks

So the storm clouds have broken and the rain's beginning. Don't panic: you're not too late. The crucial tactic for avoiding a downpour is to act fast and act rationally. When emotions are running high, not falling back into your old argument styles can be especially difficult (see 'Identifying Your Argument Style', earlier in this chapter), but remember that your goal is to change your old negative patterns of behaviour and become a negotiator. To do this you have to stick to your guns and refuse to let your partner draw you into an argument.

If the AID technique (see the previous section) has failed and tension's continuing to build between you, you have three options:

✔ **Divert:** Diverting the conversation is by far the best solution. If you've noticed your or your partner's hackles rising, but you've decided that the issue isn't something worth falling out over, do something else. Diversionary tactics include:

- Using humour: Crack a joke, mention something funny, or laugh at yourselves and the situation.

- Changing the subject: Talk about work, tell a story, discuss what to have for tea tonight or where to go tomorrow – anything that takes the focus away from the issue and back onto common ground.

- Focusing on a positive: Express something you really like about your relationship or your situation. For example, if you're about to argue in the car over directions, say how nice being able to go out together for the day is and how much you're looking forward to arriving at your destination.

- Using innuendo: Saying something sexual can instantly break the tension and get the focus back on you as a couple. It may be corny, but even the old faithful 'Wow, you're sexy when you're angry' can work a treat.

✔ **Postpone:** Consider very seriously whether now is the right time to have a productive conversation. In most cases, postponing the talk until you've both calmed down a bit is a much safer option. If one or both of you is too angry even to discuss when a better time to talk is, simply agree that it isn't now. With the postponement agreed, you now have two options:

- Use a diversionary tactic (see the previous bullet) to get you back on track.

- Have 'time out'. Time out is the best way to avoid escalation and reduce tension. Taking time out can also give both of you an opportunity to reflect on the situation and consider how to resolve it amicably. If your circumstances mean that you can't physically separate (for example, if you're on a long car journey), you can at least agree to be silent for a while and give each other some space.

✔ **Ventilate:** Sometimes, keeping the waves of emotion inside can feel impossible. If one or both of you is totally boiling about something and diverting and postponing aren't working, your final option to avoid a massive row is to ventilate. Ventilating simply means giving each of you a set amount of time, say 20 minutes, to share your feelings without any interruption. At the end of your 20 minutes, you swap over and the other person has 20 minutes to share how he feels. The aim of a ventilation session is to get difficult feelings off your chest, not to resolve the issue. So once you've both had your say, you agree to talk calmly about the issue again after some time out.

If you're doing everything in your power to stop an argument from escalating, but your partner won't or can't cooperate, insist on taking time out for yourself. Explain that you don't want to argue, and agree to talk later when you're both calmer. If necessary, use the broken record technique in Chapter 12.

Mastering the Lost Art of Negotiation

Two very distinct types of conflict exist within relationships. The first is based on differences of opinion, tastes and individual needs, the second on differences of perspective and personality. Both are fed by miscommunication and fuelled by negative thinking and blame.

To resolve both of these types of conflict, you need to start by listening and hearing how each of you views the problem, and explain your own perspective without placing blame. When you can understand where each of you is coming from, you can accurately identify the problem, agree a common goal and find a solution that works for both of you.

Chapter 8 contains loads of tips on how you can become a better listener and how you can get your message across without being antagonistic. This section focuses specifically on how you can use those communication skills to negotiate your way to a healthy resolution.

If you've been arguing about the same issues over and over again and all your efforts to find a joint resolution have failed, moving straight to Chapter 10, which explores how to break the argument cycle, may be more helpful.

Identifying the problem

When couples start bickering, the real problem often gets lost. As both partners become increasingly insistent on proving they're right, their thinking becomes more and more polarised. The objective becomes winning the fight rather than resolving the issue.

To identify what the problem is, you need to listen to one another's opinions and perspective without judgement. By putting yourself in your partner's shoes and seeing the situation through his eyes, you can discover what's really bothering him. Careful use of questioning can help you to clarify your partner's position. And you can also use similar questioning techniques to help your partner understand your perspective.

Why are we really fighting?

Maggie and Tim had a recurrent argument about how to spend their evenings. They both had demanding jobs that left them exhausted at the end of the day. Rather than focusing on how to relax together, they started to fight. Maggie preferred to relax by chatting about her day, and she wanted Tim to tell her about his day. But Tim didn't want to talk when he got home. His way of unwinding was to watch the TV or read the paper. Over the last few months they had begun to blame each other for what they perceived as selfish behaviour. Maggie accused Tim of being unsociable and unloving, and in response he retreated further into silence. Tim increasingly interpreted Maggie's need to talk as superficial and demanding. They were stuck in a stalemate position where neither met the other's needs. But when they began to drop their accusatory and defensive conflict style, they were able to see that they shared a common problem: neither of them felt able to relax.

When asking questions, retain your focus firmly on developing understanding. By keeping your tone and language within the spirit of caring enquiry, you can calm the situation down and reassure your partner that you genuinely want to understand. In Maggie and Tim's case (see the nearby sidebar 'Why are we really fighting?'), for example, saying 'How long do you want to talk about work in order to help you relax?' is much more productive than 'Do we have to talk for ages for you to relax?' or even 'I suppose we have to talk all night before you're happy.' If you're tempted to let sarcasm or subtle putdowns slip through your lips, you probably need more time before starting negotiations.

If you're in the situation where you're trying to help your partner understand your perspective, try to establish what he's struggling with or how his perspective is at odds with what you're trying to explain. Again, in Maggie and Tim's situation, Maggie can ask Tim whether he ever finds talking about work a useful way to unwind, or what about talking he finds difficult.

When using questioning in a negotiation situation, your objective's to investigate not interrogate, so keep your tone and your body language relaxed.

Agreeing goals

After you've identified the problem, agreeing the goal becomes easier. In the example in the previous section, when Maggie and Tim both realised that the problem was a difference in relaxation style, they could agree that the common goal was for them to find a way to relax together in the evening.

In almost every situation of couple conflict, the goal's a common one. Assuming that both of you are committed to being together and both of you want to live in a harmonious household, your goals are unlikely to be far apart. On the surface, you may seem as if you want different things, but ultimately they lead you to the same place.

Sometimes, one person appears to have a problem, and therefore the goal's not a common one. For example, one person may always leaves his dirty socks on the floor for the other to pick up. In this instance, the sock dropper may be tempted to say 'Get over it, it's not my problem.' While the floor full of socks may not be a problem to the sock dropper, the grumpy nagging partner almost certainly is. Therefore your joint goal may not be a sock-free floor but a harmonious laundry system.

Finding creative solutions

I'm sure you've heard that horrible expression, 'There are many ways to skin a cat.' I'm a moggie lover, so this certainly isn't one of my favourite sayings, but the sentiment's true. Often lots of different ways exist for arriving at the same conclusion, and this is particularly true in conflict resolution.

When you've both identified the problem and agreed a joint goal, your next task is to brainstorm some solutions. The key to creative brainstorming is to get off the bandwagon of thinking that you're right and your partner's wrong, and come up with one of the following:

- **Compromise:** A compromise is often the simplest solution to many problems. Both of you agree to back down a bit, and if one of you feels less strongly than the other, that partner may decide to back down more.

  The problem with compromise is that it can be a rather limited way of solving a problem, which can leave both partners feeling, well, compromised. In complex disagreements, a compromise may do little more than ease the symptoms of the problem, rather than help you reach your goals.

- **Collaboration:** When couples collaborate, the focus is on how to reach their goal. Rather than thinking about how to ease the problem, collaborating means working together to find a completely different way of attaining the joint goal that genuinely works for both sides.

- **Exchange deal:** This is backing down with a payoff, which is particularly useful when reaching a compromise seems impossible or when you can't find a third route. In an exchange deal, one partner agrees to the other one's wishes but makes a request of his own that he feels is of equal value – a quid pro quo agreement.

In practice, using these types of solution can result in several ways out of conflict. For example, Maggie and Tim (see the sidebar 'Why are we really fighting?') want to relax together in the evening, but Maggie wants to chat and Tim wants to switch off and watch TV. Here are some solutions for their problem:

✔ Compromise solutions:

- Agree a certain time to talk first and then watch TV.

- Agree to watch TV for a while and then talk together.

- Agree to alternate nights: one night they talk, the next they watch TV.

- Agree to Tim going to the pub alone to watch TV while Maggie phones a friend for a chat.

✔ Collaborative solutions:

- Agree to do something else together after work that helps them both unwind, such as ten-pin bowling, doing a crossword puzzle or having sex.

- Agree to meet at the pub to talk together and then go to the cinema or home to watch a DVD.

✔ Exchange deal: Agree to watch TV together when Tim needs to unwind, but go for a walk together every Sunday afternoon, when they can catch up on the week.

The sock rivals (see the previous section) want a harmonious laundry system. Here are a few possible solutions for them:

✔ Compromise solutions:

- Drop only one sock.

- Drop socks on the floor on alternate days.

- Pick up only one sock.

- Pick up socks on alternate days.

✔ Collaborative solutions:

- Put the laundry basket somewhere more convenient.

- Pay one of the children to collect the laundry each day.

✔ Exchange deal: Agree to sock dropping, but in exchange the sock dropper makes the morning tea.

 If you're really struggling to find a solution that works for you both and the subject isn't too sensitive, consider talking it through with a friend. Someone with an outside perspective can often see the obvious and perfect solution that's been staring you in the face.

Ensuring a win–win conclusion

After you've brainstormed as many possible solutions as you can, make sure the one you agree is realistic and achievable. Choosing a solution that's unworkable for both of you and leaves you both feeling tense may avoid that particular problem, but is likely to result in different ones.

Agreeing a review date is also a good idea. Set a time in a few days, weeks or months – whatever's appropriate to the problem – to sit down again and review whether your solution's working. If the solution you agreed is doing the job, great, but if not, go back to the brainstorm again and try something else.

Chapter 10

Breaking the Argument Cycle

Some arguments seem to go on and on and on forever, perhaps because you don't seem to find a resolution to the underlying problem, but more often because no one knows what the underlying problem even is. Constant bickering and warfare are exhausting and can take a huge toll on a relationship. As frustration grows, so does the distance between you and your partner, and the opportunities to resolve the problem can seem further and further away.

This chapter helps you work out what on earth's going on. First, you analyse what you may be doing as an individual that's fuelling the argument cycle, and how you as a couple may be unconsciously keeping the cycle going. Then you explore how your arguments may be an unhealthy way of balancing the relationship. And finally you can conduct an argument post-mortem to stop the cycle for good.

Recognising What Lurks Beneath

When arguments seem irresolvable or flare up on a regular basis, something's often going on underneath that either one or both of you aren't dealing with. This is especially true if you've normally been good at managing conflict and solving issues, or if you find yourselves arguing about things that don't really matter to either of you.

If you're bewildered by your constant rows but all your efforts to resolve the never-ending barrage of problems are getting you nowhere, you need to dig beneath the surface and find out what the real issue is.

Acknowledging personal triggers

Most people confess to having at least one or two soft spots that can trigger a row. Those soft spots may be a sensitivity from childhood or from a previous relationship, or they may reflect an insecurity you feel about yourself or your relationship. Most of the time these sensitive areas don't cause a problem; they lie hidden and dormant and may be barely recognisable. But when your partner inadvertently presses that button – bang! Your defences shoot up and your mouth snaps open.

Lots of different kinds of soft spots can develop over the years, but those that the following sections cover are the most common.

Whatever the personal trigger may be, admitting that your sensitivities sometimes make you overreact and create mountains out of molehills can be hard. But when you can recognise and acknowledge these triggers within yourself, you can work on them directly and dismantle the booby traps you've created in your relationship.

Fearing inadequacy

If you're someone who struggles with low self-esteem or you come from a childhood or a previous relationship where you were made to feel inadequate, you can easily overreact when a partner pushes that button. Something as simple as a tut or a raised eyebrow can ignite those old feelings and throw you into defensive action. You can read innocent questioning over why you've done something as an aggressive attack on your competence. And when your partner overtly points out that you've been a fool (and who isn't occasionally?), rather than take the comment as justified, your insecurity causes you to overreact.

Once you recognise your anxieties, you can choose how to manage them. That may mean boosting your own self-esteem, asking for reassurance and clarification from your partner and/or asking your partner to be more sensitive to your soft spot and approach conversations more carefully.

Reacting to labels

Often, what winds you up isn't actual words, but what you think your partner's trying to imply. Most children grow up with at least one or two labels securely stuck to them, and the unaware partner can easily reinforce those labels unwittingly. You're stupid, you're lazy, you're boring, you're selfish, you're unimportant, you have nothing worth saying, you get angry too easily, you make a fuss over nothing, you don't know what's good for you – the potential list is endless. Although you may desperately try to peel off these labels, your relationship can make them even stickier.

Think back to your childhood. Can you remember any negative labels your parents stuck on you? How many of these still hurt you and are susceptible to being triggered?

Previous couple relationships are another source of labels. If you have an ex who liked to run you down, accuse you unfairly or pick on your soft spots, you may be especially vulnerable to any hints of reactivation in your current relationship. If you're still holding on to painful labels from a previous relationship, check out Chapter 8, which helps you leave your baggage in the past.

Feeling insecure about your relationship

Insecurities about the relationship can often trigger a row. Arguing because you're scared of losing your partner is a rather ironic phenomenon but a very common one. Someone who's worrying about the viability of a relationship can become ultra-sensitive to anything that seems to challenge it. So if a partner voices a small irritation, this can feel like confirmation that the relationship's in trouble. But rather than discussing the presenting problem, you blow the issue up and distort it into an argument. These kinds of arguments can be particularly frustrating and painful, as the unconscious fear of losing the relationship becomes reinforced by the cycle of futile conflict.

Seeing how triggers cause blow-ups

Patricia and Ray came for counselling five years into their relationship. They'd only been living together for 18 months and described themselves as very much in love, but neither was sure how long they may last. They were arguing constantly about everything under the sun. They didn't have any major issues or disagreements, but in spite of this they bickered endlessly.

As we began to dig under the surface, some common themes emerged. Both had been married before, and Patricia's divorce had been particularly acrimonious. Her ex had always accused her of being controlling, which she had vehemently denied, but she was aware that the accusation had left a scar that Ray was inadvertently picking at. Ray had his own concerns. He'd grown up in a family where he'd

been affectionately nicknamed 'the plonker' because of his tendency to state the obvious. Teaming this with a fear that Patricia was a bit out of his league left Ray with deep anxieties about his value within the relationship. They were both desperate to make this relationship work, but whenever Patricia raised a minor issue, Ray became defensive and accused her of having a go at him. In turn, she would overreact and interpret his comment as meaning he thought she was being a bitch.

When Patricia and Ray began identifying their personal triggers, their relationship problems eased. Once they recognised the buttons they were pressing and the unconscious dynamic they created, they were able to stop reacting and stop arguing.

Identifying cognitive distortions

The simplest way to keep an argument going and avoid looking at what's going on underneath is to distort the reality of what's happening. By fuelling the fire and heating up the conversation, arguments become about arguing rather than about the issue. You start having an argument for argument's sake, and the goal is to prove who's right and who's wrong.

Cognitive distortion is popular psychobabble for twisted thinking. The term encompasses anything and everything humans do to skew reality to their preferred version of the truth. During an argument, cognitive distortions are the methods you use to filter conversations and arrive at your own idiosyncratic interpretation. And you can also use them outside of an argument to fuel negative thinking and sensitise triggers ready for the next row.

See whether any of the following look familiar:

- ✔ **Biased explanations:** This is a bit like mind reading but slightly more sophisticated, because psychoanalysis now complements your telepathy skills: 'The reason you said/did/felt that was because you . . . ' Many, many explanations may exist for your partner's behaviour, but you choose the one that backs up your argument.

- ✔ **Exaggerating:** 'You always do this; you never do that.' 'I've done it hundreds of times.' 'You left me waiting nearly an hour.' 'It cost almost £100.' 'I got absolutely soaked to the bone.' Exaggeration's okay if you're embellishing a story for dramatic effect and entertainment, but if you're exaggerating to win an argument, you're helping no one. Ultimately, the truth tends to come out and then you're left without a leg to stand on and your integrity in tatters.

- ✔ **Generalising:** Statements like 'everybody says', 'everybody knows', 'everybody does' are ways of backing up your arguments with generalisations that may have little relevance to your personal situation. You may use generalisations to defend yourself from attack or in an attempt to prove that you're entitled to your feelings; for example, 'Anyone would be angry if you did that.'

- ✔ **Mind reading:** 'I know what you said, but what you really meant was . . . ' Oddly, people consider themselves fantastic mind readers when they're talking about their partners' negative thinking but rarely when they're thinking nice things. Aside from the absolute impossibility of reading someone's mind, this behaviour also fuels an argument dramatically, as you force the other person into a frustrated defence rather than focusing on the issue at hand.

✔ **Polarisation:** This is when everything is either right or wrong, did you or didn't you, yes or no. You allow no shades of grey, only black or white, and only one possible conclusion – yours.

✔ **Privileging:** You remember only what you want to remember or hear what you want to hear. Or perhaps you share only part of a story or give a few of the facts. Privileging means filtering out what you perceive as unhelpful extras (unhelpful because they don't help you win). This is a particularly damaging distortion when it includes privileging only the negative things your partner says and excluding all the positive.

Cognitive distortions are damaging, not only to relationships but to you as an individual. They make finding common ground and reaching a resolution on issues impossible, and they also feed your insecurities.

Self-awareness is the first step to overcoming cognitive distortions. When you know you're prone to cognitive distortions, you can monitor your thinking and make a positive decision to stop. It's not easy to do, because many distortions become habits, but if you're serious about wanting to stop endless arguments, watch your thinking and check it's honest, fair and focused on reconciliation.

Avoiding sensitive subjects

Some couples find themselves bickering over nothing or having a full-scale row over something trivial because doing so is better than talking about what's really on their minds. When anger and anxiety are bubbling under the surface, but either one or both of you is too frightened to discuss the problem openly, the issue leaks into the relationship and finds its outlet in areas that feel safer.

The avoidance of sensitive subjects is known as *displacement*, a very common unconscious defence mechanism that redirects something that feels unsafe on to something or someone that feels more manageable. A more familiar term's the 'kick the cat syndrome'.

Almost any subject can become taboo in a relationship, but here are the most common culprits:

✔ **An affair:** This may be an affair or another indiscretion that's already been discussed, or an anxiety that an affair's happening, but neither wants to acknowledge it openly.

✔ **An unacknowledged compulsion:** That may be a drinking problem or gambling or excessive spending, or any other activity that feels out of control and too big and scary to address openly.

✔ **An unforgiven offence:** This is anything in the past that one of you still holds strong feelings of bitterness and resentment about, for example getting drunk at the wedding, forgetting an important anniversary, blocking an ambition or hobby, or a disproportionately angry outburst. Whatever the offence, both feel that it should be in the past and therefore don't talk about it. But in reality, the problem's still very much alive and kicking.

✔ **Children:** Differences of opinion on parenting can be particularly sensitive, especially concerning stepchildren. Rather than risk hurting feelings or raising deeper concerns about not sharing fundamental values, many couples avoid these conversations.

✔ **Debts:** Outstanding debts and money worries can be a source of concern for both partners, but rather than facing what may feel like an insurmountable anxiety, both partners bicker over something else.

✔ **In-laws:** Challenging your partner on her relationship with her parents or her involvement in your family can be very difficult, so many couples choose to moan about insignificant peripheral issues rather than rock the boat.

✔ **Previous relationships:** Some people feel haunted by their partner's ex, and in an effort to control their feelings they displace their anxieties and anger on to other areas of the relationship. Unfortunately, this leaves the ghosts of the past free to roam around at will.

✔ **Religion or politics:** Some say that religion and politics are contentious subjects that you should avoid in polite company. Unfortunately, these topics are also a bone of contention for many couples.

✔ **Sex:** An unsatisfactory sex life can put a huge strain on any relationship, but it can be one of the most difficult subjects to talk about. Many people find themselves blowing up over trivial things in an effort to avoid hurting their partner's feelings by discussing their dissatisfaction.

If any of these areas are sensitive subjects in your relationship, you can find more help on how you can approach these issues directly in Part IV.

Understanding Hidden Payoffs

Constant arguing may be playing a beneficial role in your relationship. I know that sounds daft, but many people maintain the argument cycle because it keeps the relationship in balance. I should quickly stress that it's not a healthy balance, and you can find many more desirable ways of keeping a relationship on an even keel. But until you know what purpose your arguing is serving, you can't begin to find better ways of meeting that need.

In a nutshell, arguing helps relationships in three ways. A good row can create an intimate connection, but if your connection's already very intimate, you may row to create distance and avoid intimacy. Or you may be arguing because it's the only way to get passion into your relationship. That may be painful passion that's hard earned, but at least it makes your relationship feel exciting.

Arguing to maintain connection

A sense of connection is an essential component of a couple relationship. In order to feel loved, cared for and valued, you need to be able to get close to your partner and feel as though your relationship's special.

Picture a typical scenario: life is busy and you're both so tired that you've slipped into the habit of collapsing on the sofa at the end of the night, with little more than a mutual grunt at communication. Nothing personal, but neither of you has the energy to do anything different. A fortnight passes and you've barely said two words to each other. You're drifting apart because of apathy, and it's driving you both up the wall. Before you know, you're griping at each other and then bang – you're having a full-blown row. But why?

Here's how arguing improves connection:

- **Creates energy:** Anger boosts your adrenalin, so suddenly you're awake and ready for action.

- **Ensures 100 per cent attention:** Most arguments mean full-on eye-to-eye contact with no distractions, so at last you get one another's complete attention.

- **Generates conversation:** You may have been silent for days, but when an argument starts, the words begin to flow. Unfortunately, they don't tend to be helpful words.

- **Improves articulation:** Lots of people find talking easier when they're angry. They get in touch with their feelings and find themselves able to express them in a way that seems totally inaccessible when they're calm.

- **Tests the relationship:** When couples are slipping into apathy, one or both partners can doubt that they still love each other. A row provides an opportunity to re-establish that at least you still care enough to fight.

When the argument's over, couples slowly drift back to their original way of being, safe in the knowledge that they can still connect. Each has aired some feelings, had the other's attention and confirmed that the relationship is still alive. But, without addressing the underlying issue of how to maintain connection in a healthy way, before long someone has to kick off another row so that the couple can get close again.

Although picking on an annoying habit of your partner's may be an effective way of re-establishing connection, a much healthier alternative is to sit down and talk about the growing distance and work together to find a resolution.

Using rows to avoid intimacy

Having an argument is a very effective way both to avoid and to regulate intimacy. While many people want more intimacy in their relationships, some feel they get too much. Too much closeness can feel suffocating, especially for someone who was brought up in a reserved family environment. And a partner who wants you to spend lots of time together, talking and cuddling and generally being nice and loving, can feel demanding and stifling.

Some people use arguing as a way of maintaining a safe emotional distance. If you've been badly hurt in a relationship before, you may be frightened of getting close again. Continuing the argument cycle eases the sense of vulnerability and ensures that you don't make a full emotional commitment.

Here's how arguing avoids intimacy:

- ✔ **Creates independence:** Everyone needs space from their relationship, so when a partner's being dependent and needy, an easy way of creating separateness is to find something to bicker about and push her away.

- ✔ **Evades serious talks:** For some people, having an intimate conversation about problems and issues within the relationship provokes more anxiety than a row does, so the latter may be a favourable option.

- ✔ **Justifies time alone:** If your partner makes a huge fuss every time you want to do something alone or see friends, if you overreact to a problem in the relationship, it can provide the perfect excuse to get away.

- ✔ **Maintains emotional safety:** If you think your partner's distancing herself from you or has a problem with the relationship, you may start a fight first to protect yourself from getting hurt.

- ✔ **Sabotages sex:** If you're really not in the mood for sex but don't want to say so, starting an argument is an excellent way of nipping any action in the bud.

If avoiding intimacy is a hidden payoff for you, put some time aside to think about healthier ways of getting the space you need. That may involve some straight talking, which may be hard for your partner, but it won't be anywhere near as painful or as exhausting as living in a war zone.

Injecting passion the hard way

You've probably heard people say that the only thing better than a good argument is making up afterwards. True, making up can be a very profound, intimate and even sexual experience, but is it really worth the pain? Can't you think of easier and more convivial ways of injecting passion into your relationship?

Some couples can't stop the argument cycle, because that's the only way they can get any excitement in their relationship. When they don't argue, life feels bland and uninteresting and they wonder whether they even love their partner, let alone share a fulfilling relationship. But when these couples argue, the emotional, psychological and physical floodgates open, they throw caution to the wind and they feel passionate again.

Here's how arguing ignites passion:

- ✔ **Creates excitement:** Yes, you may be shouting and hurling insults and being vile to each other, but at least that's exciting. Powerful negative emotions can feel better than none at all.

- ✔ **Heightens desire:** When you get angry, you produce adrenalin, and when you produce adrenalin, you become sexually aroused more easily. For some couples, a good argument is simply foreplay.

- ✔ **Lowers inhibition:** Once you've had a slanging match with your partner, you can more easily say and do things that otherwise feel out of place. Becoming vulnerable with each other at an emotional level can be a potent precursor to becoming more open sexually.

- ✔ **Rekindles 'in love' feelings:** Making up is the best bit of an argument because it allows you to feel close to your partner again. A twisted kind of logic says that if you push your partner as far away as possible, you're able to enjoy an even greater level of relative intimacy. So the bigger the row, the bigger the making up and the greater the feelings of recaptured love.

Some couples can't stop the argument cycle, because the hidden payoff of passion is too great. If you can identify with this, take a look at Chapters 4, 5 and 7 and write a list of healthy ways of increasing your ardour.

Getting Off the Argument Merry-Go-Round, Forever

No couple wants to live in a war zone. Not only is being there exhausting, it steals the joy from so much of life. Living in an argument cycle is quite simply a waste of time – time that you can spend on living and loving.

If you want to get off the argument merry-go-round once and for all, you need to analyse what's going on and address the underlying problems. And once you resolve the issues, or at least make a commitment to working on them together, you can begin to heal your relationship. Until this happens, trying to make up is like putting a sticking plaster on a volcano. Doing so may work for a short time, but inevitably the volcano blows again and you're right back where you started.

Conducting an argument post-mortem

The first step in breaking the argument cycle is identifying exactly what's going on when you row.

Go through the argument post-mortem flow sheet in Figure 10-1. This helps you see what happened in your argument and consider what the deeper issues or needs may be. You can also think about any cognitive distortions you used that may have influenced your perception, and any external factors that may be making you more sensitive.

Ideally, each of you completes the flow sheet alone and then you share your thoughts with one another. Doing this helps you take responsibility for your contribution to the argument and let go of any residual angry feelings. And with your emotions under control and your thinking cap firmly on, you're in a more positive position to talk to your partner.

If you try to share the results of your post-mortem flow sheet while one or both of you is still feeling angry, the argument can easily flare up again. So ensure that both of you are calm and ready to talk before sharing your discoveries.

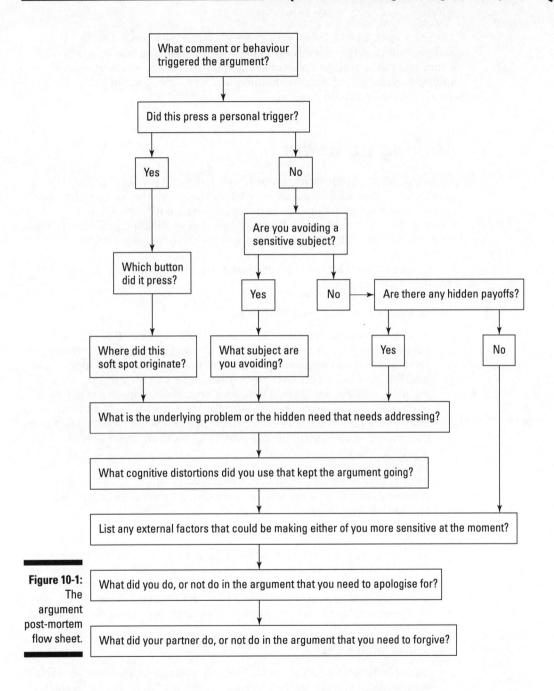

Figure 10-1:
The argument post-mortem flow sheet.

After you've completed your post-mortem, you have a much better understanding of the real issues facing your relationship and a greater awareness of the role you play in keeping the argument merry-go-round spinning. With this information in mind and a greater sense of calm, the time's come to make up properly.

Making up again

Making up after an argument can be a wonderful experience. The battle's over and you can breathe a sigh of relief and patch up the hurt and broken pieces of your relationship. But in order to make up with confidence, knowing that neither of you is harbouring any resentments, you need to make sure that the air is clear of any debris and the dust has fully settled.

To ensure that your making up isn't just papering over the cracks, follow the five-step make-up plan:

1. **Acknowledge your responsibility.**

   First and foremost, you need to acknowledge to yourself and to your partner how you were responsible for starting the argument, reacting to the argument and keeping the argument going. Try to be as specific as possible and make sure that any explanations you offer aren't justifications. For example, 'I was very tired yesterday when I got back from work and overreacted to your request to go back out and buy milk. I misread your request as being demanding and selfish and refused to let the subject drop in spite of your efforts to avoid an argument.'

2. **Apologise.**

   After you've accepted the ways in which you were to blame for the argument, it's time to say you're sorry. Not a half-hearted sorry, but a full, heartfelt apology.

3. **Forgive.**

   An apology is pointless unless the other person accepts it and forgives. If your partner has said she's sorry, your responsibility is to accept her apology and forgive. That doesn't mean that you're saying what she did doesn't matter or that you're going to forget all about, it simply means that you're willing to let go of your negative feelings towards her for the offence.

4. **Accept forgiveness.**

   If your partner has forgiven you, but you continue to chastise yourself for a mistake you made, the forgiveness was pointless. Being forgiven doesn't mean that you don't have to make an effort in the future, but it does mean that you can stop beating yourself up.

5. **Reach out.**

You can reach out to each other and reconnect in lots of different ways. You can do something special together, such as going out for a meal or a romantic stroll, or you can share a glass of wine, have a hug, or dive into bed. What you do doesn't matter as long as it helps you to get close again and enjoy the good things in your relationship.

Recovering from an argument can be physically, psychologically and emotionally exhausting and takes essential energy away from other areas of life such as parenting, work and having fun. The faster you can make up with your partner, the faster you regain your vigour for life.

After you've made up, you need to focus on the positives in your relationship and rebuild your intimacy and connection. Chapters 4 and 5 offer lots of suggestions on how you can get closer.

When making up is hard to do

The aftermath of an argument can be a tense and difficult time. With each of you nursing your wounds, you can easily retreat into silence or monosyllabic replies. You may be tempted to behave like a child. You both want to get close again, but you're feeling hurt and upset and want your partner to make everything better.

Making up may be easy, but only after you can get in touch with your adult self and leave any childlike feelings and behaviours behind. If you want to get the relationship back on track again, you need to obey the following making-up rules:

✔ **Don't sulk.** Understandably you feel hurt, upset and angry, but withdrawing into a childlike, sulky silence isn't going help you or your partner. Recognise what you're doing, let go of your stubbornness and focus on the bigger picture of getting close again.

✔ **Don't punish.** Wanting to get back at your partner is another common childlike response after an argument. Your child voice is telling you to retaliate and make your partner hurt like she hurt you. But if you go deeper inside, you find that what your child really wants is a big hug and to get close again so that you can go out and play instead.

✔ **Don't pick the scab.** After an argument you can be very tempted to keep replaying it over and over again in your head: remembering what your partner said, thinking about a better comeback, tutting and cursing under your breath at the unfairness of everything. This is another childlike response that does no more than fuel your negative feelings and postpone your healing.

When you're able to get in touch with your adult self, you're ready to let go of your negative feelings and focus on how you can heal the rift between you and resolve the deeper issues. The sooner you do this, the sooner you feel better and are able to get on with the rest of your life.

Committing to better conflict resolution skills

After you've made up, you may be tempted to leave the whole messy business in the past and not talk about it again. And while you obviously do want to reach this point at some stage, before you can do that you need to feel confident that history is not going to repeat itself.

Before you put your feet up and relax, take some time to discuss and agree the following:

- ✔ What can each of you do in the future to avoid triggers?
- ✔ Which cognitive distortions do you need to become aware of and stop?
- ✔ When can you sit down and talk about the underlying issue that's causing our argument cycle?

The last point is the most important one, because after you've dealt with this matter, the other two will disappear on their own. Having identified the root cause of your argument, you can use the relevant information in Part IV and the negotiation skills that I outline in Chapter 9 to help you find a lasting solution.

Part IV
Working Through Relationship Issues

'You knew I wasn't perfect when you met me.'

In this part . . .

Every couple hits problems in their relationship, at least occasionally. Not because the individuals are awkward or the relationship is on dodgy ground but because we're human, and sometimes things just do go wrong.

This Part starts off by focusing on the day-to-day hassles of living with another human being: Running a home, earning a living and looking after family. The next chapter explores the difficult emotional challenges that some couples face and gives some ideas for how to deal with them together. I go on to talk about the twists and turns of life and give you some tips for navigating them together. Everything you never want to know about affairs is covered in its own chapter, and then I finish with a chapter on how to recognise if it's the end of the road for your relationship.

Chapter 11

Overcoming Day-to-Day Grumbles

● ●

In This Chapter

▶ Understanding the impact of day-to-day living

▶ Developing a teamwork attitude

▶ Working together to overcome differences

▶ Protecting your relationship from contaminating stress

● ●

*I*n this chapter I look at all those minor and major irritations that couples who set up home together have to face. In the heady days of early romance, you can't possibly imagine that one day you may be fighting over a pair of dirty socks or who's meant to pick up little Billy's football boots. But unfortunately, when reality strikes, these little niggles are often what can turn your blissful home into a battleground.

Here I explore why these seemingly trivial issues are so powerful and how you can overcome them. I help you understand yourself and your partner better, and show you how to minimise the effect that life's daily stresses have on your relationship.

Homing In on Housework Hassles

Very few people on the planet actually enjoy housework. When have you ever heard someone say 'Oh please, please, let me do the washing-up' – unless, of course, you were offering some kind of reward in return. You don't call housework 'chores' without good reason. Jobs around the house are a pain, but unfortunately everyone has to do them. Even those couples fortunate enough to be able to pay a cleaner still have to find a way of getting the dirty laundry in the basket and the pots into the dishwasher. Housework's a hassle that affects everyone.

Figures vary in different surveys, but on average 26 per cent of couples argue regularly about housework, and many resort to couple therapy to try to resolve their differences. On the surface, paying someone to resolve your arguments, rather than just paying someone to do the cleaning for you, may seem crazy, but the reason housework causes so many problems is that it represents some of the most fundamental human values.

Understanding why housework matters so much

Imagine you've had an exhausting day at work and you come home to discover the house is a tip. Washing-up is left in the sink, lunch crumbs are all over the table, the milk's left out on the side and a coat's thrown on the floor. And then you walk into the living room and find your beloved engrossed in his favourite TV programme. You're unlikely to be thinking how happy you are to see him. In fact, as you either sulk, storm out of the room or begin to share your disappointment and frustration in reasonable or not so reasonable tones, you're much more likely to be thinking and feeling one of the following:

- You don't care about me.
- You don't respect me.

What started as a bit of a mess is now turning into a major commotion. Disagreements about who should do what around the house press two major emotional buttons: the uncared-for button and the disrespect button. When your partner fails to do what you see as being his fair share, you conclude either that he doesn't respect you or that he doesn't care for you, or both.

Most people are brought up to see housework as a rather menial and demeaning task, so they can easily interpret a reluctant partner's behaviour as a sign of arrogance, a signal that he believes himself to be too important for the job. So by leaving the work undone, he gives you an implicit message that the work's more suited to you. In reality, this is rarely the case: in all probability your partner forgot to do the chores or you arrived home sooner than expected. But unfortunately, when your partner has pressed your disrespect button, you can need a while to relieve the pressure.

You may also have been brought up to believe that loving someone includes looking after their physical needs. If your mum or dad showed their love by tidying up after you, packing your sandwiches, caring for your clothes and so on, then you're more likely to see your partner's withholding of these small duties as a sign that he doesn't care for you.

Annoyingly, these two viewpoints can combine to create a stalemate. One partner complains 'If you respected me, you'd put things away after yourself,' while the other retorts 'But if you cared for me, you'd want to do it for me.' Fortunately, you can resolve these crazy Catch-22 arguments when both of you recognise what you're doing and commit to addressing the tidying-up issue rather than fighting about who's right and who's wrong.

The reality is that you're both equally right and you're both equally wrong. As with most couple disagreements, you just have differences in perspective. The sooner you see the housework through your partner's eyes, the sooner you can resolve the problem. You need to confront the issue not each other.

Another dynamic sometimes underlies a couple's ongoing housework hassles: using housework as the battleground for a war that's really about something else altogether. Often the root's still respect or care, but the reason you can never fully resolve the problem may be because you're not addressing the real issue. If you've got a nagging feeling that every time you bicker about housework you're actually making mountains out of molehills, stop and consider what else may be going on. Flick to Chapter 10 for more help on unravelling the roots of your rows.

Recognising differences in tidiness tolerance

Tidiness, like beauty, is in the eye of the beholder. What I may see as ordered serenity, you may see as a cold, barren emptiness. Back in the 1950s, housewives had a media blueprint of how their homes should look, but now many different ways exist of running your home. You may like a rich, unordered, lived-in look, but your partner may prefer a fuss-free, minimalist environment. You may not care if you leave washing-up until the morning or iron shirts when you need them, whereas your partner may like to get everything done and out of the way before he relaxes.

This is another of those frustrating areas of life where no right and wrong answer exists. You can try as hard as you like to fight your corner, but the only solution is compromise. But compromise on housework is often much harder than you expect, and this is because tidiness pushes one of your most potent emotional buttons: shame.

Spend a few minutes looking at the following statements and ask yourself how many of them you heard as a child and what impact they had on you. Or, even better, do this exercise together and share your thoughts and feelings:

- Your room's filthy, you should be ashamed of yourself.
- Your untidiness is an embarrassment.
- You're slovenly and lazy.
- Cleanliness is next to godliness.
- Tidy home, tidy mind.

Shame is a powerful weapon that many parents use on children to make them tidy up after themselves. If you were one of those children, then keeping your home clean and tidy is a moral issue. If you were brought up with powerful messages about the moral importance of keeping a tidy home, you probably have a very low tolerance for mess. If you believe that the state of your home reflects your character, you're going to be incredibly uncomfortable if you live surrounded by dirt and disorder.

With housework, you're better to let your standards slip than your relationship.

Some people who were brought up with strong moral imperatives around housework go completely the opposite way. If you find yourself filling up with moral indignation whenever your partner asks you to do something, maybe you were brought up with exactly the same messages, but your way of coping was to rebel against them. You may be determined to live in the environment of your choosing, and refuse to be bullied or shamed into doing otherwise. If this describes you, then recognising what you're doing is probably enough to make you realise that the battle isn't with your partner but with your parents, and now's the time to end the war.

Showing respect and being fair

If you're arguing about housework, then today's the day to stop. That the chores need doing at all is bad enough, so why make things worse by turning housework into a tense and stressful activity?

Here's a plan to help you overcome the problem forever:

- **Understand each other's perspective.** If you haven't already done so, set some time aside to talk about how housework was handled when you were growing up. Was your childhood home dusted and hoovered every day? Were you brought up always to keep the place tidy? Or was your home a more laid-back environment where muddy shoes on the carpet were no more than a minor inconvenience? Think also about who did the work at home. Did Mum do most? Or did Mum and Dad share the work equally? Were particular chores seen as either men's work or women's work? Were the children expected to pitch in as well?

When you can understand your own attitudes and your partner's, you can much more easily accept that no right or wrong exists. You can also more easily remind yourself that your differences aren't necessarily a reflection of your relationship or of your character, but are simply differences in upbringing.

✔ **Negotiate bottom lines.** Whatever your childhood standards of tidiness and cleanliness may have been, now that you share a home, you need to agree some new benchmarks. Start by sharing the things that bother each of you most. Don't try to justify why each thing is important, focus on the impact it has on you. So if you find that facing a sink full of washing-up in the morning is really difficult, say so. And if your partner says he can't relax in a room where the bin's overflowing, accept that.

Also share anything that your partner does that you particularly struggle with, again without trying to justify it or placing blame. If your partner always puts his laundry on top of the basket rather than in it, explain to him how you feel when that happens. Your goal's to respect one another's views and feelings and agree a baseline of what's important to each of you.

✔ **Establish the contribution that each of you can make.** You can't always divvy out the chores equally, but that doesn't mean that the division can't be fair. If one of you works much longer hours than the other or has much further to travel to and from work, then expecting them to spend the same amount of time on housework isn't fair. Similarly, if one of you has additional responsibilities, for example for children or to parents, then you may have less time and energy to commit to the home.

However, this doesn't mean that the responsibility for caring for the home shouldn't be equal. Even though one of you may spend more time cleaning or cooking or doing the laundry, both of you are equally responsible for getting the jobs done. Both of you must commit to making life as easy as possible for each other, while accepting that, whether you like them or not, some chores just have to be done.

Creating a rota

A housework rota's a simple and easy solution for the many couples and families who find housework an ongoing battleground. A good rota lists everything that needs to be done on a weekly, fortnightly or even monthly basis and makes clear who does what. It also gets around the problem that some people see mess more than others. If either you or your partner is one of those lucky people who just don't see the clutter and dirt around them, then a rota's perfect because it stops you having to be permanently alert lest you miss something that your partner claims is right under your nose.

Here are some steps for making your rota:

1. **Make a list of everything that needs to be done on a daily, weekly, fortnightly or monthly basis.**

   As well as household tasks, put down things like cooking, laundry, gardening, managing finances, cleaning the car, food shopping and anything else that feels like a chore.

2. **Look at the list and tick the things that each of you enjoys and is happy to continue doing.**

   The key to a successful rota is collaboration. When both of you (and your children as well, if you have any) are involved in creating the rota, then it's far, far more likely to work. And giving people jobs they like to do balances the drudgery of the less enjoyable tasks.

3. **Now divvy up the chores that each of you dislikes.**

   Remember that negotiating is okay. So if you really, really, really hate cleaning the loo, consider swapping that chore for two others. If both of you despise some tasks, agree to rotate them. Try to think creatively as you go through the list. Can you do some activities together to make them more fun or at least more tolerable? Can you pay someone else to do some things – either a family member or a professional?

4. **After you have your final rota, agree a period over which to run with it before doing an evaluation.**

   Some things seem straightforward on paper, but in reality they just don't work. So agree together that your rota's a work in progress that's always renegotiable.

Minimising Money Maelstroms

Money may make the world go around but, unfortunately, it brings many relationships to a grinding halt. Whether you like the fact or not, money's an important and essential part of your life, so perhaps not surprisingly, it often causes a lot of stress.

People's attitudes towards money and spending vary enormously, and some are naturally better budgeters than others. But money arguments are rarely about pounds and pence: they reflect deeper issues of life values, self-worth and power.

Recognising the roots of money rows

Attitudes to money start in early childhood. Each family earns, manages and spends its money in a different way. Some people talk about money very openly, sharing how much they earn and how much things cost; for others, money may be a taboo subject. If money was tight in your childhood, then you may have grown up instinctively aware of the value of things. But if your family was more affluent, you may have no experience of ever worrying about cash flow.

Some parents see teaching their children about money as really important – perhaps by giving them pocket money from an early age and teaching them how to budget. Others prefer to hold on to the purse strings and give their children money only when required, and some parents use money as a reward.

The way your parents managed money says a lot about the values they attached to it, and you and your partner are likely to have grown up to adopt these same values for yourselves. Broadly speaking, your attitude's likely to be one of the following:

- **Money's for enjoying.** Someone who believes money's for enjoying may drive a nice car, have great holidays and see saving for tomorrow as a waste of today.

- **Money's for security.** You want to squirrel away any excess cash into a savings account. You want to be sure that if a rainy day ever comes along, you've got enough resources to deal with it.

- **Money's for sharing.** You're a generous host who always wants your guests to have the best. You enjoy buying presents for friends and family, and you may also give regularly to charity.

If you and your partner have different attitudes, you're going to run into difficulties. If you have plenty of money, then you should be able to reach a compromise – saving some and spending some. But when money's tight, perhaps the security person's a tight-fisted pessimist, the sharer has his priorities all wrong and the person who enjoys spending his money's little more than a selfish, short-sighted hedonist.

But before you sink into a pit of despair, remember that no attitude's right or wrong. When you can understand where your values have come from and can talk about and accept your differences, you can work together to find a mutually acceptable compromise (see 'Creating a couple-friendly financial plan', later in this chapter).

Before I move on from the roots of money rows, I want to look at one other very important point. And that's what money says about your priorities in life, what it says about the things you value most.

Consider this: if, out of the blue, you got a £500 tax rebate, how would you spend it? Would you treat yourself to something special? Take your best friend away for a weekend break? Buy that gift for your partner that he's always wanted? Put it in a savings account? Buy something for the kids? Put it towards the family holiday? Would you and your partner make the same choices or would the discussion end in a row?

When couples argue about how to spend money, they're not just arguing about how much things cost, they're arguing about what they're worth. If a man spends more on his mother's Christmas present than his wife's, or a woman is happy to splash out on a spa break with a friend but whinges about the cost of going away as a couple, each is speaking volumes about their priorities. How much you spend on something reveals how much you value it. And if you struggle to spend money on yourself or feel guilty when someone spends money on you, then perhaps a part of you thinks you're not worth it.

Answer the following questions to explore how your self-worth relates to money:

- ✔ When you spend a lot of money on yourself do you think:

    a. I deserve a treat.

    b. I deserve a reward.

    c. I shouldn't be spending this.

- ✔ When someone else spends a lot of money on you, do you feel:

    a. Special.

    b. Appreciated.

    c. Guilty.

If you answered *a*s, you have positive self-worth and see money as something you're entitled to enjoy. If you answered *b*s, your self-worth's fairly high but you struggle to spend money on yourself unless you think you've earned it in some way. If you've answered *c*s, you put other people and other things before yourself and may have difficulty in appreciating just how valuable you are.

Regardless of what the old saying has us believe, giving is not always better than receiving. Being able to spend money on yourself or letting others treat you without feeling guilty is a sign of positive self-worth. It shows that you value yourself. For more on self-esteem, look at Chapter 3.

If money rows are an issue in your relationship, take some time now to think about what's at the root. Do you have different attitudes on what money's for – security, sharing or enjoying? Or does the way you spend money reflect different priorities in life? Does the way you spend money affect your self-worth because you're left feeling unvalued? If any of this rings true, then the first thing you need to do is sit down and talk to your partner about how you feel, so that both of you have the opportunity to develop greater understanding and find solutions.

Dealing with issues of power and control

Unfortunately, money not only buys essentials and luxuries, it also buys power and influence. For some couples, money becomes a powerful weapon for controlling a partner. And you don't necessarily need to have a huge amount of the stuff to throw your weight around.

When one partner has control of all the money, he also controls the decisions about how money should be spent and, consequently, about the couple's lifestyle. He can decide what car to drive, what goods to have in the home, where to go on holiday, where to eat, what clothes to buy, how much to spend on children and friends, and so on and so on. The other partner may feel that she has no right to make decisions and that she's forced to depend on the grace and generosity of the other. I'm not saying that her partner may not be generous. Indeed, he may have bucketloads of generosity, showering the purse-less partner with extravagant gifts and treats, but with no opportunity to repay the kindness, the partner may feel constantly indebted.

More subtle versions of this power exist. For example, a couple may have equal access to finances, but one person is left with the responsibility to pay all the bills while the other pays for luxuries and entertainment. In this situation, both partners can commonly become resentful that the other's supporting them. Another common scenario is where one person is secretive about his spending but he expects his partner to account for every penny she spends, which, as well as showing mistrust, is massively unfair.

When one partner's using money to gain an unfair advantage over the other, arguments inevitably follow. A relationship that's going to work needs to be equal on every level. Both partners must have and accept equal responsibility for the decisions in life. That doesn't mean that both must earn and contribute the same amount, because that's often not possible, but it does mean that whatever income comes in, both partners are responsible for it.

If money represents a basic inequality within your relationship, then this is an issue that you need to tackle head on. The bottom line is this – money's a resource within a relationship that you can either share to enrich your lives or use against each other to control or maintain distance.

Creating a couple-friendly financial plan

No preset financial plan exists that works for every couple. Everyone's circumstances are different; for example, if you're a second family, then you may have other responsibilities outside your current relationship. To create your individual plan, you first need to know what sums you're working with.

If at all possible, sit down together to create your financial plan. When both of you are involved you're more likely to commit to following the plan.

1. **Get a blank sheet of paper and list all of your income.**

   Remember things like benefits, maintenance payments, rental income and any significant interest from savings, as well as salaries.

2. **On another sheet of paper (unfortunately this one probably has to be a lot bigger!) list your essential outgoings.**

   List things like the mortgage, water rates, TV licence, utilities, insurance, childcare fees, maintenance payments and so on: anything that you absolutely have to pay where the amount tends to be the same every month. You may also want to put a figure in here for savings.

3. **Look at your variable essentials.**

   This is where the fun starts! Undoubtedly, some things both of you agree are essential, such as food and petrol, but for others things – such as entertainment, gadgets, holidays, clothes or, in my case, shoes – one of you may consider something to be more of a luxury. You may find digging out a few old bank statements helpful to ensure you've remembered everything.

4. **Consider the luxuries.**

   Use your findings from the previous step to decide which items of expenditure are non-essential luxuries, and list them.

5. **Set your budget.**

   Put an agreed budget next to each essential and luxury item of outgoing on your list. This is where a bit of quid pro quo may come in handy. If one of you thinks £100 on gadgets is fair and the other thinks he should spend the same amount on shoes, then compromise and agree £50 each. And if you can't agree a figure for an item you both think is essential, haggle until you come up with something you can agree on. If you can't agree at all on some items, you may want to list these separately as things that come out of your own individual pockets.

6. **Organise your banking.**

   Most couples manage their basic income and expenditure through a joint account. You can agree to have both of your salaries paid into the same account to cover your essential costs and your joint luxuries. Then set up a standing order into your individual accounts to pay for your individual luxuries and any treats that you may occasionally want for yourself or presents you want to buy for each other.

   How much you decide to pay into your individual accounts obviously depends on how much surplus cash you have, but may also depend on the amount of your contribution to the household income. Some couples prefer to split everything 50/50, regardless of who earns the money, whereas some like to split everything in proportion to their incomes. So if one of you earns 25 per cent more than the other, he pays 25 per cent more of the bills but pays 25 per cent more into his individual account. The choice is yours.

   Finally, decide how much money you're okay to spend from your joint account without checking with each other. Rather than walking away from that bargain sale item or risking a major row for wasting money on something frivolous, agree your budget for impulse buys.

Table 11-1 shows an example financial plan, to give you an idea how the concept works:

Table 11-1	An example financial plan
Monthly joint income	£4,580
Total for essential fixed costs	£2,900 (mortgage, rates, utilities, insurance, child support payments, insurance, loans, TV/broadband package, pension plan, standing order to savings account)
Budget for variable fixed costs	£950 (food, clothing, petrol, DVD rental, presents, kids' entertainment, Pilates classes, DIY sundries)
Budget for joint luxuries	£430 (cinema, meals out, extra unneeded clothes, CDs, days out)
Regular payment to personal account	£150 each

Dealing with Toddlers, Teenagers and All Ages in Between

Parenting's a difficult job and one that can cause a whole load of headaches for couples. Whether you have a toddler going through the terrible twos or a 13-year-old intent on pushing you to breaking point, the pressure can at times feel intolerable. Parenting together is a skill that's well worth picking up as early as possible in your parenting career. The rules and roles that each of you chooses may change as your children grow, but being able to support each other needs to be continuous.

Not only is harmonious, cooperative parenting a benefit for the parents, it's also essential for children. The relationship between the adults in a home determines the atmosphere of the whole household, so making a priority of strengthening your relationship is the best investment you can make for your future family happiness. Battles with your kids may be inevitable, but war between the parents isn't.

Seeing what you picked up about parenting as a child

You discover how to be a parent from your parents, from what they say and from what they don't say. You pick up all sorts of messages about how children should behave and how childhood should be. Some of those messages are very conscious and others may be deeply ingrained in your unconscious psyche.

Often only when a situation challenges those unconscious messages do you even know that they exist. So as parents you are inevitably going to discover lots about yourselves and reflect on your childhoods in a way that perhaps you've never done before. The more you and your partner can share your childhood experiences and talk about how you were parented, the more insight you have into yourself and into each other.

Take a sheet of paper and at the top write 'Children should . . . ' Now brainstorm all the statements that come into your mind. Try not to censor yourself if things come up that you don't agree with. The negative messages can often be just as powerful if not more so than the positive ones.

CASE STUDY

Identifying and respecting differences

John and Karrie had three children aged 7, 4 and 2, and they often bickered about how to bring them up. As they talked about their childhoods, they began to see why they had such different parenting styles. John was the eldest of four boys and he had lived in a hectic home where the kids were often left to fend for themselves. As the eldest, he had always taken a responsible role. If the boys were ever naughty, his parents adopted the short sharp shock treatment. In John's experience, children should know that life is hard, and should be resourceful and responsible, respect their parents and do what they're told. Karrie's childhood had been more privileged. She was a much-longed-for only child who had always got a lot of her parents' affection and attention. Her only responsibilities were to have fun and do well at school. According to her experience, children should play, have fun, be kind and love their parents. As they discovered each other's backgrounds, John and Karrie began to respect their differences and talk about how they could collaborate to build the future for their children that they both hoped for.

If you were fortunate enough to have a happy childhood, then you may be content to model your parenting style and beliefs on how you were brought up. But if your childhood was difficult, then you may be adamant that you're not going to make the same mistakes with your children. Either way, you need to work together as a couple to develop a parenting style that works for each of you and for your children.

Agreeing the roles of parenting

Fifty years ago, life was simple. Limited, but simple. Women stayed at home and looked after the children and the home, and men went out to work. Today, many, different ways of parenting exist. Men and women, or same-sex parents, split the workload and the responsibility according to their individual circumstances and the changing needs of their growing families. You no longer have a blueprint for being a family; instead you have lots of different approaches.

When couples can't define the roles of mum and dad, arguments often follow. Those arguments can be particularly bitter because each feels that the other's not living up to their parenting responsibilities. But in reality, these rows are often more about misunderstandings and lack of communication than anything else.

Parenting roles and duties change as your children and family grow, so you have to remain flexible and continue to adapt together. Some roles are fixed because of your gender; for example, only mums can breastfeed and dads are generally better at giving 8-year-olds piggybacks. Other roles are tied to your circumstances such as your work hours. So Dad may always drop the kids at school and Mum may always collect and do tea. But the majority of duties are up to the two of you to divide according to your abilities, availability and, of course, fairness.

Some parenting duties are always the joint and equal responsibility of both parents. You must both love, protect and nurture your children. The way you demonstrate this may vary, but children must know that both parents care for them equally.

One of the easiest ways to talk about who should do what in the family is to start by creating a list of everything that needs to be done. So, get a piece of paper and start writing. List all the childcare duties you can think of, but leave out discipline issues (I cover those in the next section). Starting in the morning, work your way through an average day and also note any activities or duties that happen on a regular basis. Your list may look something like this:

Daily	*Regular*
Get kids up and dressed	Lifts to Brownies, football practice
Organise breakfast	Visiting grandparents
Get lunch boxes ready	Trips/treats – McDonald's, park
School run there and back	Dentist/doctor/health appointments
Helping with homework	Playing games
Bath	
Bed and story	

After you've completed the list, you can use this as a basis for deciding who should do what. As you divide up the difficult duties, make sure that one of you isn't getting all the fun stuff while the other gets all the drudgery. Bear in mind the amount of positive child contact time that you have available and ensure that you both get as much quality time with your kids as possible. Remember that you can share many activities or you can take some things in turns so that children get an equal share of your attention.

However you set up your system, your family needs and circumstances change over time. Sometimes, children want their mum or dad more than at other times. Your goal should be a united team with two parents that your children can feel equally close to.

Setting boundaries and maintaining discipline

Being naughty's part of growing up. In order for children to become independent human beings, they have to be allowed to flex their growing muscles and make their own decisions (even if they seem like stupid ones to you). Inevitably, they make mistakes. A parent's job is to make sure that boundaries are in place to keep children safe while they experiment, and to put them right when they're going too far.

When couples argue about discipline, they do so for one or both of the following reasons:

✔ They don't agree on the rules.

✔ They don't agree with the style of discipline being used.

To avoid these arguments, first and foremost you need to agree the rules of your home. Now, that may be easier said than done, but remember that your children absolutely must have clear, consistent boundaries that they know both of you support. Good parenting means being on the same side and making sure that your children know that.

The rules you put together need to be reasonable for the age of your child or children. If your children are old enough, you may think about including them in coming up with the rules for your home. Consider the following areas as you put your list together:

✔ Bedtimes

✔ Courtesy to others

✔ Home times

✔ Housework

✔ Meal times

✔ Schoolwork

If you really can't agree on something, then you must compromise. As a general principle, if the rule's about safety, then respect the parent with the strictest opinion, because he gets most stressed if he has to back down. But on all other things, remember that whatever you're arguing about doesn't matter anywhere near as much as presenting a united front.

The next thing you need to do is agree what the consequences are if a child breaks a rule. Again, the consequences need to match the age of the child, and you should never be angry or abusive. The goal should be to teach not to punish.

Finally, you must both be committed to sticking to the rules and following through with any consequences, and, perhaps most importantly, setting a good example to your children through your own behaviour.

For more on parenting, treat the family to *Parenting For Dummies* by Helen Brown (Wiley).

Facing the challenges of step-parenting

Becoming part of a step-family is a big step for everyone – parents and children. Understanding how you and your partner feel and discovering how to manage everyone's concerns helps the two of you create a positive atmosphere for everyone involved.

Helping children adjust

Becoming part of a step-family almost inevitably means the breakdown of an old one and, because most children want their parents to live together happily ever after, they often have a lot of emotions that they find difficult to handle. Some children can feel afraid that a new step-parent may get in the way of their relationship with the absent parent, or they may feel disloyal to their absent parent if they like their step-parent too much. Some can resent a new step-parent for damaging the closeness and attention that they enjoyed with their single mum or dad. And some may feel particularly resentful if they have to share limited resources with new step-siblings. Nearly all children worry that they're not going to get as much love and attention as they used to, but in spite of this, most do want to get on with their step-parent and any step-siblings.

A common problem within step-families is that any difficulties with the children are assumed to be because of the family change. But in reality, growing up's a difficult and stressful experience, and nearly all children go through difficult times. Any problems you're having may just be normal kid stuff, and nothing at all to do with being part of a step-family.

What children need is reassurance that although family life has changed, they are just as important as they ever were and that your love never diminishes.

Protecting your relationship

Children aren't the only ones with worries and anxieties about change. Parents can feel particularly concerned about making sure that their kids don't feel pushed out by a new partner, and step-parents can worry about their role. Many step-parents put a huge amount of pressure on themselves to love and get on well with a new partner's children, but in reality loving a step-child as if he were your own may never be possible. Step-parents who are separated from their own children can also feel guilty that they spend more time with someone else's children than they do with their own.

If you're a step-couple, then you haven't had any time alone together to build your relationship before children entered the scene. If only one of you has children, then you may feel guilty that you can't give either your partner or your children 100 per cent of your attention. And if both of you have children, then both of you have other priorities and commitments competing for your time.

The biggest issues that step-couples face are to do with loyalty and jealousy. The bond between parent and child is very strong, and some couples struggle with feeling pushed out by this. Remember that children always hold a very special place in a parent's heart, and this is quite different from the feelings a parent has for a partner. Children also grow up and move away, so a parent's attention isn't divided for ever.

Another common area of tension is ex-partners. If exes are still involved in parenting (which hopefully they are), then you can't completely move on from the past. Some new partners can struggle with this, but if you can remember that the relationship's changed and the common ground is the children, not anything else, then you can more easily maintain perspective and work with your partner in the best interests of the children.

Here are some general tips to help you run a smoother step-family home:

✔ Sit down together and set clear roles and responsibilities for yourselves and the children.

✔ Make sure that you spend time alone with your own children and time alone with the step-children too! Also encourage children to spend time with their absent parent. This ensures that children know that you respect all these different relationships.

✔ Don't attempt to discipline step-children until you've built a relationship with them.

 ✔ Try not to take negative feelings personally – children often dislike the step-parent's role, not the person themselves.

 ✔ Grab every opportunity you can to spend time alone as a couple and continue to build on your relationship with each other.

A healthy couple relationship takes time and commitment, and sometimes letting your relationship slip is easier, because you're torn by so many other conflicting demands. But any investment's well worth making – for you and for your children.

Juggling Parents, In-laws, Friends, Work and Other Stuff

Relationships would be so much easier if you could just be left on your own, but unfortunately everyone has to deal with life as well. On top of the complexities of running a home and having kids that I explore in the earlier sections, you have other family members to look after and visit, friends to keep up with, hobbies and leisure interests to maintain and, of course, work to do.

All of these things can put pressure on a relationship, not just in terms of time but also your priorities. When couples lead busy lives they have to work together to keep their relationships top of the agenda.

Understanding how 'everything' affects couples

Take a look at the life wheel in Figure 11-1. This represents how your relationships are both the hub, in the centre of the wheel, and the tyre around the outside. The spokes are all the different duties, responsibilities and activities that you bring into your relationship – things that affect your day-to-day life.

Relationship

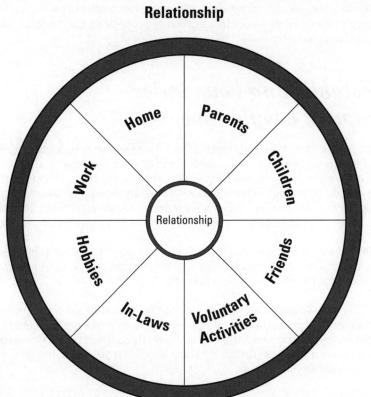

Home
Parents
Work
Children
Relationship
Hobbies
Friends
In-Laws
Voluntary Activities

Relationship

Figure 11-1:
The life
wheel.

For a wheel to function properly, you have to look after the hub, the tyre and the spokes. If one of the spokes is damaged or not working, then you're in for a bumpy ride.

The same is true in a relationship. If you've got problems with your children or your in-laws, or at work or down the club or in the Brownie pack you run, then they're going to affect both of you as a couple. Even if the problem doesn't take time away from your relationship, it almost certainly diverts your energy. And if the problem's something that the two of you don't agree on or that creates stress for you both, then the impact can be very detrimental.

When a couple can understand how everything affects their relationship, they're more likely to confront external problems together and put measures in place to protect it.

Establishing boundaries around couple time

The most successful relationships are those where couples make a priority of spending time together. Like a plant without water, a relationship can wither and die if you don't have regular time together. To stay connected as a couple, you need to feed your relationship with time: time to share your hopes and dreams as well as your fears and failings, time to keep in touch with what's happening in your everyday lives, and time to have fun.

Chapter 4 explores ways in which you can prioritise your relationship and make time for each other. After you create time to spend together, you must be careful to protect those moments.

Other people and other activities can often impinge on your time with your partner, and resentments often begin to build if one person seems unable to put boundaries around their time. If you have parents or in-laws or friends who have a habit of turning up uninvited, then you need to agree as a couple how you can handle this.

Most people do respect the importance of a couple having time alone, but unless you tell them, they may not know that they're getting in the way. One simple solution is to say that you're not available on certain days of the week or at certain times of the day. You can make this time even more secure by switching off your mobile and agreeing not to answer the phone.

Another problem can arise when one of you doesn't stick to the couple time that you've agreed, perhaps regularly going to the pub on the way home from work or arriving with a friend when you're looking forward to time alone. When this happens, the other partner can feel as though the relationship isn't important or that his partner prefers being with someone else than alone with him.

All couples have different needs for intimacy, and some people genuinely don't need to spend much time with their partners to feel connected. But two of you are in this relationship. So rather than take the issue personally, you need to share honestly how you feel and find a compromise that you both agree to stick with to ensure that both of your needs are met.

Accepting interruptions to your time

At some periods of your life, other things take up time that you want to be spending as a couple; for example if you're starting up a business or have just got a promotion, if your children are going through a particularly difficult or demanding patch, or if you have elderly parents you need to care for.

Unfortunately, you can't schedule life to fit into your diary; sometimes life just happens and you have do whatever you can to cope. But that doesn't mean that you can't continue to make your relationship the priority. If you know that when the chips are down, your partner always put your needs first, you can much more easily be relaxed when other things take his attention away from you.

Accepting your circumstances is the first step towards working together. When both of you can acknowledge, without blame, that life's tough at the moment, you can work as a team to get through your challenges.

Chapter 12

Handling the Bigger Difficulties

*E*motions and mental health problems are tricky things – not only for those experiencing them, but also for those who have to live with them. Some emotions are harder for couples to work through than others, especially if they're deep rooted and persistent. While the emotional partner is struggling to manage her difficult feelings and fluctuating between remorse and justification, the other partner is left to look after his own needs while balancing empathy with frustration.

This chapter starts by staring the green-eyed monster in the face and untangling the grip that jealousy and insecurity have on so many relationships. I then move on to focus on the difficulties of living with depression, anxiety and any kind of addiction or compulsive disorder, and offer support and advice for how you can recover together as a couple. Finally, I look at the destructive power of anger within a relationship – overt rage and also its quieter but equally devastating cousin, passive aggression.

I don't have enough room on these pages to go into depth on all of these issues, but I hope you find sufficient information to help you recognise and minimise the impact these powerful emotions may be having on your relationship. Wherever possible, I signpost you to other resources where you can get further help to overcome the problem for good.

Understanding Jealousy and Insecurity

Saint Augustine said, 'He that is not jealous, is not in love.' An odd thing to say perhaps, especially for a celibate bishop, but he did have a point. Jealousy, unlike envy, only exists when you face a threat – real or imaginary – of losing something you care about. So if you're genuinely in love, you almost inevitably feel at least some occasional discomfort in situations where you think that your relationship, or the quality of your relationship, may be under threat.

To a certain extent, occasional feelings of insecurity are also inevitable. Unless you have exceptionally high levels of self-esteem, or perhaps I should say arrogance, sometimes you question whether you're good enough for your partner. But like jealousy, in a healthy relationship this insecurity is a fleeting emotion that you can quickly manage and reassure. However, if you're unable to manage these feelings, then both jealousy and insecurity can become poisons that kill the very thing you most want to preserve.

Jealousy and insecurity are inextricably linked. The more secure you feel about your relationship and the more confident you are that both of you are fulfilled in that relationship, the less jealous you feel.

Knowing why a little jealousy is good for relationships

Many psychologists believe that jealousy is an innate part of being human. Evidence suggests that babies as young as 5 months old can experience jealousy if given the right (or rather the wrong) trigger. In some ways, jealousy's like grief. Not to feel grief when someone you love dies is odd to say the least, or even indicative of a mental health problem. Similarly, to feel no jealousy at all if your partner announces she's fallen in love with someone else is also weird.

Jealousy is nature's way of protecting relationships. It's a natural by-product of your desire to keep your relationship intimate and intact. In the early days of a relationship, when the overwhelming ardour of infatuation isn't yet balanced by the security of commitment, jealousy tends to be strongest and most easily triggered. You're more aware of rivals, both present and past, as you endeavour to secure your position as the apple of your lover's eye. Then as love matures and security increases, jealousy slips into the background. But like grief, it's always there, waiting in the shadows of love.

As well as protecting the existence of a relationship, jealousy also protects the quality of it. This is why people can feel jealous of a partner's ex, even after an acrimonious divorce when they know that the partner can't bear even to speak to her former partner. It's also why someone who's perfectly happy in a new relationship can feel jealous when an ex gets a new partner. Everyone wants to feel that their relationships are special and unique, or in the case of an ex, were special and unique. The appearance of another partner, old or new, raises questions of how you match up. Did the partner offer, or will she offer, something that you never can? Was or will the relationship contain something special that's missing from the two of you?

If you're tempted to try to make your partner jealous in order to add a bit of extra spice to your relationship, tread very, very carefully. A pinch of occasional flirting may not harm some relationships, but in others it's enough to burn trust to cinder.

A little bit of jealousy stops you taking your relationship for granted and ensures that you continue to show your partner how much you value her. A little bit of jealousy can heighten emotions, making love feel stronger and sex more passionate.

Seeing how jealousy can get out of control

Some say that jealousy isn't really an emotion, but a complex combination of many thoughts, behaviours and feelings. The experience of jealousy can include some, or if you're really unlucky all, of the following components:

- **Behaviour:** Difficulty sleeping, being shaky and trembling, feeling faint, flushing, loss of appetite, palpitations, stomach complaints
- **Feelings:** Pain, grief, anger, envy, fear, helplessness, humiliation, anxiety, panic, doubt
- **Thoughts:** Being inferior, self-pity, possessiveness, self-blame, resentment, being left out, being beaten, planning revenge, being suspicious

As you can see, experiencing jealousy is no fun at all, and that's why people want to stop it as fast as possible by getting their relationship back onto solid ground. It's also why a few people resort to extremes of behaviour such as stalking a partner, harassing a rival, or even murder to get rid of the pain.

Befriending the green-eyed monster

Ellie would never have described herself as the jealous type until she met Rob. She came for counselling alone, because she thought her behaviour was extreme and out of control. She felt acutely embarrassed by the lengths she was taking to keep tabs on Rob and to attempt to curb her horrendous doubts about his fidelity. A new female colleague had just joined Rob's company, and he talked about her endlessly. She was witty and attractive, and he described her as an inspiration to him. Although Ellie had no evidence that Rob was having an affair, she was terrified of him falling in love with the new colleague, the same way he'd fallen in love with her at work ten years previously. Ellie tearfully confessed that she was checking Rob's phone and email, and that once the kids were at school, she was spending every lunch hour hanging around Rob's offices to see whether he was going to lunch or, even worse, was with the new colleague. She was shocked and horrified by her behaviour and didn't understand what was going on.

Ellie's story isn't unusual. Jealous behaviour can become extreme, but if the threat is real, and assuming that no one's being hurt or abused, it's a natural response to protect your love. But often the threat isn't real. You imagine the threat or blow it completely out of proportion. Then jealousy isn't a natural and healthy response to protect love, but an irrational emotion that can wreak havoc on an otherwise healthy relationship.

Recognising unhealthy jealousy

Knowing whether jealousy's justified and therefore healthy, or unwarranted and therefore unhealthy, isn't always easy. If your partner's never been unfaithful and has always been devoted to you, but you still feel jealous, then you're probably being irrational. But if your partner has been unfaithful or constantly puts down your relationship, your feelings are understandable. If the previous sentence describes you, you can find more help in Chapter 14 as well as later in this chapter.

Comparing healthy and unhealthy jealousy

Table 12-1 lays out some of the key differences between normal, acceptable jealousy and jealousy that's moved into the realms of damaging your relationship.

Table 12-1	Healthy Versus Unhealthy Jealousy
Healthy Jealousy	*Unhealthy Jealousy*
Inspires couples to become and stay committed	Distorts emotions and focuses on the negative
Reminds you of the good things in your relationship	Creates conflict and emotional distress for both partners
Makes your partner more attractive and more valuable	Wastes time that could be spent on enjoying each other
Encourages you to improve your relationship	Feels embarrassing, confusing and restricting
Maintains excitement and increases passion	Drives couples apart

Identifying the signs of irrational jealousy

If you experience anything more than just a brief flutter of jealousy in response to the following situations, the chances are good that your jealousy's unwarranted and may be damaging your relationship:

- ✔ Your partner receives a text message but doesn't open it and read it in front of you.
- ✔ Your partner looks admiringly at a beautiful passer-by.
- ✔ Your partner says that she fancies a movie star.
- ✔ Your partner enjoys an intimate conversation with a mutual friend of yours of the opposite sex.
- ✔ Your partner talks fondly about an ex.
- ✔ Your partner suddenly announces that she has to work late and then doesn't come home until gone midnight.
- ✔ Your partner has a close same-sex friend whom you know she confides in.
- ✔ Your partner enjoys going out in the evening with single friends.
- ✔ Your partner talks with regret about being unfaithful to a previous partner, many years ago.
- ✔ You try to phone your partner but you can't get through for hours.

Unwarranted jealousy can be devastating to relationships. With nothing but vague, circumstantial evidence to support the anxiety, the jealous partner feels like she's going crazy, and the innocent partner lives under a cloud of suspicion and unfounded accusations. The jealous partner's burdened with a constant nagging insecurity, either that her partner may leave her, or that she may be unfaithful or secretly love someone else more than him. But her never-ending drive to gain security through persistent pleas for reassurance and her checking up push the partner away, creating conflict, distance and more insecurity. And so the jealousy becomes worse, the demands increase and the cycle continues.

For both partners, unwarranted jealousy feels unbearable and impossible to beat. Both feel helpless and powerless to stop the cycle, and both can begin to question the viability of a relationship that seems so fragile.

Defeating the green-eyed monster

If you're struggling with jealousy and you want to overcome it, the first step is to identify the root cause. Most people with irrational jealousy have a whole list of issues feeding into the problem. By separating out these contributory factors, you can deal with them one by one and begin to conquer your insecurities.

Whatever the root of irrational jealousy, you can beat it. But doing so takes the commitment of both partners. Many couples make the mistake of assuming that jealousy's just one partner's problem – something the partner has to get over alone. But like many other difficulties, when the problem affects the relationship, it becomes a joint problem – one that both partners need to take responsibility for fixing.

Working through old baggage

Look at these two specific areas in your past and see whether any wounds exist that need healing:

- **Your childhood:** If either of your parents was unfaithful or suffered from jealousy, you may have picked up negative messages about relationships. If you also experienced rejection from a parent, you may find trusting the security of a relationship harder, and perhaps your jealousy's a way of pushing your partner to prove that she'll never leave you.

- **Previous relationships:** If you've experienced infidelity in a previous relationship, you may be hyper-vigilant to any signs of betrayal and ultra-sensitive to anything that's not 100 per cent open and honest.

Facing up to your own fidelity

An uncomfortable possibility, but one that's true for some jealous partners, is that some irrational jealousy is a projection of doubts about their own ability to be faithful. They may have had an affair, be involved in an affair or secretly want one, but rather than face that fact, they project their weakness onto their partners and tell themselves 'they're no better than me'.

If this strikes a chord with you, it's time to reappraise your relationship and be honest about the validity of your jealousy.

Working through old baggage can be hard work. Sometimes simply becoming aware of your history and recognising that it's the past you're reacting to, not the present, is enough to help you reframe your thinking. But for other people, counselling is the best way to leave the past behind and stop it contaminating their current relationship. You can find more on counselling in Chapter 2.

Changing the environment

Jealousy can breed and grow in the wrong environment. If you're struggling with low self-esteem and/or you have difficulties within your relationship, this can massively affect how secure you feel about your partner's commitment. If you have low self-esteem, you may struggle to believe and trust in your partner's love, and constantly worry about her finding someone else. This is further compounded if previous experiences of rejection or betrayal accompany the low self-esteem.

Overcoming jealousy's much easier after you address these fundamental issues. Working through this book helps you to improve your relationship. If you know you also struggle with low self-esteem, invest in the excellent *Boosting Self-Esteem For Dummies* by Rhena Branch and Rob Willson (Wiley).

Managing triggers

A variety of events or situations can trigger jealousy – from your partner not answering her phone to seeing her chatting to someone at a party, or passing her ex in the street.

Here are five things you can do to minimise the impact of the trigger and, over time, eliminate it altogether:

- ✔ **Avoid the trigger.** I know this isn't always possible, but if you have some particular triggers that cause problems, see whether you can avoid them. For example, ask your partner always to call if she's going to be late, don't go to places where you know an ex may be, and avoid contentious topics of conversation. This may be limiting as a long-term solution, but in the short term it can help you get your confidence back.

✔ **Do a reality check.** When you feel your jealousy being triggered, take a good look at the situation and ask yourself how realistic the threat really is. What solid evidence do you have that your relationship's in danger or that your partner's thinking negatively about you? Are your feelings genuinely appropriate in the present or are they a symptom of the past?

✔ **Use positive self-talk.** When you start feeling the tinglings of jealousy, immediately give yourself a good talking to. Remind yourself that your partner loves you, is committed to you and respects you. Focus only on the positives in your relationship and pat yourself on the back for being the beautiful, loveable person that you are.

✔ **Admit your feelings.** Although you may be tempted to blame a partner when jealousy erupts, this only makes the situation worse. By taking responsibility for your feelings and sharing them, you can make your partner an ally in overcoming your jealousy, rather than an enemy.

✔ **Seek reassurance.** After you've been open about your feelings, you can ask for reassurance. This is one of the most powerful ways of nipping a jealous outburst in the bud. Without nagging or bullying, ask your partner to give you bucketloads of reassurance and to help you let go and move on from the trigger.

Helping a jealous partner

Living with a jealous partner can be totally exhausting and, at times, can feel massively unfair. You may find yourself constantly in the firing line of unfounded accusations and extreme emotional behaviour. You have undoubtedly tried many times to offer reassurance, but if your efforts seem to get you nowhere, you may find yourself giving up and stubbornly refusing to help your partner with 'her' problem at all.

The most important thing to remember about living with an irrationally jealous partner is that the problem's not about you. Your partner's jealousy is almost certainly linked to previous experiences, but because of the profound effect it has on your relationship, the two of you need to fix this problem together. That may feel very frustrating at times, but if you genuinely love your partner and value the relationship, investing time and energy in eradicating irrational jealousy is more than worth the effort.

The advice here assumes that your partner's jealousy is unfounded. But if you've had affairs in the past and your partner's jealousy is to do with rebuilding trust, please look at Chapter 14.

Here are some techniques that can help you to help your partner as well as yourself:

✔ **Reframe the problem.** Remember that jealousy is a sign of love. When you're tempted to become defensive rather than supportive, tell yourself that if your partner didn't value your relationship, you wouldn't be having this problem.

✔ **Check your behaviour.** If particular behaviours trigger your partner's jealousy, avoid them, at least in the short term until your partner has overcome the problem. Stick to agreements you've made, allow yourself to be accountable, and don't make promises you know are impossible to keep, such as *always* being contactable.

✔ **Build your partner's confidence.** Take every opportunity to tell your partner how much you love her and why you don't want to be with anyone else. Pay her lots of compliments and talk about the wonderful future you're looking forward to, in which the two of you are together.

✔ **Maintain your boundaries.** If your partner's asking you to do things you think are unreasonable, such as not going out with friends, not wearing certain clothes or not talking to an ex about parenting issues, don't give in. Although you should do everything you can to alleviate your partner's jealousy, bending to unreasonable demands makes maintaining perspective harder for her, and creates bitterness and resentments that can damage your relationship.

✔ **Manage your frustrations.** Make sure that you have support in place for yourself. Sharing with your partner how difficult you find her behaviour's okay, but when you really need to let off steam, find somewhere or someone you can do this with who is outside your relationship.

✔ **Celebrate successes.** As jealousy begins to subside and you manage new situations together that in the past may have triggered a jealous outburst, be sure to celebrate your success. You can just hug or offer a few words of recognition, but whatever you do encourages both of you to continue working in the same direction together.

Coping with Depression, Anxiety and Addictions

I'm not going to pretend to be able to solve these major issues in just a few pages. Trying that would be foolish and outside the remit of this book. But to write a book on improving your relationship without at least mentioning the significant strain that depression, anxiety and addictions can have would be a serious omission – an omission that may compound the isolation of so many couples who have to cope with these conditions.

If either you or your partner suffers from depression, anxiety or an addiction (or any other compulsive disorder), you know how hard it is. Both the sufferer and the loved one, who often feels she has no choice but to watch helplessly, know that these problems can affect every part of a relationship.

Understanding the impact on relationships

Ideally, a couple relationship consists of two equal adults who make a mutual commitment to create and maintain an intimate and fulfilling life together. Unfortunately, when one half of the couple is unwell or going through a personal crisis, she's unable to contribute her share. This either leaves the relationship depleted of essential resources or means that the other partner has to make up the difference. Either way, the balance of the relationship is affected.

All couples go through times when one person, usually through no fault of her own, has less to offer. But these periods are normally short lived and the balance is soon restored. In a successful relationship, the other partner's happy to go the extra mile and provide additional support during his partner's hour of need, not least because he knows that one day he may need the favour returned. But when one person's suffering with a long-term condition, couples can experience a roller-coaster of emotions such as:

- ✓ **Confusion:** Because depression, anxiety and addictions are often so difficult to understand, both partners can struggle to make sense of what's going on.

- ✓ **Guilt:** The sufferer can feel huge guilt about the pressure she's putting on the relationship, while the partner feels guilty about being unable to resolve the problem and about the inevitable frustration this can cause.

- ✓ **Hopelessness:** When a condition's long standing, both partners can begin to feel helpless and hopeless about getting life back to normal.

- ✓ **Inadequacy:** While the sufferer beats herself up about not being able to conquer her problem, the partner can blame himself for not being able to solve the problem.

- ✓ **Isolation:** A strong desire not to burden the other with their feelings can leave both partners trying to cope alone.

These complex emotions, on top of the actual depression, anxiety or addiction, can take their toll in every area of a relationship. Everyday situations like maintaining a home, parenting, socialising with friends, earning a living, going on holiday and relating to extended family members can all be affected. The more intimate side of a couple relationship can also suffer as couples find themselves fluctuating between withdrawing into their own separate worlds and desperately needing more intimacy.

Couples do survive the pressures that these conditions put on relationships. In fact, many couples say that such a problem makes their relationship stronger and brings them closer. When you can recognise that the condition is a common enemy, you can fight together to overcome it. And in the process, you discover more about yourselves and more about each other, finding new hidden strengths that neither of you knew you had, and deepening your love for each other.

Protecting your relationship from contamination

Although depression, anxiety or addiction may touch every part of your relationship, they don't have to spoil it. Here are some ways to protect your relationship:

- **Talk.** The most powerful weapon you have for protecting your relationship is communication. Talking openly and honestly about how you feel is the only way to beat the isolation and remind yourselves that you're both in this together. Conversations may be difficult or even painful at times, but sharing your thoughts and feelings helps you step into one another's worlds, understand each other and provide empathy and support. See Part III for more on communication.

- **Maintain perspective.** When someone's going through a particularly difficult patch of depression or anxiety, or during times when an addiction feels like it's taken over, you can easily feel overwhelmed by the problem and think that the situation is hopeless. Remembering that this phase will pass and things will get better again can help you get through the difficult times.

- **Keep sight of the person in the problem.** The condition may seem dominant, but it's only one facet of a person. Someone who's struggling with depression, anxiety or an addiction is still the same loving, caring, fun-loving, confident, competent, beautiful person she always was. Those personality traits you admire and love may temporarily be hidden, but they don't disappear. Holding on to this reality can help both of you fight off despair and look forward to good times together again.

Recovering as a couple

Depression, anxiety and addictions are not life sentences. The time you take to overcome the problem completely depends on the severity of the condition and whether any additional complications exist. But as long as both of you are committed to resolving the problem, you can.

Here are some thoughts that may be helpful for recovery:

- **Understand the condition.** You can't fight a problem together unless you know what it is. Look up information on the Internet, read books, go to support and advice agencies, and get all the information you possibly can so that you know what you're up against. In the Appendix is a resources section with details of other helpful books and agencies. Do also look at *Overcoming Depression For Dummies*, *Overcoming Anxiety For Dummies* (both by Elaine Iljon Foreman, Laura L. Smith and Charles H. Elliott) and *Addiction and Recovery For Dummies*, by Brian F. Shaw, Paul Ritvo and Jane Irvine. All three are published by Wiley.

- **Get professional support.** If your GP hasn't already done so, ask for a professional referral into your local mental health services to find out what services and resources they offer. Also search the Net for local support agencies and groups and find out what they provide. You may also find help by getting individual and couple support through a private counsellor or psychotherapist.

- **Know your medical options and treatments.** Researchers discover new methods of treatment every day. Even if you've had your condition for some time, do keep on top of the latest medical and psychological developments. Pharmacological interventions may not have been suitable or appropriate for you six months ago, but something new may now be on the market that's perfect for you.

- **Be solution focused, not problem focused.** Wherever possible, try to focus your energies on what you can do, not on what you can't. If your problem is stopping you from socialising, concentrate your attention on the things you can do alone together and/or within the home. If it's affecting your sexual relationship, transfer your energies to enjoying conversation and affection.

- **Grab opportunities to enjoy times together.** When you're going through a good time, make the most of it. Rather than dwelling on how rare these occasions may be, ensure that you maximise the opportunity and have fun. The more positive experiences you build, the easier you find maintaining perspective and the more encouraged you feel to fight for more.

- **Socialise with other couples.** Spending time with other couples can help you to keep in touch with the big wide world and maintain your perspective. If possible, have friends you feel comfortable enough with to talk openly about your problems and gain support. And also enjoy the company of friends with whom you don't talk so intimately, who can simply entertain you and give you some respite.

- **Focus on progress, not perfection.** Recovering from a long-term mental health problem or addiction can take a long time, and you have good days and bad days. As life improves, remember to look at how far you've come and celebrate your successes rather than looking only at the journey ahead.

What to do when you just can't cope

Unfortunately, not everyone recovers from addictions, and a few people are buried so deep by depression or anxiety disorders that they can't find their way out. Some partners find this an impossible situation to live with and may feel that the only way they can ever gain happiness for themselves is to leave the relationship. Ending a relationship is never easy, but under these circumstances the decision can be exceptionally difficult to make. If you feel that you may be coming to the point where your relationship can't work, take a look at Chapter 15.

Some couples get stuck in collusive relationships where one or both partners are unable to let go of the problem. The sufferer may unconsciously see her problem as essential to keep the love of her partner, and the partner may be so used to playing the role of carer that taking away the problem leaves him redundant. If this describes you, seek the help of a couple counsellor who can help you to break this negative pattern.

Dealing with Rage and Passive Aggression

Anger's a natural and healthy emotion that's essential for your survival. When your basic human rights are threatened or violated, anger helps you fight for your safety and security. Anger's also a natural response to frustration, and provides the emotional and physical energy to resolve problems. Feeling angry isn't wrong – and as couples jostle together through the twists and turns of life, inevitably both partners sometimes experience anger.

When you express anger healthily, it's a positive and constructive force that enables you to stand up for yourself and negotiate your needs. But when anger boils up as rage, leaks out as passive aggression or flares up inappropriately or disproportionately to a situation, the results can be devastating to relationships. When a partner's open about her feelings of anger and demonstrates them in an assertive way, you can quickly resolve the problems. But when a partner expresses anger unhealthily through aggression or manipulation, she compounds the original problem.

Looking at unhealthy expression of anger

People who have a problem with anger generally fall into one of two camps: those who rage and those who let their anger leak out in less obvious ways.

Recognising the signs of rage

When anger blows up and is expressed as rage, it's unpredictable, aggressive, hurtful, destructive, threatening, bullying and sometimes violent. Here are some common signs:

- Shouting and physical aggression such as pointing fingers, fist shaking, taking up personal space, shoving or violence
- Using abusive language and put-downs
- Accusing, blaming, being spiteful, punishing or withholding
- Using illogical, irrational arguments such as 'I don't care if it makes sense'
- Driving dangerously, damaging property, drinking too much
- Making threats to personal safety or to things or people a partner cares about

Identifying passive aggression

Passive aggression is far more subtle than rage, but equally destructive. Someone who expresses her anger passively often denies that she feels angry at all, but her behaviour doesn't fit with what she says. Here are some telltale signs you may recognise in yourself or your partner:

- Secretly stockpiling resentments and grudges that leak out in normal conversation or as sly digs or sarcasm; or using someone else, such as a family member, to convey negative messages
- Being silent, avoiding eye contact, shoulder shrugging, muttering under your breath, being physically non-responsive and/or sexually withdrawn
- Provoking an angry outburst in another and then taking the moral high ground
- Being a martyr in order to make a partner feel guilty, refusing to engage in any conflict, taking all the responsibility for situations
- Being a pessimist, making fatalistic comments, deliberately not enjoying the good times

Unrelenting anger causes serious damage to relationships. For some couples, this leads to constant arguments, often over trivial matters. Those who suppress their anger may find that they're suppressing positive emotions as well. Anger can also lead to physical and emotional distance, sexual problems, infidelity and ultimately to the break-up of a marriage.

Because anger and frustration are an inevitable part of living with another human being, you have to manage them healthily. Simply avoiding anger leads to the avoidance of confrontation, which may make improving your relationship impossible.

Identifying the root of hostility

Both rage and passive aggression are responses to anger that are cumulative. In other words, the unhealthy response isn't created by individual triggers but by a history of unresolved anger that builds and builds and builds. A partner may see each event as separate and individual and undeserving of such an exaggerated response, but for the angry person, the reaction's the result of a constant build-up of pressure.

The roots of long-term anger can go deep – deep into an individual's life story and deep into the relationship. In order to let go of this anger and begin to enjoy a peaceful and fulfilling relationship, you need to identify the roots and dig them out.

Take a sheet of paper and head three columns as follows: 'My family made me angry when . . . ', 'Life made me angry when . . . ' and 'My partner made me angry when . . . '. Now write down everything that comes into your head as you look at each heading. Try not to censor yourself but let your thoughts flow free. When you've finished, look back at what you've written and consider the impact that each factor may have on your relationship. The following sections may help you think more about these areas of your life.

Family roots

You first get to know about anger in your family. The ways in which your parents expressed anger and responded to your toddler tantrums are hugely influential. If you come from a background where you witnessed rage, you may have discovered how to respond similarly or become so frightened of anger that you suppress and deny it and it comes out as passive aggression. If you lived with a passive aggressive parent, you may have experienced anger as wrong and felt guilty whenever you felt the emotion. So you copied your parent and let it leak out. If your parents let you down, this may also have left you with wounds that you protect with anger.

Life experiences

Events in life take their toll. If you feel that life hasn't treated you fairly, you may react more strongly to events that trigger this awareness. Or if you've lived with genuine threats to your human rights, you may be ultra-sensitive to any hint of repetition. Any incident of bullying or times when someone misused her authority, whether that happened in childhood, adolescence or in your adult life, can also create deep feelings of anger.

Relationship resentments

Long-term feelings of hostility are often a response to hurtful situations within the relationship that remain unresolved and unforgiven, such as an affair or being abandoned or let down at a crucial time. For others, an ongoing sense of something missing within the relationship, such as a lack of affection, attention, respect or fairness, creates a permanent feeling of being hard done by.

Here are some common relationship hurts that can cause long-term resentments:

- **Deliberate hurts:** You can much more easily let go of anger when an accident caused the pain. People make mistakes and most can find a way of forgiving, but if the hurtful action was calculated, premeditated or even malicious, you find letting go much harder.

- **Unexpected hurts:** When a partner does something that comes as a complete shock, you can require a long time for the feelings of anger to go. In these circumstances, anger may be accompanied by feelings of confusion, self-doubt, betrayal and long-term distrust.

- **Repeated hurts:** If someone hurts you and in spite of explaining and expressing it she does the same again and again and again, anger grows and can be accompanied by powerlessness and exhaustion.

- **Unacknowledged or unrepented hurts:** Perhaps this is the most difficult hurt to let go of – when a partner refuses to accept either that she was responsible for the hurt or that you've any right to feel hurt.

Managing your own anger

If either you or your partner is struggling with rage or passive aggression, this isn't only damaging your relationship but also poisoning you, physically and emotionally:

- When you get angry, chemicals flood your body so that you're ready to fight or run away from the threat. You can cope with this heightened physical response for a short period, but if it continues, your body remains in a high state of emergency and you can end up with health issues such as high blood pressure, headaches, stomach problems and a lowered immune system.

✔ Emotionally, staying angry keeps you trapped in the past and takes away your power to change the present and the future. Anger can also damage your self-esteem as you feel helpless to overcome the emotion and guilty about its expression.

Dealing with your anger in a healthier manner requires two significant changes: letting go of resentments in the past and managing triggers positively.

Letting go of resentments

Resentments create a trap that keeps you immobilised. Negative thinking, which can dominate your mind and leave you plotting revenge or expectantly waiting for further offences, only feeds the resentment. Choosing to let go is first and foremost something you do for yourself, not for the offender. You're not doing it to let her off the hook, because the hurtful action doesn't matter any more, or because you weren't justified in your anger, but because you want to move forward in your life and your relationship.

Letting go of anger doesn't mean that other relationship problems disappear overnight, but it does mean that you have more energy to deal with them. You can find more help on letting go of anger in *Anger Management For Dummies* by W. Doyle Gentry (Wiley).

Managing anger triggers

Figure 12-1 shows the firework model, which people commonly use to manage anger flare-ups more effectively. In the diagram, you see that the match indicates the triggers, the fuse is your thoughts and feelings, and the barrel's your behaviour.

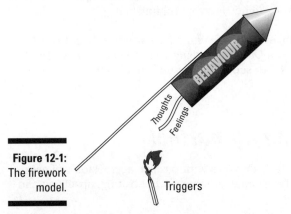

Figure 12-1:
The firework
model.

Ideally, try to avoid triggers. If you know that certain situations make you angry, talk to your partner about them and try to avoid them. But if you can't do this, your next defence lies in your thoughts and feelings. Negative thinking fuels anger; for example, thoughts like 'She did it on purpose,' 'She wants to hurt me,' 'She has no respect for me' and 'I've been made to look bad.' By challenging this thinking and reframing it to 'She didn't mean it; her intentions were good' or 'We have a good relationship and I can resolve this,' your feelings become more positive and you can control the behaviour.

Once the flame has hit your barrel, how you behave is up to you. You may not always be able to control the trigger, and your thoughts and feelings may occasionally get the better of you. But ultimately, you and only you are responsible for how you behave. When your firework's been lit, you need to ensure that your behaviour's assertive rather than aggressive or manipulative.

Assertive anger is:

- **Direct:** Calmly say that you're feeling angry and explain why without placing blame on the other person.

- **Enquiring:** Ask for clarification of the comment or situation or whatever triggered your emotion to check whether you misunderstood.

- **Honest and honourable:** If you feel that your anger is justified, explain why in a non-aggressive and non-manipulative way and ask for what you need.

- **Persistent and focused:** If you feel that your partner's fobbing you off, stand your ground, don't get side-tracked, and continue to ask for what you need.

- **Forgiving:** When you've reached a resolution, or at least agreed to differ, forgive your partner. The offence is over and finished.

Overcoming an unhealthy anger response can take a lot of work and effort. As well as investing in a copy of *Overcoming Anger For Dummies* by W. Doyle Gentry (Wiley), look on the Net to see whether you can join any local anger management courses.

Living with an angry partner

Living with a partner who either simmers with passive aggression or flares into a rage at the slightest thing can be confusing, frustrating, upsetting and frightening and very, very tiring.

Understanding where your partner's anger originates helps you to maintain perspective and address the problems that you can, and to feel less responsible for the problems that you can't. If resentments or problems exist within your relationship, working through this book helps you to work through any backlog of anger and improve your communication and conflict-resolution skills. If the root of the problem lies before your relationship, encouraging your partner to get counselling may also be helpful.

In the meantime, the following tips help you to minimise the destructive effects of anger on you and your relationship:

- ✔ **Address anger immediately.** When you first start noticing the signs of anger, ask your partner what's happening. Leaving an angry person to nurse her hurt makes things worse, not better.

- ✔ **Keep calm.** Anger fuels anger, so the calmer you can remain, the quicker your partner's anger subsides. Shouting at a partner in a rage escalates her anger, and joining a passive aggressive partner in sulking can make the situation continue for ever.

- ✔ **Acknowledge your partner's feelings.** Openly saying 'I can see you're angry' and, if appropriate, 'I understand you're angry about . . .' prevents your partner from feeling that she has to *prove* how she feels either by throwing her weight around or retreating into silence.

- ✔ **Show that you're listening.** People often continue to be angry because they don't think they're being listened to or taken seriously. You can use the active listening techniques in Chapter 8 to be sure that your partner feels heard.

- ✔ **Share your feelings.** If you're feeling angry too, then say so. If you're feeling nervous, upset or frustrated by your partner's anger, then share that also. This is especially important with passive aggression, when a partner may want to deny that her behaviour has any impact on you.

- ✔ **Be conciliatory.** Behave in a way that demonstrates that you want to make peace. That may mean saying you're sorry or acknowledging your role in a problem, or reaching out physically.

- ✔ **Use the broken record technique.** Someone in the middle of a rage often jumps from one point to another without taking time to listen to what you're saying, and someone who's passive aggressive may continue to make the same jibe over and over again. The broken record technique can help you to stick to your guns, and to the point. Simply repeat, calmly but assertively, what you want to say. For example, 'This was a misunderstanding, I didn't mean what I said the way you heard it' or 'I know you're angry, but I can't change my work commitments.'

✔ **Try fogging.** This is a helpful technique to fend off unreasonable criticism, whether that's through the nagging of passive aggression or in the midst of an angry outburst. Rather than arguing with your partner, you take the wind out of her sails by agreeing in part, or *fogging*. For example, if your partner's accusing you of being selfish all the time, say, 'I agree that sometimes I don't think about the impact things have on you and I should try harder.' Or if she's angry with you for being late, you can say, 'I'm sorry I was unavoidably late, and I should have rung you earlier to let you know.'

✔ **Make a negative assertion:** When criticism's deserved, however it's expressed, you may often be tempted to become defensive or try to justify yourself. Negative assertion stops an argument in its tracks by calmly and seriously agreeing with what's been said. You say, 'You're right, I was wrong, I shouldn't have . . . '

If your partner's in the middle of a full-blown rage, trying to talk to her about the problem is a waste of time. When a person loses her temper, she's not rational, so trying to use reason is pointless. The only goal available to you is to try to calm the situation down and, when the anger's passed, arrange a time to sit down together and resolve the issue.

Knowing when things have gone too far

Living with an angry partner is one thing; living with domestic violence is another. Estimates are that one in four women experiences domestic abuse in her lifetime, and an increasing number of men are also encountering violence from partners.

Defining domestic violence

Although violence or a threat of violence towards the partner or towards themselves is a common feature of domestic violence, it's not always present. This can leave some people wondering whether their situation really is 'domestic violence' or just an angry partner whom she should, or could, get used to. You need to understand that domestic violence isn't fundamentally about anger but about control, so while an angry person may be more likely to be violent, you may still be living in an abusive situation even if your partner's never raised her voice to you.

Domestic violence, or *domestic abuse* as it's also known, can be defined as a relationship where one partner controls and manipulates her partner's behaviour through physical, emotional and psychological coercion.

Recognising the signs

Although every situation is unique, some common signs indicate that a relationship is abusive:

- Exhibiting ongoing destructive criticism and verbal abuse

- Demonstrating bullying behaviour such as threatening to do or actually doing things such as: withholding money; removing your mobile phone; telling you what to wear, who to see, or where to work; taking the car away; lying to friends or family about you; forcing you to drink or take drugs

- Refusing to let you be involved in joint decisions or make any decisions for yourself

- Lying and withholding information that keeps you in the dark and unable to predict or know what's happening

- Harassing you by following you; checking your mail, email and text messages; questioning where you've been and insisting on being with you whenever you go out

- Intimidating you through physical aggression; destroying possessions; punching walls; threatening to harm you, people you care for or family pets; threats of suicide

- Carrying out acts of sexual violence: using force, threats or intimidation to make you have sex when you don't want to or perform sexual acts you're not comfortable with

- Inflicting physical violence: punching, slapping, hitting, biting, pinching, kicking, pulling hair out, pushing, shoving, burning, strangling

- Denying that the abuse exists or saying that you're responsible for the abusive behaviour

- Being gentle and loving in public but completely different when you get home

- Promising that the abuse will never, ever happen again and being as passionately sorry as she is abusive and controlling

Getting out of violence – safely

People often stay in abusive relationships out of fear, shame and anxieties about housing, money and children. Many think, hope and pray that they can do something to make the situation better. But research shows that unless the abuser can admit her problem and get professional help, things grow worse.

If you're living in an abusive relationship, you deserve a better life, but getting free is sometimes a long process that, in the short term, may escalate threats of violence. Therefore you absolutely must get the right professional help to keep you and your loved ones safe.

You can get support and advice from the National Domestic Violence Helpline on freephone 0808 2000 247. They can give you the emotional and practical advice you require to make an informed decision about your future, and all the information you need to help you to leave safely and build a secure and happy life.

If you're in immediate danger, always call the police, dialling 999 and telling them it's an emergency. They have a duty to protect and help you.

Chapter 13

Managing Major Life Changes

*L*ife's full of ups and downs. Some are predictable and pleasant, but others hit you like a steam train and leave you floundering at the side of the track. Managing life's challenges as a couple builds teamwork and strengthens relationships, but doing so is not always as easy as it sounds.

In this chapter you can find advice and information on maximising the joy of life's planned changes such as having a baby, moving home and retirement. And I also look at the bombshells that so many people have to face, such as redundancy, ill health and bereavement.

Adjusting to Parenthood

How you adjust to becoming a parent largely depends on how prepared for it you are. If the pregnancy is planned and falls into your schedule for life, and if you've got friends or family who've let you practise a bit with their kids, then chances are you're good to go. But if the pregnancy was unplanned or didn't happen as you hoped, the adjustment is often greater.

Whatever the circumstances of your bundle of joy's arrival, becoming a parent is a big deal. Becoming a mum and becoming a dad both mean a change in your personal identity. Depending on your own experience of childhood, you may have a very positive idea of what being a mum or a dad means or you may have a more negative image. But to be honest, you can't know how you may feel until you're actually a parent.

Planning for a baby

Deciding to start a family is a major decision, one that affects every area of your life. It affects how you feel about yourself, how you spend your time, how you manage your day-to-day life, how you plan for the future and how you interact with friends and family. But perhaps most significantly, the decision to become a parent affects the relationship between you and your partner for the rest of your lives. You're no longer just partners – you're parents.

Most couples expect to have children one day. The expectation's passed on from parents and from society. But before you get stuck in to baby making, you must be sure that it's the right move for both of you and that now's the right time.

Before you make the final decision, sit down together and answer the following questions, honestly and frankly:

- ✔ Are we both ready to become parents?

- ✔ How do we expect life to change when we have a family?

- ✔ What sacrifices do we need to make and are we ready to make those sacrifices in our lives?

- ✔ Can we see any advantages to postponing starting a family, or any advantages in starting now?

- ✔ Is either of us tempted to have a baby to fix something else that's missing in our lives?

- ✔ Do we have any problems in our relationship that we should resolve before starting a family?

The final question is perhaps the most important one. Some couples start a family because they hope that doing so brings security to their relationship. But in reality, unless your relationship's already strong, becoming a threesome's more likely to create pressure. A new baby can be a powerful bond in a happy relationship, but it can break up an unhappy one.

Having a baby's a lifetime commitment. It's an irreversible decision that has major consequences for both of you, and for your child. Feeling nervous about such a major decision is inevitable, but if either of you is definitely against it, now's not the time to start a family.

Coping with fertility issues

After you've made the decision to start a family and handed the practicalities over to mother nature, discovering that one of you has a fertility problem can be a devastating shock.

Infertility affects an estimated one in seven couples around the world. Although an increasing number of treatment options are available, the processes are lengthy and can be exhausting both emotionally and physically. Throughout investigations and treatment, many couples experience a seesaw of highs and lows as emotions swing between hope and anticipation, and failure and disappointment.

Infertility challenges even the healthiest of relationships as each of you tries to manage your own feelings at the same time as supporting one another.

Although every situation and every individual is unique, the following guidelines may help you to help each other:

- Remember that you both have different personalities and that no right or wrong ways exist for coping with the frustrations of infertility.

- Encourage each other to keep up regular routines as much as possible rather than putting your lives on hold.

- Share your hopes and disappointments with each other and support one another when you're down, without feeling that you have to try to make things better.

- Make time to have fun together doing things you don't have time to do when you have a baby.

- Keep your sex life exciting and intimate and don't forget that sex isn't just for procreation.

- Don't lose focus on all the rest that life has to offer, and remind yourself of the advantages of being child free.

Surviving the turbulence of infertility takes patience and determination. You can get a lot more practical advice and information in *Fertility and Infertility For Dummies* by Gillian Lockwood, Jill Anthony-Ackery, Jackie Meyers-Thompson and Sharon Perkins (Wiley).

Living with a new baby

Okay, you need to get one thing straight right away – from now on, your baby's in charge. You can throw your plans and schedules out of the window, because a newborn baby waits for no one. Your baby's needs are immediate and, like it or not, for a while he has to come first.

For most couples, becoming parents is a joyful time. You spend many hours staring dewy-eyed at your new creation, marvelling at those perfect little fingers and toes. Each new development's a milestone to share: the first smile, the first bottle, the first solids – the first night's sleep! Becoming parents can be a bonding experience.

But with the joys come the trials. The biggest problem by far is the lack of sleep. Exhaustion can leave you feeling physically ill, mentally drained and emotionally raw, which can make even the smallest disagreements seem huge and the bigger disputes feel insurmountable. Here are some of the most common issues that arise:

- ✔ **Time:** Finding enough time for your baby, for each other, for your job and for yourself becomes an ongoing battle. If you have twins, it's twice as hard.

- ✔ **Money:** As well has having less money, the financial balance changes if one of you chooses to give up work or go part time. Being the sole breadwinner can be a heavy responsibility, and being totally reliant on another's income requires a new level of trust. (Chapter 11 offers more advice on money.)

- ✔ **Sex:** If you ever manage to find the time and energy for sex, you've still got to muster the enthusiasm. Eighty per cent of new mothers report lowered desire in the first months. (If you want some tips to turn up the passion, see Chapters 6 and 7.)

- ✔ **Household chores:** One tiny baby can cause an amazing amount of havoc in a household. Daily routines like cooking, cleaning, shopping and doing laundry seem to take twice as long when you're exhausted.

- ✔ **In-laws:** Other people can walk a thin line between helpful involvement and interference, and the balance often depends on what mood you're in at the time and whose relations they are. (You can get more help with in-laws in Chapter 11.)

Keeping the lines of communication open when you're both exhausted and the baby's crying can be difficult. But to stop minor issues becoming major problems, you need to keep talking.

If you can, try to find at least an hour a week when you can talk through how things are going. As well as ironing out any practicalities, talk about how you feel about being a parent: what you're enjoying about your new baby, but also what you're finding most difficult. Share how you're feeling about yourself and how you're feeling about your relationship.

Keeping up your coupledom

Although your newborn baby's needs may seem to be hogging the agenda at home, that doesn't mean that your needs and your relationship's needs aren't equally important. In fact, you can argue that looking after yourself and your relationship now is even more important. A healthy parent makes a healthy child, and a happy relationship makes a happy family.

The best investment you can make for your child's future is ensuring that you make time for yourself and time for your partner.

Making time to be a couple can be difficult. You need to be more flexible and more creative than ever before. First, you need to realise that all couple time counts, whether it's a two-minute hug or a weekend away. As a couple, both of you need to watch out for and grab every opportunity you can just to sit and talk or to do something more intimate together. That means when the baby's asleep, when Grandma's around and can look after him for 20 minutes, or when he's asleep in the car or in the pushchair. Make every moment count. Writing a list of things you used to enjoy and working out which you can still do when the baby's around and awake may also be useful.

For most new parents, resuming a regular sex life can seem particularly impossible. On top of the lack of time and the general exhaustion that caring for the needs of a newborn 24/7 brings, the mother's sex drive is reduced. For the first few months, a woman's hormones are pre-programmed for feeding and nurturing, not making more babies.

The most important things you need to do during this time are:

- **Keep touching.** Just because you don't feel like being lovers doesn't mean you can't be affectionate.

- **Share how you feel about sex.** Either partner may feel guilty about wanting or not wanting sex. Talking helps you to support each other and to maintain intimacy as a couple.

Moving Home

Most people move home for positive reasons such as wanting a nicer home or a better location, or as an investment. Unfortunately, moving home can sometimes be a negative experience, for example if you're downsizing because of financial difficulties or having to relocate for employment. Either way, moving can be stressful. In fact, some people liken the stress of moving home to that of a relationship breakdown. Personally, I don't think those people have ever been through a divorce, but the two situations do have some similarities.

Aside from the stress of strangers stomping around your house passing judgements, and trying to find somewhere to live that you like and can afford, moving involves inevitable losses that can put a strain on relationships.

Recognising losses

Whatever your reason for moving, leaving your old home means saying goodbye and closing a door for good. Before you do that, knowing exactly what you're saying goodbye to is useful. That way you can wave a fond farewell rather than waking up in a few weeks feeling like you've misplaced something but you can't work out what it is.

For many people, home is where the heart is. Home is not only a physical base but also an emotional and psychological base where you feel secure and grounded. Moving home doesn't just involve transporting all your worldly possessions but also transporting your stability, which is a bit of a contradiction in itself.

Dealing with impending loss is simpler once you acknowledge exactly what you're going to lose. Here's a list of things you may miss:

- **The bricks and mortar:** Some people are more attached than others to the style and layout of their house. If you've always liked particular features such as your inglenook fireplace, which you can snuggle up in, that may be something you're going to miss.

- **The contents:** Although you almost certainly take most things with you, inevitably some items never find the same 'right place' as they have at your current home.

- **The trimmings:** Although you can redecorate your new home in exactly the same style if you want to, moving often means saying goodbye to some well-loved and often hard-worked trimmings such as those curtains you spent hours making to fit the alcove window perfectly or the landscaped garden you've lovely created and tended for years.

✔ **The view:** What you see out of your kitchen, study or top room window may be something very special that you're sad to lose (although if you've recently found yourself overlooking the new superstore car park, this may be the very reason you're moving!).

✔ **The location:** Being close to the shops and nightlife may have been a real bonus for you, or being near the school or office. Or perhaps you've been in the middle of the countryside, just a few steps from good walks or the sea.

✔ **The company:** Friends and family are often the biggest loss when moving house. Yes, you can keep in touch, but not having them on your doorstep for an impromptu coffee or pint can make the distance seem vast.

When you know what you're going to miss, you can much more easily work together as a couple to plan how to make up for the shortfall. Forewarned is forearmed, so the more you can think and plan in advance, the less chance of finding yourselves feeling cast adrift.

Getting stuck in to new challenges

New home equals new challenges: some exciting and energising, some a pain in the backside. Quite aside from having to work out how to get your six-seater corner sofa into your cosy new living room with its narrow door, and transferring your insurance policies and redirecting the post, you also face the emotional challenge of making a strange place feel like home.

How you face new challenges in life is all about attitude. The more positive you feel about the future and the more you focus on what you hope to gain, the more you achieve.

Here are some tips for facing the challenge of moving with optimism:

✔ **Talk to your partner.** Share your hopes and fears for moving and take time to discuss the challenges you face and how you want to manage them.

✔ **Write lists.** I'm a great fan of writing lists for helping life to feel more under control. As well as having practical lists of what you need to do, also have a wish list of non-essentials that you can refer to.

✔ **Set time goals.** Your most urgent priority is getting through moving day, but think also about the weeks and months ahead and plan what you want to achieve and by when.

✔ **Research.** Visit your new location, and also look online to find out what's available close to your new home. As well as the practical resources such as plumbers and locksmiths and the post office opening hours, also check out what social networks are around. Find your nearest gym or sports club, residents' association, hobby club, church, book club, evening class or whatever you're into.

- ✔ **Schedule friends.** To make the transition easier, book dinner dates and visits with existing friends into your diary now, either going back to theirs or inviting them to your new home.

- ✔ **Meet the neighbours.** When you've got a definite moving date, consider inviting your neighbours over for an informal drop-in 'hello' drink and nibbles or tea-and-cake afternoon.

- ✔ **Prioritise decorating.** If a room in your house is particularly important to you, such as your bedroom, kitchen or study, make sure that you get this room organised first.

- ✔ **Be ready for emergencies.** You inevitably feel more insecure in a new place, but if you know that you're ready for any minor or major emergencies, you can relax much more easily. Find out where the stopcock and fuse box are, register with a GP and a dentist, and locate your local A&E and vet's practice if you have pets. And change the address on your driving licence and/or passport quickly in case you need to prove who you are or forget where you live!

- ✔ **Involve the kids.** If you've got children, get them involved in the whole moving process as early as possible and plan ahead for their physical and social needs. Happy kids make life soooo much easier.

Settling into a new home takes time, and you and your partner may possibly work on different schedules. One of you may join a new social circle quickly but still be missing the garden, while the other loves your new home but finds making new friends difficult. No rights and wrongs exist, so if feeling settled is taking one or both of you longer than you hoped, don't give yourself a hard time.

Building a harmonious home together

Moving home often marks a new stage in life, an opportunity to leave old habits as well as old haunts behind you. This is as true of your relationship as of anything else. For many couples, a new home provides an opportunity to address and resolve any problems that may have been niggling at your relationship. For example, if you've often argued about housework or money, a new home can mark a new beginning. Or if one of you has had an affair, moving home may be an important emotional and psychological step towards leaving the painful past behind and starting afresh.

Your new home may coincide with changes within your family, such as a new baby or children leaving home. Or you may be starting a different career or retiring. Whatever the life change, now's a chance for you to work together and face a fresh future as a team – building your home into a place where both of you can feel comfortable, relaxed and secure, and also building your relationship into a place where both of you can feel fulfilled.

If you want moving home to mark a new start in your relationship, sit down and share with your partner all the things you want to change. As well as practical changes you may like to make in the way you run your home, think also about any changes you want in how you spend your time together, especially new opportunities you can create for building communication, companionship and intimacy.

Coping with Redundancy

As I'm writing this book, unemployment figures are on the rise again and more and more industries are affected. No one's safe in his job any more, and if you've been fortunate enough not to be affected by redundancy, chances are you know someone who has been.

Redundancy can have a significant impact on relationships. Not only does it create financial anxieties, it can also affect self-esteem, shift the balance of power between couples and raise doubts about the future. And if you struggle to find work and your home comes under threat, you can feel as if the very foundations of your family are being ripped away.

Understanding the emotional impact

For many people, being made redundant comes as a huge shock. Even if you know that the threat of layoffs is hanging in the air, discovering that you're one of the chosen ones still comes as a shock.

In organisations where mass redundancies occur, managing the 'Why me?' questions is easier, but if only a handful of staff are made redundant, or if you're the only one, you may experience great difficulty in not taking redundancy personally and you may struggle with feelings of anger and self-doubt.

Both the person who's been made redundant and the partner can feel knocked sideways by redundancy. Common emotions for both include shock, anger, confusion, embarrassment, fear and anxiety. On top of this, you and your partner are likely to struggle with additional emotions of your own:

- ✔ **The person made redundant:** If you're the person who's been made redundant, you may feel hugely responsible for finding another job as soon as possible and restoring the status quo. But this is happening at a time when concerns and anxieties about your employability are at their highest. You may feel shame that you were unable to keep your job, and rejection may be particularly acute if other redundancies or personal rejections occurred in the past. You may think 'What's wrong with me?'

  If job hunting is fruitless, feelings of powerlessness and despair can creep in under the avalanche of repeated knockbacks. And if you don't have other friends or colleagues who are also unemployed, life can begin to feel lonely and pointless. If your partner's still working, you may feel envious that he continues to have an emotional, physical, intellectual and social outlet outside the home.

- ✔ **The partner:** If your partner's been made redundant, you can have powerfully conflicting emotions. First, you feel sympathetic and want to be supportive and encouraging, but these emotions are equally matched by feelings of anxiety for the future, resentment at the impact on you and perhaps questions like 'Why you?' Although all those feelings are natural, sharing your own concerns with your partner can be particularly hard when you know he's struggling so much with his own.

If losing a job turns into longer-term unemployment, feelings of resentment can grow further, accompanied by feeling powerless to change the situation and perhaps being isolated from friends who aren't in a similar situation.

Whenever a crisis hits any couple, open and honest communication is essential for maintaining intimacy, sharing support and avoiding miscommunication. Take a look at Part III for tips and advice for improving your communication.

Adapting to changing roles

When one of you is involuntarily unemployed, the established roles within a relationship change. When one or both partners are out at work all day, you build your routines around that reality. Who cooks the meals, cleans the house, does the laundry and looks after the kids are all based on who's physically available. When that changes, the rules and the roles you've lived by get shaken up.

On top of that are the changes in your financial contributions. If one person has suddenly become the main breadwinner, the balance of dependency changes. Relying on someone else and trusting that your decisions are still important can take a lot of humility. And if your only option as a couple is to both be on benefits, you may be sharing a new level of equality you've never had before.

The biggest change to many couple relationships after redundancy is time. Most couples spend at least eight hours a day apart, and this forced separation can give both partners the opportunity to enjoy their independence and autonomy. If one partner doesn't work, then his partner's redundancy means having more time together. And this can leave many couples struggling to balance their needs for intimacy and together time with their needs for autonomy and independence.

Here's a list of the key areas to consider and talk about to ensure that you both get your needs met and know where you stand:

- ✔ **Finances:** While your financial situation's still in flux, agree any changes that you need to make in spending and decision making. You can find more help on this in Chapter 11.

- ✔ **Running the home:** Think about what changes you need to make in your regular routines to ensure that the division of labour's still fair. If you have children, also discuss how you can divide the duties of care as well as how both of you can continue to get quality time with the kids.

- ✔ **Time alone and apart:** Consider how you can both continue to get the time you need on your own. That may mean agreeing times when you go out to visit friends alone or just times when you can be alone to read, watch TV or enjoy an activity or hobby. If you're spending a lot of extra time in one another's company, also schedule special couple time when you can be more romantic and intimate.

Maintaining optimism

Redundancy has its advantages. For some, it's an opportunity to re-evaluate a career and maybe retrain or launch out alone in a new business venture. And others are fortunate and find that redundancy's accompanied by a lump sum that can pay off debts, be invested in the home or splashed out on something special. Redundancy also provides an opportunity to do the chores you've been putting off for ages. And if money's an issue, you may find that a reduced income can help you refocus on the many joys that money really can't buy.

Here are a few more upsides you may not have considered:

- ✔ **Increased creativity:** You have time on your hands, and less money can motivate a new creative streak you never knew you had – making things for the home, recycling things you normally throw away and learning 101 dishes with tuna.

- ✔ **Rekindled romance:** With fewer distractions to take up your time, now's an excellent time to do the little things that matter.

- ✔ **Improved sex life:** The one hobby in life that really is 100 per cent free! If you can't afford to go out, make your own entertainment and grab the chance to experiment and revitalise your sex life.

- ✔ **Stronger relationships:** Busy work lives often leave you with little space for the people you really love. A period of unemployment is a great opportunity to spend more time with friends and extended family members.

Whatever your individual circumstances may be, redundancy can be an opportunity to re-evaluate your priorities in life and invest more time and energy into your relationship and family. Pulling together as a team towards a common goal can create a special bond that lasts long after the crisis is over.

Overcoming 'Empty Nest Syndrome'

Psychologists coined the term 'empty nest syndrome' to describe the psychological condition that many parents, especially mums, suffer when their children leave home. Releasing your children into the big wide world is a scary time – not just for them, but also for you.

For the first time in perhaps 20 or more years, just you and your partner are at home. And if your current partner isn't also the parent of your children, this may be the first time the two of you have ever lived alone.

Parenting takes up a huge amount of emotional and physical energy, and chances are your children have been the centre of your life. All decisions revolve around their needs, from what you have for tea and where and when you socialise, to where you go on holiday and how you spend your money. Becoming child free can change your life, and your relationship, very quickly. Whether those changes are positive or negative is up to you.

Allowing yourself to grieve

Many parents experience profound feelings of loss when their children leave home. The role they played as nurturers and protectors has gone and this can leave them feeling lost and redundant. Some also have regrets. Too late now to wish you'd played more of a hands-on role or spent more time together. Many parents wonder whether they've done enough: did they get close enough, teach enough, encourage enough?

For some people, children leaving home makes them feel older and greyer than their years. The endless activities of their offspring energise many parents, so that when they're gone, they feel empty and tired. You may find yourself looking at younger families with envy, reminiscing about the good times with fond affection. You may also finally realise that those words muttered by old ladies as they cooed over your newborn were true – 'They grow up so fast and they're gone before you know it.'

Here are some other very common symptoms of the empty nest syndrome:

- ✔ **Anxiety:** What does the future hold? What do I do with my time, my life? Should we downsize? Move away? What may happen to my relationship? When one chapter in life ends and another one opens, you can expect feelings of anxiety.

- ✔ **Confusion:** In the first few months after leaving home, some children fluctuate between needing or even demanding lots and lots of contact and then complaining that you're suffocating them when you call too much. This is about them finding their feet, and contact soon settles into a regular pattern.

- ✔ **Craving:** Many parents find themselves sitting in their child's empty room, hugging his favourite stuffed toy and yearning for him to call. These powerful feelings are natural and gradually fade in time.

- ✔ **Loneliness:** If you spent a lot of time in your children's company and were particularly close, you miss them and may be surprised at how often you find yourself alone.

- ✔ **Purposeless:** If being a parent's an important part of your identity, losing that role can leave your life feeling rather pointless.

- ✔ **Rejection:** Inevitably, children find their own lives and sometimes they forget to call, or send only a brief text message rather than the promised email. Realising that you're missing your children so much more than they're missing you can be tough.

✔ **Unvalued:** A person's self-esteem is often closely linked with parenting, so when that role goes, some parents feel that they have little or nothing of value to offer society.

Alongside the feelings of loss and doubt is the excitement of impending freedom: this is a time when you can focus on your own needs and desires rather than having to think about the best interests of the wider family. And on a practical level, the workload decreases enormously. You have less tidying up, less laundry, fewer people to cook for and no taxi duties. When you go home at the end of the busy day, the house looks the same as when you left it, food doesn't disappear from the fridge and you can use the computer whenever you like. Most people have mixed feelings: freedom and loss, pain and pleasure.

All of the feelings associated with empty nest syndrome are normal and healthy reactions, and people experience them in varying degrees. Your partner almost certainly reacts in his own unique way, and that doesn't mean that one of you loves your child more, it just means that you're different.

Here are some tips for dealing with empty nest syndrome:

✔ **Keep in touch.** Get on the Internet, on Facebook, MSN or whatever your child's into, and get to know the lingo so that you can keep in touch easily and quickly.

✔ **Allow yourself to cry.** In fact, allow yourself to cry and weep and be soppy and sentimental. Missing your child is okay; it proves how much you love him.

✔ **Talk.** Make sure that you're sharing your feelings with your partner, friends and family. And if you feel you need more support than they can offer, consider seeing a counsellor. Talking reduces isolation and helps you work through feelings and find solutions.

✔ **Treat yourself.** Give yourself a boost by treating yourself to some of the things you were never able to do when the kids were around. Go out more, spend hours in the bathroom, have sex on the sofa, go away for the weekend and, if the fancy takes you, watch an uninterrupted series of mind-numbingly boring history or nature programmes.

✔ **Focus on the future.** You really do get soooo many advantages from the kids leaving home. Make a list of all the things you've always wanted to do but haven't been able to, and get ready to start ticking them off.

Empty nest syndrome often coincides with age-related hormone changes, which can compound a predisposition towards depression. If feelings of loss continue for many months and you find that you're losing motivation to do anything else in life, visit your GP to check that you haven't developed depression.

Recognising replacement activities

When something major goes from your life, you naturally want to replace it. Doing that is absolutely not wrong, as long as you know that's what you're doing and it doesn't have a detrimental effect on the replacement object. As you gradually get more and more used to your kids not being around, you need to make sure that you don't regret what seemed to be logical decisions in the early days.

Common replacement activities include:

✔ Putting all your energy into other children who are still at home, to the point where they feel suffocated and overwhelmed

✔ Becoming more dependent on a partner or beginning to treat him as the child you've lost

✔ Emptying your child's bedroom and renting it out to lodgers

✔ Buying a dog or another pet to transfer your affection to

✔ Taking a volunteering role or making commitments to a community or political project to make life seem purposeful

✔ Downsizing, relocating or doing major DIY around the home to mark a new start in life

✔ Taking up a new hobby or evening class simply to kill time

With the exception of the first two replacement activities, none of these things is necessarily a problem. And indeed, many of them are positive ways of adapting to change. But be sure that you're ready to make the commitment that's required and that it's something you've always wanted to do, not a flash-in-the-pan idea to relieve the pain of a temporary situation.

Re-establishing your couple identity

Sadly, many couples find that they have little in common when their children leave home. Being parents together is a significant bond, but with that hands-on role over, some couples become almost like strangers. And now that people live longer and healthier lives, you can have another 20, 30 or even 40 years of child-free married life ahead of you.

Sometimes children are a useful distraction from problems within the relationship. With all energy focused on the children, you can avoid other issues. You may even have made the conscious decision to stay together for the children. Other couples simply find that having spent so many years with the children around, they've never really considered their relationship or put any effort into maintaining it.

If the children leaving home has highlighted long-standing problems within your relationship, you can use the information and advice in other sections of this book to help you resolve your difficulties. And if you're finding that somewhere over the past parenting years you've lost the intimacy and connection you used to have, take a look at Part II for ideas on how to create it again.

Finding yourselves suddenly alone can be both exciting and daunting. Some couples love the new-found freedom and opportunities, and others take time to adjust and have to rediscover how to be a couple. Either way, now's a time of new beginnings.

Exploring your future

In many ways, this stage in life looks similar to when you first met. Just the two of you are deciding how you want your life and your relationship to be. But you need to remember that both of you have grown and changed since you first met and now you must look forward, not back.

With the wisdom of years, time on your hands and hopefully a bit more cash in the bank, you and your partner can begin to explore a whole new life together. How you choose to use your time is now totally up to you. The world's your oyster.

As well as working out what you want to do as a couple, also think about what you want to do individually. Focusing on your own needs as well as your couple needs gives you more to offer your relationship. You also have the chance to discover new things about yourself and enjoy sharing your discoveries with your partner.

Take a sheet of paper and divide it into three columns. Head the first column 'Partner 1's hopes and dreams', the second 'Partner 2's hopes and dreams' and the third 'Couple hopes and dreams'. Now brainstorm a list of thoughts and ideas under each heading. If possible, do this exercise together, but if you do it alone, make time to share your findings with your partner.

For some people, thinking back to all the things they wanted to do but have never had time to try is helpful, as well as using the Internet and local directories to find ideas.

Dealing with Ill Health and Disability

The traditional marriage ceremony asks couples to declare their intention to stick together 'in sickness and in health'. When you're both young, fit and healthy, that's an easy promise to make, but the reality can be much tougher.

When one of you is diagnosed with a long-term health problem or forced to face a disability, it affects both of you. Managing the practical and the emotional impact together is a test for even the strongest relationship.

Love can grow in sickness and in health if you both commit to sharing your feelings, no matter how hard that may be, and you both adapt as your circumstances change.

Coping with shock, loss and anger

Serious illness or disability is always a shock, especially if it strikes in youth. Many people feel as if life is cheating or short-changing them, because not only the person with the illness but partners as well have to make huge adjustments.

Some people liken the effect of a sudden onset of illness to a bereavement. After the initial feelings of shock pass, you may encounter times of immense anger at the unfairness of the world. This rage is sometimes accompanied by anger at yourself or your partner for things that may not have been achieved earlier in life. Both partners can also feel regret and guilt over things left undone: the holiday they always said they'd go on, the family they postponed starting or the better sex life they'd enjoy when they had time. Gradually these feelings change into those of sadness and loss.

Trying to deal with these emotions alone can leave couples feeling isolated and resentful. But when you're able to talk openly about these emotions, you can support each other and grow closer together.

Coping with terminal illness

When an illness has been diagnosed as terminal, the time remaining can be a heady mixture of bittersweet moments. People can react very differently to the news. Some want to make the most of every moment that's left, some want life to continue as before, and others feel swamped by despair. Some couples find themselves slipping back to earlier feelings of intense connection, but others may have a distressing sense of growing distance. Knowing that soon they will be alone leaves some people unconsciously separating in preparation for the inevitable ending. Fortunately, the days of 'stiff upper lip' have gone and many support networks are available for couples facing the most challenging time of their lives. Ask your health team for details of local services.

Moving from partner to patient

A long-term illness or disability changes the roles within a relationship. Up until now, you may have cared for each other equally, perhaps in different ways, but at the end of the day your roles were equal. When one partner is diagnosed with an illness or disability, he commonly takes on the role of patient and the other becomes the carer. Some couples find this change difficult to adjust to, because a patient–carer relationship can feel more like parent–child than equals.

Here are some ways you can keep the dynamic equal:

- ✔ **Make decisions together.** Continuing to share decision making is an important way of keeping the relationship equal. Even though the carer may be doing more, that doesn't mean that the decisions can't be joint.

- ✔ **Be adult in your discussions.** Keep communication at an adult level and avoid slipping into childlike exchanges.

- ✔ **Maintain a sense of independence and autonomy.** The ability to do this varies enormously, depending on your individual circumstances, and you may have to be creative and enlist the support of others to make it possible. But even having a few separate hobbies or interests around the home that you do alone helps you to respect each other's individuality.

- ✔ **Reverse roles.** Swapping the roles of carer and patient occasionally can help both of you to continue to feel appreciated. That may be something simple like the patient giving the carer a foot rub, making the morning tea or cueing up the DVD for a film.

Caring for each other

Whatever your individual circumstances and your practical abilities, you still care for each other emotionally. And contrary to what some people may think, illness and disability don't mean that you have to give up on your sex life. In fact, the increased creativity required to fit around bodily limitations can make sex better than it's ever been before.

If you experience sexual problems as a result of your condition or medication, a wide range of medical interventions are available today, so do speak to your GP about appropriate options.

Continuing to talk to each other about your thoughts and feelings and making new plans for your future keep you connected, and you can continue to be romantic and sensual together in many ways.

Here are some additional tips for keeping your relationship strong:

- ✔ **Talk.** Share how you're feeling on a regular basis, even the difficult stuff. It's the only way to break through feelings of isolation and understand and accept each other.

- ✔ **Be romantic.** Romance doesn't have to go out the window, but you may have to be more creative. Take a look at Chapters 4 and 5 for more tips.

- ✔ **Be sensual.** Share a bath or hugs, or enjoy your sensuality through taste, sight, smell and sound.

- ✔ **Share memories.** Recollect and enjoy talking about old times.

- ✔ **Plan for the future.** Your plans may have changed but you can still have them, large or small.

- ✔ **Remember to laugh together.** I know it's a cliché, but laughter really is the best medicine. Try to OD on it every now and again.

Adapting to Retirement

When you're 40, you can't wait to retire. When you're 50, it can't come soon enough. But when you're 60 you think, 'WHAT! Where have the last few years gone?' Although everyone knows they're going to retire one day, the event still creeps up on many people. A lifetime of structure, schedules and a reason to get out of bed every morning suddenly disappears and endless amounts of free time replaces it.

For couples, retirement poses a number of challenges. Unless both of you have experienced long-term unemployment, it's the longest time you ever spend with each other in your lives. It's probably also the first occasion when you're wholly responsible for your time and free to make all of your own decisions. Work is called the 'legitimate mistress' because it gives couples an alternative outlet for their needs and emotions. With the mistress lost, couples may find that they only have each other to turn to.

Embracing a new way of life

Some people love retirement. They long for it, plan for it and greedily embrace it in both arms. But for many, the time's a mixed experience of loss and gain as leisure replaces meaningful activity. How you face your retirement years depends on your expectations. If you anticipate great things, you can expect to find them, but if you expect retirement to be miserable, chances are you're right.

Thinking positively and planning positively as a couple ensures that you adapt to this new stage of your life and enjoy it. That doesn't mean that you have to hide or deny the anxieties that you feel, but that you look them squarely in the face and work out together how you can deal with them.

Take a sheet of paper and divide it in two. In the first column write down all the things you're looking forward to in retirement and are hoping to do. Your list may include activities you want to pursue, a skill you want to grasp, building new or stronger relationships with friends and family, visiting new places or relaxing more, and also things you're looking forward to in your relationship such as spending more time together, being romantic or overcoming a particular difficulty. In the second column write the things that you're worried about, for example anxieties about getting bored or feeling directionless, or perhaps money concerns or worries you have about your relationship. When you've finished, share your list with your partner and discuss how each of you can achieve your dreams and manage your anxieties.

Facing the challenges of aging

One very understandable anxiety about retirement is the fast and growing awareness of aging. Retirement marks the final phase of life, and shortly after that you're at the end of your life. Gulp! No one wants to think about their own or their partner's death, but during the retirement years, the reality that you're both getting older and will one day die becomes increasingly apparent.

For some couples, facing this reality enables them to make the most of the years they have left together. They know that their bodies may be getting a bit weaker and slower, but that's not going to stop them having fun.

Perhaps the biggest challenge of retirement is debunking the myths of aging. A hobby of the young and the media is to deride aging and laugh at the 'wrinklies'. But most of what's thrown at older people is rubbish – unless, of course, you choose to believe it and let it control your life. Here are some of the most common myths about aging, and the reality:

- ✔ **When you get old you get more boring.** Generally a comment from people who've never said more than two words to someone over 60, let alone got into a conversation. A wealth of knowledge and experience, as well as plans for the future, accompany old age – none of which need be boring.

- ✔ **Old people become ill and frail.** A few do, but most people stay in good health until close to the end of their lives. Physical responses do get slower and muscular strength declines, but a regular exercise routine can make a dramatic difference, and some retired people say that they're fitter than they've ever been.

- ✔ **An unsound body equals an unsound mind.** Old age heralds a slow and gradual decline in some cognitive functions such as memory, but unless you're unfortunate enough to develop Alzheimer's, you still have as many marbles as you have now.

- ✔ **Old dogs can't learn new tricks.** They can, just ask a dog trainer. The problem is that most old dogs can't be bothered. Retirement is an excellent opportunity to get to grips with something new, whether that's playing a musical instrument, discovering a new sport or speaking a foreign language.

- ✔ **Old people are lonely, depressed and bad tempered.** Well, that's not surprising when everyone gives them such a hard time! Apparently, your personality changes very little after the age of 30, so if you were a happy 30-year-old, your luck's in.

- ✔ **Old people don't want or enjoy sex any more.** Absolutely untrue. Sex drive diminishes very slowly, and orgasm may feel a little weaker, but research shows that a significant percentage of the population are still having sex well into their 70s and enjoying it more than ever.

- ✔ **Old age means getting wise.** I know you want this one to be true, but in all honesty, you do get some stupid older people. Yes, older people have a wonderful wealth of experience that can increase their capacity to assess the world and make decisions, but not all of them use it.

Living in the third age

For many couples, retirement is a time when they get closer and closer. You have more time than ever to focus on each other and on your relationship. The first age of childhood is long gone, the second age of family and career is finally completed and now you're in the third age – the rest of your life.

Every year, the proportion of third-agers to other age groups is increasing and, consequently, more and more services are available to them. Now is probably the best time ever to be retired, so you really have no excuse not to maximise your opportunities and enjoy it.

Just because you're getting older doesn't mean that you have to feel older – or so says the jacket of *Healthy Aging For Dummies* by Brent Agin and Sharon Perkins (Wiley). If you want to know how to make sure that you continue to look and feel good, no matter what age you are, get a copy of the book and follow its 'proven strategies to slow down the aging process'.

A passion and purpose in life can easily compensate for the minor niggles of aging.

Supporting Each Other Through Bereavement

Unexpected bereavement can rock even the strongest of relationships. As individuals, you can feel as though the bottom has fallen out of your lives. As one of a couple, you have to work out how to support your partner when you may also be struggling with your own despair.

The relationship that you and your partner had with the lost person, and also the suddenness and perceived 'timeliness' of the death influence the depth of pain from a bereavement. However painful the grief may be, it affects your relationship.

Understanding the stages of grief

Recognised stages of grief exist that are common after any kind of loss. Understanding that the emotions you feel are natural and healthy can help you to accept them and work through them more quickly.

1. **You feel shock and disbelief.**

   You may feel little more than numbness as you try to take in the news. Disbelief sometimes extends to denying the degree of the loss as a way of trying to ward off the inevitable pain of grief.

2. **You feel anger and you protest.**

   'Why, why, why?' is a common proclamation from someone who's experienced a loss. Anger often accompanies the questioning: anger at the world, at medical staff, at family members, at yourself and even anger with the bereaved for leaving you. Although the anger stage can feel particularly painful, some unconsciously choose to stay stuck in their anger as a way of feeling energised and defending against moving into the next stage.

3. **You feel yearning and sadness.**

   This is undoubtedly the most painful stage of the cycle and, depending on how close you were to the person you've lost, it's a stage that can continue for a long time.

4. **You move on.**

   Fortunately, grieving does come to an end. Although you may always feel as if you have a hole in your life where your loved one used to be, the space around it increases, allowing you to focus more attention on the rest of life.

Doing grief differently

The stages of grief vary hugely from individual to individual: the intensity differs and so does the length of time spent during each stage. No right or wrong way to grieve exists. Every person's a unique individual, and the way each person mourns is also unique.

But for couples, these differences can create additional distress. At a time when you desperately need to share your grief and feel close, you may not be able to understand why your partner isn't reacting in the same way as you. Some of the differences originate from personality, with some people naturally being more introverted and introspective, and others more expressive and reaching out towards other people. Other differences can result from childhood experiences of loss, and family messages about how to manage grief.

Different types of bereavement also bring their own challenges:

✔ **Losing a parent:** Everyone's relationship with their parents is different, and partners can sometimes struggle to comprehend the sense of loss and their reaction. Because the partner who was the child is likely to be struggling more, he may rely on the other partner for support. The supportive partner needs to continue to be aware of special anniversaries that may reawaken feelings of loss.

✔ **Losing a baby:** A pregnancy or newborn baby arrives with great joy and expectations, but unfortunately, sometimes things don't go to plan. Genetic difficulties force some couples to make agonising decisions about terminating a pregnancy; others experience inexplicable miscarriages, and others lose a baby at birth or in the first few months. The symbiotic bond between mother and baby often leaves a mother feeling the grief much more than her partner. A partner may struggle to understand the depth of emotion, and the mother may hear heartfelt words of comfort such as 'We can try again' as empty platitudes. But the situation's hard for fathers too, and some feel cut adrift in the mourning process, with little support and understanding of the unique loss they have also experienced. You need to find ways as a couple to comfort and support each other through your mutual loss.

✔ **Losing a child:** Most people agree that this is greatest and most shocking of bereavements any human has to face. After such a loss, the world can seem such an unsafe and unfair place. With both parents sharing the grief equally, accepting any differences in the mourning process can be difficult. Not uncommonly, one partner is in the anger stage of grieving while another is stuck with the sadness. Understanding that both stages are a natural part of the grieving process is essential. One partner may also often take the coping role, being responsible for holding life together, while the other disintegrates into his grief. Encouraging one another to share the roles and experience each equally is important.

Holding hope for each other

When you've had a significant bereavement, you may feel as if the world can never be the same again, and life can feel meaningless and hopeless. You may find that the two of you fluctuate between feelings of despair and optimistic determination. And at times, both of you may be caught in despair.

Although every grief situation and individual is unique, you may find the following guidelines helpful for getting you through:

✔ Accept that you are both different and no right or wrong way exists to cope with loss.

✔ Make time to be together when you can share feelings and talk about the future.

✔ Help and encourage each other to keep as many regular routines going as possible.

✔ Create opportunities to do pleasurable things together, such as going for a walk or watching a film.

✔ Encourage your partner to take time for himself and be kind to himself.

✔ Don't make any major changes in your life for at least 12 months after a bereavement.

✔ Allow yourselves to be upset together or angry together without feeling that one of you must lift the other up.

✔ Give one another plenty of physical affection.

Whatever their loss has been, couples find themselves having to adapt to new circumstances. The nature of grief is for individuals to feel isolated, but once healing begins, couples often find that they feel closer than ever before.

You can find a lot more advice on coping with bereavement in *Grieving For Dummies* by Greg Harvey (Wiley).

Chapter 14

Surviving an Affair

Affairs make blockbuster movies and gripping television dramas, but they tear relationships apart and devastate people's lives. In a couple relationship you can commit no greater betrayal than giving your love or your body to another person. It breaks the rules of commitment and exclusivity that form the backbone of a stable, loving relationship.

But relationships can and do survive an affair. In almost every case, an affair's a symptom of unresolved or sometimes unspoken relationship difficulties, an external sign of an internal desire for change. Something in either the person's life or the relationship isn't okay, and the affair creates the trigger for change.

In this chapter I explore how to survive what may feel like the end of the world: how to cope with feelings of anger, self-doubt, regret and remorse; how to make the agonising decision about whether to recommit to the relationship; and, if you do decide to work at your relationship, how to rebuild trust and affair-proof your relationship for the future.

An affair always signals a turning point in a relationship, but it doesn't have to signal the end.

Coping with the Discovery

When one of you first discovers or confesses an affair, your relationship's instantly transformed. The circumstances of the affair and how the discovery's made are significant to how you respond as a couple.

If you find your partner in your bed with your best friend, and discover that their clandestine relationship's been going on for ten years, this is very different from hearing your partner tearfully confess a one-night stand that happened five years ago. And a first offence that happened during a time of difficulty between you feels very different from listening to an indifferent partner telling you she's slipped up, yet again.

The most significant factor that affects the outcome of an affair is the level of threat it poses to the relationship. If a strong physical and emotional connection exists with a lover whom either partner perceives as being better than the betrayed partner, then the threat's high. And if considerable deceit has stretched over a long period, the betrayed partner may feel that she doesn't know her wayward partner and that the relationship she thought she had never existed at all.

If the circumstances of an affair feel overwhelming and you're seriously doubting whether you have any chance of saving your relationship, please continue to read the rest of this chapter. Whatever the future of your relationship, you still need to cope with your feelings and find a positive way of moving forward with your life. Understanding why an affair happened can help you rebuild your self-esteem and face the future with confidence.

Identifying the five common types of affair

People have affairs for many different reasons; in fact, probably as many reasons exist as people, because every circumstance is different. People generally assume that affairs are always sexual, but some affairs are purely platonic. With the Internet being the fastest-growing arena for infidelity, no physical contact may take place at all. Some say that without sex, an affair's not real, but relationship experts agree that any intimate activity between two people that breaches the trust of a partner is an affair.

The following sections outline the five most common types of affairs. You may find that your circumstances fall neatly into one of the types or they may be a combination of a few.

The exit affair

When a relationship's in dire difficulty, an affair can be a way of bringing it to an end. The unfaithful partner may not have made a conscious decision to end the relationship in this way, but the affair brings the problems within the relationship into sharp focus and forces a decision.

For some, the decision to end the relationship may have been made a long time before, but fear of being alone has kept them in the relationship way after it stopped working. In effect, the affair partner becomes a replacement who makes leaving the relationship possible. In these situations, the unfaithful partner commonly leaves for the lover, but these relationships rarely last. After the affair serves its purpose, it's likely to come to an end as well.

An exit affair may occasionally be triggered by the faithful partner who's looking, consciously or unconsciously, for a reason to end the relationship. The faithful partner may withhold sex and affection and offer only hostility or indifference, so the emotionally starved partner finds solace in another person. Although the betrayed partner may be outraged and upset, secretly she's relieved to have a good excuse to end the relationship without acknowledging responsibility.

The thrill affair

Thrill affairs are fun. If they weren't, people wouldn't have them. True, the price to pay is too great for many people, but for some the illicit nature of an affair brings a powerful adrenalin rush. Add to that the excitement of sex with someone new and the romantic trimmings that accompany all new relationships, and an affair can seem irresistible.

The thrill affair is the one that's most about sex and least about problems in the relationship. It may happen more often in a long-term relationship where sex has lost its sparkle or to individuals who need a buzz in their lives. When the unfaithful partner is discovered (and she rarely confesses), she's likely to plead in her defence 'it was only sex' and be surprised that her heartbroken partner doesn't understand. A common response from the bewildered partner is 'How can you hurt me this badly and jeopardise our relationship for something that means so little to you?'

The angry affair

Two types of anger can trigger this kind of affair: a conscious anger that results in an affair being taken as revenge, and an unconscious anger made up of years of bitterness and resentment over unmet needs. Ironically, an angry affair's most likely to happen between couples who dislike and avoid conflict.

When a partner's feeling seriously hurt by her partner but unable to express, manage and overcome those feelings within the relationship, an affair can be an unconscious way of forcing issues into the open. These affairs are often quickly uncovered, because the purpose of the affair was always to bring the couple's difficulties to a head and resolve them.

Sometimes both partners within a couple may be angry at how much they're drifting apart, and not until an affair happens does either realise how bad things have become.

The safety affair

People who engage in safety affairs are likely to repeat the pattern of behaviour for many years, either through multiple affairs or with one long-term lover. Committing to one person may feel like a terrifying prospect, so rather than putting all their emotional eggs in one basket, they keep part of themselves separate for someone else.

Partners who engage in these kinds of affairs may have been deeply wounded by rejection in the past and may struggle to trust the love and commitment offered in their relationships. They desperately crave intimacy and security, but, ever fearful of not receiving it, they sabotage the very thing they desire with infidelity.

Safety affairs may help a couple relationship, because the unfaithful partner may use the lover as an emotional outlet for difficult feelings that she can't express in the primary relationship. But in the long term, deceit and secrets damage intimacy, and the unfaithful partner, the betrayed partner and the lover all get hurt.

The platonic affair

Although a platonic affair may seem harmless on the surface, it takes away a level of intimacy that's normally reserved for the couple. The affair may start as 'just good friends', but as the emotional lovers confide more and more in each other, they share less and less with their partners. And the risk of the affair becoming sexual is always present and may add an additional, exciting tension to the relationship.

The Internet and close workplace relationships have caused a rise in platonic affairs. People who may feel they're being betrayed can find confronting their partners difficult. This is especially true where the whole affair is conducted online. Cyber-affairs are common in online communities and within virtual worlds. The visual anonymity provided by these environments allows a level of self-disclosure and intimacy that's hard to replicate in the offline world, and people can maintain the fantasy of the perfect relationship and protect it from reality.

A common reason for this kind of affair is a lack of intimacy within the primary relationship or feeling stuck in a dead relationship but unable to leave, perhaps because of children. These affairs can continue for many years, spurred on by fantasies of being together 'properly' in the future. In the meantime, distance grows in the primary relationship and any hope of repair may be lost.

Looking at the reactions of the betrayed partner

For almost everyone, discovering that a partner is having or had an affair comes as a massive shock. Even if you had your suspicions for some time and the revelation was the result of many months of detective work, after the affair is out in the open, the emotions can still feel overwhelming.

Discovering an affair is probably one of the most traumatic experiences anyone can go through. Whether you're told by a partner, by friends, by the lover or you find out for yourself, you never forget the day. As the next few days and weeks pass, many betrayed partners find themselves going through similar experiences to those that characterise post-traumatic stress disorder: numbness, anger, depression, sleep and eating disturbances, hyper-vigilance (being overly alert), irritability, anxiety and obsessively thinking about the details of the affair.

In the early days after a discovery, wanting to make a decision about the future of your relationship is natural. But in the middle of such emotional turmoil, reaching a rational decision is difficult. Your first priority is to look after yourself and get the support of friends and family who can help you through this crisis phase.

Here's a list of common emotions you may experience if you're the betrayed partner:

- **Anger and rage:** Discovering an affair is a common trigger for violence within a relationship, and crimes of passion are still frequent occurrences. The anger you experience – directed at the partner or at the lover, or both – can feel totally overwhelming.

- **Confusion:** 'Why?' questions commonly go around and around after you discover an affair. In the early days, you find yourself desperate for information and details: why did she do it, who was the lover, what is he like, where did they go, who else knows, how long has this gone on, why didn't I notice, why didn't she tell me, does she still love me, do I still love her . . . and so on.

- **Disbelief:** You may have difficulty believing that what you're being told is actually true at all and wonder whether your partner, or whoever told you, is lying. You may find yourself wanting to believe your partner's plausible explanations for those hotel receipts you found, or keep telling yourself that the affair didn't mean anything.

- **Embarrassment:** Feeling profoundly embarrassed by an affair is common, especially if it's revealed publically or the affair was with someone you knew. But even if no one else knows, you may still wonder what people would think if they did know and wonder how the affair reflects on you.

✔ **Fear for the future:** An affair changes the future of a relationship for ever. Even if you're confident that you can rebuild your relationship, you commonly worry about what's ahead.

✔ **Jealousy:** Jealousy's a common emotion experienced by those whose relationships are under threat. The depth of jealousy varies depending on the type of affair, and is particularly acute if the lover is still around and available. You can find more on jealousy in Chapter 12.

✔ **Loss:** The feelings of loss can continue for a long time after you discover an affair: loss of what you thought your relationship was, loss of who you thought your partner was, loss of what you thought you shared and enjoyed together. Realising that your relationship as you knew it was never what you thought it was and never can be again is intensely painful.

✔ **Rejection:** An affair's a personal rejection. Many people try to reassure their heartbroken partners that their love for them never changed and that the affair was no more than a stupid mistake. That may be true, but it doesn't take away the feeling that your needs weren't important enough to stop the affair happening.

✔ **Self-doubt:** Trying to understand your role in the deception can lead to profound feelings of self-doubt. 'What did I do to deserve this?' is a common refrain for the betrayed partner. Self-esteem and confidence can be profoundly damaged when you find out that your partner has chosen to be with someone else in spite of the pain that causes you.

✔ **Shock:** You see affairs on TV or read about them in magazines, but you don't expect one to happen to you. You may never have thought that your partner was 'like that', or be shocked by her level of deceit or choice of lover or how long the affair has gone on. You may be shocked that you never saw the affair coming or had any inkling of what was going on.

✔ **Suspicion:** No matter how much your partner tries to convince you that the affair's over, believing that's true is hard. After all, she lied before. Once trust has been broken, you may suspect that your partner is lying about other things too.

In the first few days and weeks after discovering an affair, you can feel overwhelmed as you see-saw between all the different emotions. All you can do during this early phase is look after yourself and take one day at a time. Get as much support as you can from close friends and family, and give yourself the space you need to come to terms with the news.

Exploring the reactions of the unfaithful partner

Society often has little sympathy with the guilty partner in an affair, but the emotions she experiences can feel just as overwhelming as those of the betrayed partner. And without acknowledgement and empathy, moving forward positively can be difficult.

If you were the one who was unfaithful, you may not be able to understand what you're going through. You may feel preoccupied with your partner's emotions and think that you're not entitled to feel pain of your own. But when your partner discovers your affair, you may be devastated, not just because you've been caught but because you too must now face the consequences.

Here's a list of common emotions experienced by the unfaithful partner:

- ✔ **Confusion:** If a partner reacts differently to how you expected, you can be very confused. Most people who've had an affair have thought through what would happen if they were discovered. They may be ready for anger and retribution and find tears and self-reproach. Or they may expect their partners to be prompted to resolve issues within the relationship, only to find that they're walking out the door. Occasionally, a partner goes into denial, saying that the affair doesn't matter, which can be extremely confusing and frustrating for the unfaithful partner who sees the affair as a trigger for change.

- ✔ **Defensiveness:** When an affair is a symptom of a problem within the relationship, or if a partner had an affair in the past, if the other partner accepts no responsibility for what has happened then feeling defensive is common. If the affair is over, feeling defensive at ongoing accusations of continued contact is also usual.

- ✔ **Fear for the future:** When an affair's discovered, most unfaithful partners want the relationship to continue. But in the days and weeks following the revelation, they may be powerless to influence any decision. Waiting to find out whether a partner's going to stay or go can be agonising.

- ✔ **Guilt:** Seeing the pain an affair causes can create devastating feelings of guilt. Even if you know your partner may take the knowledge badly, having to sit and watch his heart break with the news of what you've done is heartbreaking for you too.

- ✔ **Mourning:** If an affair has been long or particularly intense, the partner commonly and naturally misses the lover. This can be extremely difficult to talk to anyone about, because you may feel you have no right to experience loss and know you may receive little sympathy. Mourning the end of the affair is often a guilty and secret pain that you handle alone.

- ✔ **Relief:** Many people who have an affair are hugely relieved when it's finally discovered or when they confess to what's going on. Maintaining an affair can feel like being split in two, and the guilt can be very hard to live with. Once it's out in the open, the affair has to end and you can begin to work on any issues within the relationship. Although most people regret the pain caused by an affair, many don't regret the affair itself if it brings issues to the surface of a relationship that may otherwise have gone unaddressed.

- ✔ **Shame:** *Guilt* is an emotion you experience when you know you've *done* something wrong; *shame* is what you feel when you think that you as a person *are* wrong. Many people who have affairs never thought they were capable of doing so. They may have been judgemental about people who cheated on their partners, but now they must face the fact that they're one of those people. Remorse and self-reproach can feel so overwhelming that the unfaithful partner thinks that she should end the relationship because she's not worthy of her partner's love.

When an affair's just been revealed, you may be tempted to go straight into fix-it mode. But make sure that you also take time to come to terms with what's happened. Before you can move forward, you need to give yourself time to grieve the ending of the affair and rebuild your self-worth. If you can, find someone you can talk to whom you can trust with your feelings, and be kind to yourself.

Deciding whether to tell others

People react very differently to discovering an affair, and this is normally a reflection of how private the couple has been in the past. Some feel hugely embarrassed and don't want anybody else ever to know, regardless of what decision the couple makes for the future. But others want to shout it from the housetops so that everybody knows what a so-and-so their partner's been.

Before telling anybody, considering what your motives are and what the consequences may be is essential. Seeking revenge and wanting to shame an unfaithful partner are common and natural urges, but they can seriously backfire. Similarly, wanting to be honest with friends and family about the problems in your life may be admirable, but you need to consider their reactions as well.

Take some time. Before you tell anybody else, consider the following:

- How do you think this person may react? Can she be a positive support for you or may she make things worse?

- Can the person you're thinking of telling influence the decision you eventually make about your relationship's future? Can she continue to support you and your partner, whatever decision you make?

- Do you trust this person not to tell anyone else?

- Are your motivations purely coming from anger and spite? If so, how do you feel about making an irrevocable decision based on this?

- May the news hurt the person you're thinking of telling? Is she able to cope? And can you live with the responsibility of knowing what pain you may have caused her?

Many couples regret telling other people about an affair, especially if they later decide to work at the relationship. Other people may have very strong opinions about what you should and shouldn't do, and telling them may damage their relationship with you as a couple for ever. This doesn't mean that you shouldn't tell anybody, but make sure that if you do tell someone, she's a person you can really trust and who can support you in the long term.

Telling children that one of their parents has had an affair can be devastating and can damage their relationship with Mum or Dad for ever. It unfairly drags them into your problems and forces them to take sides. Whatever happens to you as a couple, you're still parents who need to put your children's needs first.

If someone else has made the affair public, you may decide that telling people close to you is better before they hear it from someone else. If this describes your situation, sit down as a couple and agree what needs to be said, and if possible tell people together.

Navigating the Aftermath

Once the dust's begun to settle after discovering an affair, both partners can find themselves dealing with very different emotions. While the betrayed partner's still in the midst of powerful feelings of shock, anger and loss, the guilty partner may be desperately trying to make amends and mourning the loss of the affair. These differences can leave partners feeling isolated from each other and make talking about the future of the relationship difficult.

The person who's had the affair may be ready to move on and start rebuilding the relationship as soon as possible. She may want to put the whole horrible mess behind her and get on with life. For the person who's been betrayed, this can feel like a minimisation of the affair and an attempt to pretend that it never happened. In reality, it simply reflects the different places the partners have reached on the journey of recovery.

Before you can make any decision, understanding why the affair happened and accepting your share of the responsibility are both essential. Fully grasping the meaning of an affair takes time and, depending on the length of the infidelity and the level of deceit, this can be weeks or months. Finding a way to work through this time together can help you avoid making snap decisions that you may later regret.

Understanding why the affair happened

Whatever you're thinking about the future of your relationship, understanding why the affair happened helps both of you to comprehend and manage your emotions and move on positively. Living with 'whys' is exhausting and keeps people trapped in the past, unable to enjoy the present or have hope for the future.

When you understand why an affair happened, each of you can take responsibility for the role you played and ensure that it never happens again – whether that's within your future relationship as a couple or in new relationships in the future.

Getting to the bottom of the cause of an affair requires open-heart surgery. Doing so means asking yourselves some tough questions and being honest in your replies. It doesn't mean finding excuses or throwing blame, but it does mean accepting responsibility and finding understanding.

Here are three lists of questions – one for the betrayed partner, one for the unfaithful partner and one for both of you – to ask about your relationship. If your partner can't or won't do this exercise with you, you can still read through her questions and consider how you think she may reply.

Questions for the betrayed partner:

- ✔ Have I been withholding emotionally from my partner?

- ✔ Has my partner tried to talk to me about issues that I've ignored?

- ✔ Am I aware that my partner's been unhappy, but been reluctant to talk about it?

✔ Have I had an affair in the past?

✔ Have I withheld sex from my partner or refused to explore her needs?

✔ Have I done anything I'm aware of that's seriously hurt my partner or damaged her trust?

✔ Do I treat my partner with respect?

✔ Do I demonstrate how much I love my partner?

✔ Have I become complacent about my relationship and been preoccupied with other things in life?

✔ Have I been a friend and companion to my partner?

✔ Have I provided support and empathy to my partner in times of need?

Questions for the unfaithful partner:

✔ Am I generally bored and feeling unfulfilled by life?

✔ Do I struggle with low self-esteem and concerns about aging?

✔ Did my lover provide something important that was missing in my relationship, and is this something I've asked my partner for?

✔ Do I crave more excitement in my sex life?

✔ Am I holding on to anger and resentment towards my partner that I haven't expressed?

✔ Do any unresolved issues exist within our relationship that I avoid talking about?

✔ Have I tried to talk about problems, but my partner's refused to acknowledge or address them?

✔ Do I find difficulty in getting emotionally or physically close to my partner?

✔ Do I believe that my partner respects and cares about me?

✔ Do I believe that my partner loves me and is committed to our relationship?

Questions for both of you:

✔ Have we been drifting apart recently?

✔ Do we still share hopes and dreams for the future?

✔ Have we both avoided talking about issues between us?

✔ Do we struggle to support one another when we're going through stressful phases of life?

✔ Are there problems in our sex life that we've failed to address?

✔ Do we make time for each other as individuals?

✔ Do we make time for ourselves as a couple?

✔ Do we still enjoy being intimate in non-sexual ways?

When you've answered all the questions, you should have a good idea of what was missing from your lives and from your relationship. This absolutely does not justify the affair, but it can tell you what created the environment where an affair can happen.

Accepting responsibility

Accepting responsibility for what has happened leading up to an affair can be difficult, especially if you're the betrayed partner. But doing so not only helps you to manage your feelings healthily, it also empowers you to prevent an affair happening again.

If the reasons for the affair were nearly all to do with your partner's unexpressed needs for excitement, or as a way of escaping other problems in her life that weren't to do with your relationship, you may genuinely find that you have little to blame yourself for. If this is the case, your decision about the future is based on your ability to forgive and on your partner's ability to change.

If you were the unfaithful partner, your guilt may encourage you to take all the blame on yourself. Or, in an attempt to avoid facing the devastation that you've caused, you may try to lump all the blame on your partner. You need to accept total responsibility for having the affair and the deceit involved, but you may be only partly responsible for the circumstances leading up to the affair. If problems existed in your relationship that you avoided talking about, you also need to accept responsibility for allowing an affair to happen because you weren't ready to open up.

Blaming the lover for an affair and making him the scapegoat for what's happened to your relationship can be tempting. Doing this prevents you from facing up to problems in your relationship and affair-proofing it for the future.

Affairs are a symptom of problems in the relationship. This means that both of you need to share the responsibility for what was happening between you, how you talked about your problems and how you avoided dealing with them.

Working through the early weeks and months

The first few weeks and months after an affair is out in the open are often the most difficult time a couple ever face. In many cases it's still too early to make a decision about the future of the relationship, because both partners continue to work through the implications of what's happened. If the affair went on for a long time, the betrayed partner may continue to have many unanswered questions, and both of you still need to decide whether and how you want to resolve any underlying relationship issues.

These tips can help you to survive the aftermath:

✔ **Be prepared to listen to painful feelings.** Both partners need to hear what has happened from the other's perspective. This means that the unfaithful partner needs to hear how much pain she's caused and cope with the tears and anger. The betrayed partner may also have to listen to some painful home truths about what was missing in the relationship and led to the affair.

✔ **Put boundaries around conversations.** When an affair happens, it can seem to take over everything else in your life and you can be tempted to talk about nothing else. You find that your conversations are more constructive if you limit them to times that are convenient for both of you, when you both have the energy to cope. How often you choose to talk is up to you. You may decide that you want to put some time aside every day or two or three times a week. Either way, agree the time in advance and don't talk for longer than two hours at a time. Anything longer than two hours is likely to stop being productive.

✔ **Write down your thoughts and feelings.** As well as sharing your thoughts and feelings with each other, you may find writing things down helpful. This helps you to manage your emotions between your conversation sessions and ensures that you don't forget anything important that you want to say.

✔ **Think before asking and answering questions.** The betrayed partner commonly has hundreds of questions. What did the lover look like? What was the sex like? Where did the lovers go together and what did they do? Was the lover more intelligent, funnier, easier to talk to? The big questions underlying many of these are 'Was he better than me?' and 'Did you share something we don't have?'. Before asking these questions, make sure that you're ready to hear the answers. The reality is that perhaps the lover was better looking, younger, more intelligent and shared your partner's love of opera. But is that information really going to help you? If you were the unfaithful partner, be honest with your answers but be sensitive, and if you really feel that an honest answer may be painful, check that your partner really does want to know.

✔ **Agree and accept accountability.** Most betrayed partners can't even consider rebuilding a relationship until they're 100 per cent convinced that the affair is over. This means that the unfaithful partner must become ultra-accountable for her time and behaviour. You should agree to be open about emails, texts and bank statements, and contactable on your mobile phone at any time. Some activities, such as going out with friends or playing sport, may be limited or checked with others for authenticity. This can be incredibly uncomfortable for both partners, because the betrayed partner feels that he has to play detective, and the unfaithful partner has no privacy. But the measure is short term until trust is restored, and is the price you pay for infidelity.

✔ **Give yourselves time.** No right or wrong amount of time exists over which to navigate the aftermath of an affair. What's most important is that you don't rush yourself or each other. Over time, you find that your emotions become less overwhelming and the questions become fewer, and while you may both be desperate to make a decision about the future, that decision affects both of your lives for ever, and, if you have children, theirs too.

✔ **Get professional help.** If you haven't been for couple counselling before, now may be an excellent time to go. A counsellor doesn't rush you to make a decision but does help you both to focus on working through the emotions of the here and now and gaining further insight into what's happened. If you find that your conversations are going around and around in circles or are too painful to bear, a counsellor can also help you to manage the process more comfortably.

Many couples find agreeing not to make a decision for a set period helpful. For example, you may say that you're not going to talk about the future or ask one another what you're thinking for another two months and then either make a decision or postpone further. This can give both of you the space to work through your feelings now, rather than worrying about the future.

Choosing Your Future

At some point, you have to decide whether you want to try to rebuild your relationship or walk away. Your decision depends on the reasons for the affair, how strong your relationship was in the beginning, and your own individual motivations.

If the affair highlighted irreconcilable differences between you and your partner – for example if one of you wants more intimacy than the other or wants to choose a different lifestyle – you may decide to separate. And if your relationship was already in difficulty, the affair may be the last straw. If a considerable amount of deceit was involved or your partner had an affair with someone you know, you may decide that ever trusting again is impossible. But if you have children, you may both have more motivation to work at the relationship, in spite of your differences.

If you're still very unsure about the future of your relationship, you may find reading Chapter 15 helpful, as well as the rest of this section.

The first step towards making the final decision is to look at the damage that the affair has caused and consider whether salvaging your relationship is worthwhile.

Assessing the wreckage

Discovering an affair stops any relationship in its tracks and forces couples to re-evaluate what they have and what they want for the future. If cracks have always existed in your relationship, now they're more like craters. And if you've been papering over the cracks for many years, now you're forced to look at them full on and decide what you want to do, and can do, about them.

Deciding whether your relationship's worth saving isn't an easy or quick task. It takes time, but time that's an important investment in your future.

The relationship scale exercise can be really helpful for people trying to work out whether enough is still left in the relationship that they want to save. You need a pen and paper so that you can make a note of your scores.

1. On a scale of 1–10, rate how good your relationship was before the affair.

2. On the same scale, rate how good your relationship is now.

3. Now ask yourself what's currently keeping you from 0. In other words, what good stuff is left that is stopping you from knowing that your relationship's over?

4. Ask yourself what needs to change in order to get you back to how you felt before.

5. What do you want to work on to get you closer to 10? (Remember that no relationship's permanently on 10!)

When you've completed the exercise, discuss your findings with your partner. If you're both in agreement on the areas you want to improve, and both of you are willing to work on those areas, then the chances of saving your relationship are good. Indeed, more than that, as well as getting your relationship back to where it was, you can commit as a couple to making it even better.

Using the relationship scale exercise

Karen and Tim used the relationship scale exercise to help them decide their future after Karen confessed to a ten-month affair with a colleague at work.

Karen rated her relationship before the affair as a 6, and now as a 3. Her list of things that were keeping the relationship from 0 were their shared sense of humour, good companionship, parenting their children, shared ambitions for the future and her love of Tim's personality. To get back to where they were before, Karen knew that she had to work at rebuilding Tim's trust and also getting their sex life back. To make things even better, she wanted to build more intimacy into the relationship and improve communication, which were two of the key things that she felt contributed to the affair.

Tim rated the relationship before the affair as an 8, and now as a 1. As is common, Tim had rated their relationship higher than Karen before the affair. He hadn't realised that problems existed or at least, he definitely hadn't seen them as being as important as Karen had. As the betrayed partner, for him the relationship was now much worse, but keeping him from 0 were their shared sense of humour, companionship and their shared plans as a family. To get back to 8 where he thought they were before the affair, he had to believe that he could trust Karen again and that she really loved him and wasn't looking for someone else. He also wanted to feel more confident as a lover again and regain the intimacy he felt that they'd shared in their sex life. To get closer to 10, he also wanted to work at communication and intimacy. He had always agreed that this was a problem area, but had never before realised how much of a problem it was for Karen.

You may also find looking at Chapter 2 and completing the relationship health check-up questionnaire really helpful. The chapter helps you to analyse the strengths and weaknesses in your relationship and prioritise the areas you want to improve.

Making the decision to forgive

Whatever your final decision, forgiveness is essential to recovering from an affair. All the time you hold on to bitterness and resentment over what happened, you continue to lock yourself in the past, weighed down with pain and anger. When you forgive, you free yourself from those painful emotions and give yourself the chance to live again.

Forgiveness is a rather old-fashioned thing that people don't talk about very much, but psychologically speaking it's one of the most powerful tools for healing the human heart. People are often confused over what forgiving really means, and this confusion can mean that they can't understand why they'd ever want to forgive. Hopefully, the following sections clarify what forgiveness is all about.

Defining what forgiveness isn't . . .

Forgiving does not mean forgetting, and it definitely doesn't mean that the wrong doesn't matter any more. Forgiving also doesn't mean that everything's going to be all right between you in the future.

Forgiveness isn't excusing someone or condoning something that's wrong. It doesn't mean that you're willing to tolerate something that's unacceptable or that you don't protect yourself from being hurt again in the future. Forgiveness also doesn't let someone off from the consequences of what they've done. It's not a pardon, nor does it reduce the sentence: the price still has to be paid.

Forgiving someone for hurting you, but still making the decision that you don't want to be close to her again, is quite possible. Forgiveness doesn't mean reconciliation. You can forgive your partner for the affair and still decide to separate.

. . . and seeing what forgiveness is

First and foremost, forgiveness is a conscious choice that the offended person makes. It's a choice that you can make in response to genuine remorse and a sincere apology from the unfaithful partner. If a partner isn't sorry, then forgiveness may be a one-sided transaction, purely for the benefit of the offended party – something he does to help him move on. But when a partner's truly sorry, the apology and forgiveness create a foundation on which to move forward, alone or together, in the future.

Forgiveness is a process, not a single event. If someone says sorry for standing on your foot, you can instantly forgive her. But when she's had an affair, something that's broken down the fundamental bond of fidelity between you, forgiveness takes time. Forgiveness means slowly and gradually letting go of anger, giving up the desire to retaliate and moving forward.

Without forgiveness, rebuilding the relationship isn't possible. With forgiveness, reconciliation becomes a real possibility if both of you want it and are willing to change behaviour and improve your relationship.

Forgiving your partner

The most obvious person to forgive is, of course, the unfaithful partner. To do this, you need to be clear what the offences are and that the unfaithful partner has shown appropriate remorse for each offence. Sleeping with someone else or getting intimate with someone else is probably the first offence that comes into your mind, but also consider apologising for not talking about a problem sooner, for lying and misleading, for the time taken away from the relationship when the affair was taking place, and for all the emotional pain that you've caused.

If the affair was a symptom of particular problems within the relationship, then the betrayed partner may also seek forgiveness. For example, you may apologise for not listening to your partner when she said she was unhappy, or not taking her complaints more seriously.

To help you facilitate the forgiveness process, each of you can write a list of the things that you're sorry for and give it to your partner. Try to go into as much detail as possible and avoid using generalisations such as 'I'm sorry for hurting you.' Instead, list the individual emotions you've evoked; for example, say 'I'm sorry for causing you embarrassment, damaging your memory of special events, and causing so much anger.' After you have completed and exchanged your lists, tell your partner if you're ready to forgive her for some offences while you need some time for others.

Forgiving yourself

If the affair was a result of problems within your relationship that both of you have ignored, you may both be beating yourselves up for things left undone. And if you were the one who had the affair, you probably feel particularly bad about yourself. Forgiving yourself is an essential part of moving forward from difficult times. That doesn't mean telling yourself that the affair didn't matter or it wasn't your fault, but allowing yourself to gain from your mistakes and resolving to improve.

Some unfaithful partners can find forgiving themselves difficult, even after their partner's forgiven them. When this happens, one partner's left feeling forever in the other's debt, and as she tries continually to make amends for what she's done, her partner loses an equal partner in the relationship.

Forgiving the lover

This is perhaps the hardest part of forgiveness, and some may feel that it's unnecessary. But forgiving the lover means that you can stop being tied to him by anger and jealousy. All the time you harbour negative emotions towards the lover, you keep him in your life. But when you can let go of those emotions and stop thinking about how he hurt you, you can leave him in the past with the affair.

Recognising blocks to forgiveness

Forgiveness isn't easy. It's a long process of letting go of painful emotions and choosing to move forward rather than being tied to the past. Here are three of the most common blocks that people can face when working through the forgiveness process:

✔ **Wanting justice:** Affairs aren't fair, and something that was rightfully yours was taken away. Of course you're angry and want justice for yourself, perhaps by punishing your partner or constantly reminding her of the pain she caused. But no one can change the past, and whatever you do doesn't change the fact that you were treated unfairly. Forgiving is your opportunity to leave your painful feelings in the past and seek justice in the future. Not allowing yourself to do that is an even greater injustice.

✔ **Wanting control:** Trust is extremely fragile after an affair, and one way of managing this is to continue to demonstrate how hurt you are and ensure your partner's undivided attention and compliance. In the short term that's okay, but if you want to move on from what's happened, you need to get back to the place where you're equal partners again. That doesn't mean that you can't ever talk about the affair again, but it does mean that you allow your feelings to soften with forgiveness and you stop using your emotions to manipulate your partner.

✔ **Wanting safety:** When you've been badly hurt, you can take a long time before you feel emotionally safe again. After an affair, people commonly think that if they forgive their partners, they may cheat and hurt them again. In reality, not forgiving fuels your insecurity, because it means that your damaged emotions never get the chance to heal. By forgiving, you become strong again and you have more energy and motivation to ensure that you build a relationship – with your current partner or a new one – where you're confident that you can trust.

Forgiveness doesn't mean forgetting or saying that the affair didn't matter, it means letting go of painful emotions and looking ahead rather than back. It takes time, and sometimes you feel like you're moving forward and then suddenly like you've gone back to square one. But with persistence, you can leave the affair in the past and focus on your future. You may always bear the scars of the affair, but you don't have to live with gaping wounds.

Re-establishing commitment

If you've decided to work at your relationship again, you need to commit to each other to make your relationship stronger and rebuild the trust that you've lost. This may seem like a huge expectation when you have no guarantees of success, but without at least some level of commitment, neither of you has the motivation to give your relationship 100 per cent.

The individual circumstances of the affair, how long it lasted and the amount of deceit involved are key factors in agreeing together what you're committing to. Other factors that also influence your decision are how good your relationship was in the first place and your family and financial situation. Some couples choose to recommit to the relationship because divorce simply isn't a viable option.

You can consider three levels of commitment:

- ✔ **Commit to couple counselling to decide what to do next.** That means postponing the decision about whether your relationship can work until you've spent time with a couple counsellor exploring all the issues.

- ✔ **Commit to working at the relationship for an agreed amount of time.** You may agree 3, 6 or perhaps 12 months. Or if a particular milestone is ahead, you may agree to commit until your 40th birthday or until your children have finished exams or left home. The essential point here should be that you agree that you're *working* at the relationship, rather than waiting to see whether things get better. If you're only willing to do the latter, take a look at Chapter 15. When you reach the date you've agreed, you may be ready to move on to the following level or decide to set another period of time.

- ✔ **Commit for the long term.** If you're already working well through the forgiveness process and you're both clear on what needs to change within your relationship, you may be ready to commit to your relationship indefinitely. To do this takes a reasonable degree of confidence that you can restore trust and solve the issues that contributed to the affair.

Once you've made a commitment to work at your relationship for whatever period, you may find completing, as a couple, the relationship health check-up questionnaire in Chapter 2 and agreeing where to focus your attention helpful.

Rebuilding Trust

No relationship can survive without trust. To feel secure, you need to know that your partner's committed to you and to the relationship, that she's the person you believe her to be and that she's there for you and with you through thick and thin.

Trust is something that builds over time, and for people who've come from a background where trust was often violated or frequently absent, it can take years to develop. Unfortunately, trust can be broken and lost in a few thoughtless seconds.

Research has shown that the affairs that are hardest for couples to survive are those where the deceit's been significant and ongoing. When a betrayed partner discovers that her partner's been lying to her over an extended period, not only does this devastate her belief in her partner, she may also doubt herself. When she didn't suspect the affair and an unfaithful partner has succeeded in living a double life, the betrayed partner wonders whether he can trust his own judgement any more.

After an affair, you need to be rebuild trust in four areas:

- ✔ **Your partner's integrity:** Can I believe again that my partner's an honest and decent person with whom I want to share my life?

- ✔ **Your partner's motivation and intention:** Can I believe again that my partner wants and intends to be faithful and will never intentionally deceive or hurt me again?

- ✔ **Your partner's consistency:** Can I believe again that my partner's words and behaviours are honest and true and will continue to be so in the future?

- ✔ **Your own judgement:** Can I believe again that I will recognise truth and in time trust my partner again?

Unfortunately, no quick and easy ways exist to rebuild trust. Doing so is a gradual process that takes time. After an affair, nobody goes from 'I don't trust you' to 'I trust you' without passing through painful phases of partial trust and then crushing doubt. All you can possibly hope for at first is to discover how to live more comfortably with uncertainty.

Agreeing absolute honesty

Trust is built on absolute honesty – something that's not always as easy as it sounds. Affairs block honest communication, not just about the existence of the affair but also about the state of the relationship. Affairs are nearly always a symptom of unspoken relationship problems – difficulties that either one or both partners haven't been honest about. You must establish a new level of open communication in order to rebuild trust. In that way, not only can the betrayed partner grow in faith that her partner isn't deceiving her, but both can grow in confidence that an affair won't happen again.

Being honest if you were the unfaithful partner

If you were the one who had the affair, becoming absolutely honest about the details of your day-to-day life is essential. Anything that can be interpreted as secrecy or deceit can wreck everything you're trying to rebuild with your partner. Where you go and what you do need to be 100 per cent transparent. This means:

- ✔ Allowing your partner access to your email, mobile phone, Internet community sites, browser history bar, bank statements, credit card bills and phone bills

- ✔ Saying where you are when you're not together and being contactable at that location

- ✔ Always phoning immediately if you're late and explaining why

- ✔ Not having *any* contact with the affair partner

- ✔ Disclosing if the affair partner contacts you in any way

This last point's especially important. Disentangling yourself from an affair doesn't always happen instantly, and ex-lovers often send an occasional text or email. If the affair's really over and you want to rebuild your relationship, your partner must know if you have any contact and that you're doing everything in your power to discourage and end any communication with your affair partner.

You also need to become honest about your thoughts and feelings within the relationship. If something's bothering you, speak up. If an issue you've struggled with in the past happens again, highlight it and try to resolve it. In the past, you may have used the affair as a place to hide from your relationship difficulties – now you need to demonstrate that you're ready and willing to address them head on.

After an affair, the guilt that some unfaithful partners feel makes speaking up about problems within the relationship difficult for them. If this describes you, remind yourself that the problems contributed to your affair and that talking about them honestly is a sign of commitment to your partner and the future of your relationship.

When you're able to talk openly about difficult and painful emotions, doing so makes your loving words and reassurances more believable. Many betrayed partners have difficulty in believing well-intended reassuring words, fearing that they're only motivated by guilt. But when you can share the bad stuff as well as the good, your partner can more easily trust your integrity.

Being honest if you were the betrayed partner

When you discover that your partner's had an affair, you experience many different emotions and find yourself questioning your partner, your relationship and yourself. Talking about what's on your mind and sharing how you feel with your partner helps you to rebuild trust. For some betrayed partners, this comes easily, but others try to push negative thoughts and feelings into the background in an attempt to avoid them.

Some also find talking about other problems within the relationship difficult, feeling that they have enough on their plates coping with the affair. But not talking about problems that may have contributed to the affair leaves them unresolved and fuels fears and doubts for the future.

Being honest about how you're feeling also gives your partner the opportunity to understand the impact of the affair on you and to show empathy. And when you share your anxieties and difficulties in an open way, your partner can more easily give you the reassurance you need.

Feelings of doubt, suspicion and insecurity are normal after an affair. The best way to work through these feelings is to share them openly with your partner and ask for reassurance.

Taking risks again

Trust can't exist without risk, in the same way as hot can't exist without cold. If no risks existed in relationships, you wouldn't need to trust. But the harsh reality is that at some levels you never truly know your partner (or yourself) or can concretely predict what she may do in the future.

Building trust and becoming more confident in your relationship again just isn't possible without risks. In the early days, when trust is very fragile or even non-existent, pushing yourself too far and perhaps agreeing to your partner going away alone for the weekend is foolish to consider. But as time passes, allowing more freedom and autonomy is the only way to test your faith.

When maintaining accountability begins to feel intrusive and upsetting, start to extend the time between checks. If you've got into the habit of looking at your partner's mobile every evening, extend that to every other day or once a week, and use positive self-talk in between. Similarly, if your partner's lunchtime phone calls are beginning to serve more as a reminder of the affair than a reassurance that it's over, suggest sending a text instead.

When couples take transparency and accountability too far and extend them for too long, they can block recovery, because they're only reminding themselves of the trust that's been broken. Beginning to let go of the control reins may feel uncomfortable at first, but in this way your trust strengthens and you can begin to leave the affair in the past.

Refocusing on the positives

As you begin to rebuild your relationship, you spend a lot of time thinking about the affair and the problems in your relationship that led up to it. To balance this, make sure that you also spend time focusing on the positive aspects of your relationship that keep you together. If you've always enjoyed the same sense of humour, get in more funny movies and spend time having a laugh together. And if parenting's always been a place where you've shared common values and purpose, book plenty of family days out.

The paradox may seem bizarre, but many couples say that their sex lives significantly improve after an affair's been revealed. The betrayed partner, who may have had low libido before the affair came to light, may suddenly find that her sex drive goes through the roof. Evolutionary psychologists explain this as nature's way of re-establishing an individual's territorial rights and re-bonding the couple to each other. Whatever the explanation, you can enjoy this time and use it to strengthen you both.

Part II of this book is all about boosting your relationship by improving your intimacy, romance and sex life. Take time with your partner to look at some of the suggestions and advice in this part, and make getting closer a priority.

Affair-proofing for the future

After the dust of devastation settles following an affair, some couples are confident that they've gained from the experience and that it will never, ever, ever happen again. The damage may have healed, but each partner still carries the scars, and this may be enough to ensure that neither person makes the mistake again.

For other couples, an affair increases their vigilance and any idealised fantasies that 'it can never happen to us' disappear. Knowing why the affair occurred (see 'Understanding why the affair happened', earlier in this chapter) can help these couples avoid the particular circumstances that triggered the affair, but anxieties may remain that something else may go wrong in the future.

Whatever your feelings for the future, agreeing to abide by the following rules as a couple can help you both feel confident that an affair can't happen again:

- ✔ **Rule 1: Stay close.** Building and maintaining emotional and sexual intimacy in your relationship makes you strong as a couple and less likely to seek closeness with someone else.

✔ **Rule 2: Don't let problems fester.** If problems or difficulties exist between you, talk about them and resolve them quickly before they can fester and become resentments that make you drift apart.

✔ **Rule 3: Be open.** Keep your partner in touch with what you're doing and who you're meeting in your daily life, and ask the same of her. If you're ever tempted to keep something a secret, ask yourself why and deal with it immediately.

✔ **Rule 4: Agree boundaries.** Make sure that you both know what is and isn't okay in relationships with other people. Agree whether flirting is ever okay, and with whom and in what circumstances. And if you have close friendships on- and offline, discuss what contact you're both comfortable with and respect your partner's views. When you both know exactly where the line is, inadvertently crossing it is much harder.

✔ **Rule 5: Stay alert.** Feeling attracted to other people is part of being human, but if you find yourself wanting to act on those feelings, refocus on your partner and on your relationship, and either stop or minimise any contact with the other person before anything has a chance to develop.

Chapter 15

Recognising That It's Over

*I*ncluding a chapter on how to know whether your relationship's over may seem just a tad defeatist in a book about how to improve your relationship, but unfortunately not all relationships work out. Many reasons exist for why relationships fail: some relationships are doomed from the start, others crumble beyond repair after years of neglect, and a few are wiped out by one devastating blow. Most ultimately fail because partners can't agree on what a good relationship is and consequently find themselves pulling in separate directions.

In this chapter I look at how you can tell whether your relationship's at the end of the line rather than just at another turn in the road. If you decide that the end is nigh, I offer guidance on working through the painful decision to leave. Finally, I explore how you can get through your break-up and set out on a new path alone.

Spotting the Signs of Relationship Bankruptcy

In Chapter 1, I explain how a relationship's like a bank account. Instead of depositing money, however, you deposit love, kind words, thoughtful deeds and all sorts of other warm, fuzzy stuff. But when a relationship goes through difficulties, your care and consideration withdraw from the account. And if you're not careful, you find yourself overdrawn with a debt to pay.

Debt seems to be a fact of life nowadays, not just in finances but in relationships as well. As long as you've got a good credit history, you can top up most accounts and make them healthy again. But if one of you can't or won't pay back the debt, then you may find your relationship account empty and bankrupt.

Only you can decide whether your relationship's bankrupt or just in debt. No simple quiz or equation can help you work this out, no 'Congratulations, you scored mostly *C*s: your relationship's okay.' Making the decision is a difficult and painful process and one you can't undertake quickly or lightly.

The following three sections help you analyse how you feel and what you think about your relationship. Read each section slowly and thoroughly and make notes on any statements that stand out for you. If one or two things really hit you between the eyes as being true, don't make a decision based just on those but consider how they balance with the other statements. Most importantly, take as much time as you need to consider everything in depth, especially anything you're not sure about. This is a decision that affects the rest of your life, so give it your fullest consideration.

Looking at reasons to stay

Here's a list of statements that may help you make the decision that your relationship's still much too good to leave. They're not in any particular order of importance, because only you know what's important to you and what makes you happy. Answering an enthusiastic yes to some of them doesn't instantly transform your relationship, because you still have the issues to work through that brought you to this page. But hopefully, you can find new motivations to keep on improving your relationship.

- ✔ **You both still love each other.** An obvious one to start with I know, and unfortunately love doesn't conquer all, but if you still have love between you, then you definitely still have hope.

- ✔ **You both understand and acknowledge the problems between you and are willing to accept responsibility for working them out.** Whatever your difficulties may be, however large, if both of you are aware of them and willing to work on them together, now's not the time to end your relationship. If your efforts fail, perhaps you may think again, but until that time the game's not over.

- ✔ **You're still able to talk to each other and enjoy each other's company.** If, in spite of your problems, you're still able to communicate in a healthy and meaningful way and you continue to enjoy being together, then you have a good solid basis from which to grow.

✔ **You can't bear to throw so much away.** If your relationship's always been good in the past and something that's given you fulfilment and happiness, maybe the current situation's merely a block in the road. It may be a massive great boulder that you can't see around, but if you begin to hack away at it, the view may become clear and you can move forward.

✔ **You have a great sex life.** A good sex life is a major bonus to any couple and can help you to stick together through the trials of life. Right now, that may not be enough, but it's a unique bond that many couples don't have and one you may regret losing in the future.

✔ **You can't imagine not being with your partner.** If life without your partner is something that's too difficult or too painful to think about, you're not ready to leave. True, sometimes a relationship can just become a habit or a dependency, but if being around your partner still means the world to you, keep fighting for your relationship.

✔ **You would lose something really special if you weren't together.** Couples share many things together that bring satisfaction and give their life meaning. That may be parenting, a beautiful home, a shared love of opera, a dedication to a political cause or something else you both value. This may not be enough to resolve your differences, but it may give you sufficient motivation to try harder.

✔ **You don't know why you want to go.** If you haven't got to the bottom yet of why you're considering leaving your relationship, you need to work harder at uncovering the core issues. When you've done so, you may find that the problem is something that's relatively easy to resolve.

✔ **You're willing to give more and change more.** If, in spite of your problems, you've still got more to give and are willing to change yourself if required, leaving now may leave you with regrets. Ending a relationship is always painful, but even more so if you leave knowing that you may have been able to do more to save it.

Exploring reasons to leave

You may notice that the following is the longest list of statements in this section. That's not necessarily because you have more reasons to leave than to stay, but because your reasons to leave may include things that are out of your control, such as your partner. Ultimately, making a relationship work always takes two people, so you may find that in spite of agreeing with many of the reasons for staying, you still decide to leave because your partner doesn't share your motivation or optimism.

As before, these reasons are in no particular order of importance; you need to decide what really matters to you:

- ✓ **Your partner refuses to accept that a problem exists.** If as a couple you can't agree on what the problems are within your relationship, resolving them is impossible. If that's the case for you, consider whether the problem is something that you can accommodate or whether it crosses a bottom line that makes you want to leave.

- ✓ **Your partner doesn't want to change.** Sometimes a partner can acknowledge a problem and even go so far as to understand it from your perspective. But out of indifference, inability or just plain stubbornness, he refuses to make the personal changes necessary. Many people find they can't live with this situation without growing resentment and therefore choose to end the relationship.

- ✓ **You don't want to change.** Perhaps you're the one who's being stubborn or who feels that he can't change. If so, consider how both of you are going to feel living in this ongoing situation. If the future feels unbearable, you may decide to leave.

- ✓ **Staying means sacrificing something really important to you.** Not all change is healthy. If staying in your relationship means you giving up something that's really important to you, such as having children, living in a certain place or having sex, you may decide that the relationship isn't worth the sacrifice.

- ✓ **Staying means compromising your values.** This is similar to the preceding reason, but goes even deeper. If the only way to make your relationship work is to change your value system – for example by continuing to be with someone who breaks the law, works in an unethical industry, asks you to give up your faith or has very different parenting standards – you may decide that ending the relationship is the only way for you to maintain your personal integrity.

- ✓ **You no longer respect or like your partner.** Love is an emotion that ebbs and flows, and many couples go through times when feeling love is hard. But if you no longer have any positive feelings towards your partner and can't respect him as a human being, your relationship has little chance of surviving.

- ✓ **Your partner no longer respects or likes you.** If your partner no longer wants to spend time with you, values your opinions or respects you as a person, you're probably wondering why he's not leaving you. Some partners have very selfish reasons for not wanting to end a relationship, but if you're being made to feel bad about who you are, you have the right to walk away.

✔ **Violence or domestic abuse has occurred within your relationship.** Okay, having said that these were in no particular order, this statement does deserve the warning symbol. Evidence shows that domestic violence and abuse normally gets worse over time, not better. So if any violence or emotional, sexual or psychological abuse has happened within your relationship, then seriously consider leaving now. Chapter 12 helps you find support.

✔ **You can't or won't forgive your partner.** If you've had a significant event or breach of trust in your relationship that you can't or won't forgive your partner for, your future's likely to be full of resentment and bitterness. Forgiveness is a long and painful process, but without it you're shoring up more problems for yourself in the future.

✔ **Your partner can't or won't forgive you.** Perhaps you were the one who committed a major offence and, in spite of your remorse and apology, your partner refuses to forgive you. If the offence happened more than a year ago and your words and acts of penance have made no improvement, the time may have come to consider moving on rather than living in debt for ever.

✔ **You're bored.** This may seem an odd statement, but I can't think of a better word than 'bored'. Some people just want out. They don't have any particular problems, massive issues or major disagreements. The relationship's okay and they share love, respect and affection. But in spite of that, one partner just doesn't want to be there any more. That's a very difficult reason to give for ending a relationship, but sometimes it's the kindest thing to do for your partner.

✔ **You're in love with someone else.** This doesn't automatically mean the end of your relationship, especially if you've only recently got into a relationship with someone new. The early days of any new relationship are always passionate and exciting, but in time your feelings mellow to the familiar affection you probably share with your existing partner. If you have no problems in your relationship apart from this, then I strongly advise personal therapy before walking away, to ensure that you're making the decision for the right reasons.

✔ **You're just waiting for someone else.** This maintains the fantasy that someone better exists. And indeed, he may do. If you have lots of problems in your relationship and that's why you're waiting for someone else, but are only staying because you're scared of being alone, leaving now may be fairer on your partner. But before you make the decision, make sure that you've done everything you can to improve your relationship.

✔ **You just don't care any more.** Indifference is the biggest killer of relationships – not flaming rows and constant bickering, but reaching that point where you can't be bothered to argue any more and you just don't care what your partner thinks of you. If you've reached this situation, then the only thing keeping you in the relationship may be the lack of energy to do anything else.

Considering reasons to give the relationship more time

The previous two sections look at reasons to stay and reasons to leave, but one other option exists: you can postpone making a decision and give your relationship more time. The time you allocate doesn't have to be an indefinite period. You may decide to give the relationship a few more months or another couple of years; the length of time really doesn't matter as long as you're genuinely working at the relationship until that point. Passively waiting for a more convenient time to separate can be agonising for everyone within the home, so if you do decide to give your relationship more time, make sure that you invest everything in trying to make it work.

This list of statements may help motivate you to give your relationship another chance. They're in no particular order, and if something jumps out at you as particularly pertinent then allow yourself time to mull it over and, if appropriate, discuss it with your partner and/or close friends.

✔ **Reading the preceding two sections didn't help at all.** If you've worked through the reasons to stay and the reasons to leave but are none the wiser, then now isn't the right time to make a decision one way or the other. So in the meantime, you may as well keep working at the relationship and see whether the future becomes clearer with time.

✔ **You're angry, upset, discouraged and disillusioned.** Your emotions guide your decision about the future of your relationship, but you shouldn't base your decision on them. If you're in a state of high emotion, give yourself time for those feelings to subside before making a decision.

✔ **You both share the same goals for your relationship.** If, in spite of your problems, you both still want the same things from your relationship, you have hope. You may be struggling to reach the place you both want to get to, but while you're heading in the same direction, keep working.

✔ **You can see signs of improvement, however few and however slow.** Some relationship difficulties take a long time to change, and you may feel as if you're getting nowhere slowly. But if, on reflection, your relationship has improved, persevere until you either get there or reach the end of the line.

✔ **You want to stay together for the children's sake.** Staying together for the sake of the children is a controversial decision. As well as considering the impact of separation, you also need to think about what your children are discovering about relationships by seeing you stay in a broken marriage. But if you feel strongly that separating now would be detrimental to your children, this can be a powerful motivator to work at the relationship and hopefully overcome your problems for good.

✔ **You can't split, because of financial considerations.** Some couples simply can't afford to separate. Although staying together because it's the cheaper option may not be the most romantic of reasons for staying, it may buy you more time to resolve your differences.

✔ **You haven't been totally honest with your partner about the issues.** If you haven't yet disclosed to your partner some issues within your relationship, you can't possibly resolve them. Sharing exactly what's on your mind may be the final straw that leads to separation or it may provide the impetus for the change you need. However difficult doing so may be, talk to your partner and give yourselves the chance to make things better.

✔ **You really should read more of this book.** If you've turned straight to this section of the book, chances are your relationship's already in dire straits and you're eager to make a decision. But before you decide, work through the chapters in the book, especially Chapter 2, and give yourselves at last six months' concerted effort at improving your relationship.

✔ **You haven't tried couple counselling.** Ideally, couple counselling isn't a last resort, but if you've tried everything else and failed, why not give it a go? An outside view can often help to provide fresh insights into your problems and give you new ways of moving forward together.

If, after reading the statements in this section, you still feel unsure about the future of your relationship, keep reading. Sometimes the only way to make the final decision is to look the reality of separation full in the face. When you know what leaving entails, you may decide you don't want to do it, or you may discover that the proposition is not as scary as you thought and start packing your bags.

Trial separation

Some couples find that a trial separation for an agreed amount of time gives them the distance they need to clarify their thinking. Moving out of a highly charged emotional situation may provide both of you with the space you need to calm down and reflect on what's gone wrong and what needs to change. If you choose this option, make sure that you're both clear about what you hope to gain from the time apart and agree whether and how you can communicate during the break.

Working Through the Decision to Leave

One of the struggles many people have when considering the end of their relationship is picturing themselves going through the separation process and being alone. This is especially difficult for people who've been married many years and have built a home and a family together. The prospect of going through the legal and financial battles of divorce, separating children from a parent and losing a home can seem so terrifying that some people are too scared to leave. And others who don't consider how painful separation can be may end up regretting starting a process that was avoidable.

Over the next few pages I look at what separation really entails: how you can expect to feel emotionally, the practical decisions you have to make and the impact on your children.

Separation is a major decision with many repercussions, but working through it in a healthy and positive way is possible. To do that, you have to know what you're likely to face.

Counting the emotional cost of separation

If you've been in your relationship for only a short time, then the changes you face ahead may be relatively small, but if you've been together many years, you're choosing a new direction in your life that you haven't walked in for a long, long time. Either way, separation's undoubtedly an extremely stressful time that challenges people in every way possible. Along with the loss of a partner, you lose the dream of living happily ever after. You may also lose your home, economic stability and regular contact with your children. By anybody's standards, that's a huge amount of loss.

The emotions you go through when a relationship dies are the same as those you experience when you lose someone through death. Many therapists use a model of stages of grief, originally devised by Elisabeth Kübler-Ross, to help people understand the many emotions they're likely to experience during separation. Chapter 13 outlines the emotions you move through following a death: shock and disbelief, anger and protestation, yearning and sadness, and finally acceptance. The emotions you go through when a relationship dies are the same as those experienced when you lose someone through death.

How you react and how you cope during the stages of grief depend very much on your character and personality and also on your individual circumstances. No two people are the same and no two divorces are the same either; therefore, no right or wrong way exists for managing the roller-coaster of emotions. How long you take to work through the stages also depends on the degree of loss you're experiencing. If your relationship's been long and one that you were very happy in, then you may take a few years to work through the stages fully. But if the relationship was shorter or one where you were unhappy for a long time, you may take only a few months.

Moving through the stages of grief isn't a purely linear process. Unfortunately, you don't go through each step neatly, finishing one phase then going into the next without a backward glance. Regressing to a previous stage is common as you work through the different losses. For example, finding out that your partner's met someone new may throw you back into anger. Slipping back is a normal and temporary blip in the process, and you rarely go back to a stage with the same degree of severity.

On top of these emotions, many people also struggle with feelings of doubt, guilt, loneliness and low self-esteem. But in spite of this, separation's a process that most survive, and for many it's considerably less painful than staying in a broken relationship.

Deciding on the practicalities

If you're considering separating from your partner, you have to make significant and difficult decisions in five (or six if you're married) key areas:

Where do you live?

Deciding new living arrangements depends on your individual circumstances. If you have children, your priority's thinking about what your children need and how you can maintain as much of the status quo as possible for them.

Money also plays a key role in your decision, as do any other commitments to work and other family members. You may decide to sell your home and move into separate bought or rented properties, or you may opt for just one of you to leave the house (if so, you also have to decide who).

In the current economic climate, many separating couples are finding that they can't sell their properties and are forced to continue living in the same home for months or even years after they've agreed to separate. Hopefully that won't be the case for you, but if it does happen, you need to consider how you manage this.

Some couples split up because someone else is on the scene, and the most sensible solution may appear to be moving straight in with the new partner. Although this may seem like the best option for you and your soon-to-be ex, it's often the worst scenario for children, especially if you want the children to live with that parent.

How do you look after your children?

You can come to many different arrangements for your children. You may go for shared residency in one home, where you take turns moving back in, or shared residency in both of your homes. Or you may opt for solo residency with agreed contact times or, if your children are older, ad hoc contact that suits the kids. Whatever decision you make needs to provide maximum quality contact with both parents, but is also influenced by financial resources.

Most parents agree the new caring arrangements between themselves without any legal intervention. The more you can agree as a couple, the easier you find it to maintain flexibility and change plans as your children's needs grow. Agreement also demonstrates to your children that you're still able to cooperate with each other in their best interests.

How do you cope financially?

Most people are worse off financially after a separation, and some are considerably worse off. You need to think about how you'll split any equity and investments that you have, how you'll financially support new living arrangements and children and how you'll live on a tighter budget. If you have children, you're best to use a solicitor to write up a formal financial agreement that will protect their current and future welfare.

Becoming broke, even if temporarily, is a significant extra burden on top of the loss of your partner, your home and your dreams for the future. Most people get used to their limited income fairly quickly, but you can take many years before you reach the same level of economic stability.

How do you split your possessions?

You also need to consider how you split the household contents in a way that's fair for each of you, but also fair for the children. Both of you, and your children if you have them, still need to feel that you have a home and have access to familiar surroundings. You inevitably lose some things you value and care about, and making this adjustment is often more painful than people think.

How do you manage living or parenting alone?

As soon as you're separated, you have to cope with the day-to-day pressures of living alone or, if you have kids, of parenting alone. You have a home to run, housework, laundry, general home maintenance, gardening, cooking, shopping, looking after pets, school runs, homework, out-of-school activities, supporting elderly relatives if you have them and generating an income. Life alone is harder, and often not until your partner has gone do you realise just how much he did to keep life running smoothly.

How and when do you start divorce proceedings?

If you're married, divorce is on the cards. Some people want to get the legal procedure of divorce underway as soon as possible, while others see this purely as a formality that can wait until many years after the relationship's ended. Neither is right or wrong. One thing that's worth considering, though, is the cost of divorce. If a lot of acrimony still exists between you and your ex, then a divorce is more likely to be long and drawn out, and therefore expensive. Waiting until emotions have calmed down may make the legal process smoother and cheaper for everyone involved.

When you're ready to proceed, you can either go through a solicitor, use one of the many online services or do it yourself by buying a divorce kit.

Considering children's needs

If you've got children, the decision to separate affects their lives for ever. The bottom line is that you're making a decision that they're forced to live with, whether they like it or not. Getting through a separation and adapting to the inevitable life changes it brings is a tough enough task for adults, but for children it can be even harder.

A secure family unit forms the foundation for a child's healthy psychological and emotional development. When you remove that structure, the impact can be devastating. As an adult, you know that many of the changes associated with separation are temporary and that you can put a new structure in place, but children have a limited capacity to understand time and its passing, so they initially assume that the current feelings of destruction and devastation are permanent.

Kids do survive separation. Recent research shows that children are most adversely affected by conflict and inadequate contact with both parents. Although a child's struggles are significant, as a parent you have the power to minimise the negative effects and help children to survive and thrive in spite of your family change.

If you choose to separate, then you as a parent are responsible for behaving in a way and making decisions that are always in the best interests of your children, in spite of what you may be feeling emotionally. The relationship with your partner may be coming to an end, but your relationship with your children is for life.

Breaking Up without Falling Apart

Separation is a mega thing to go through, whether it's your choice or not. But if you do decide it's the only option left open to you, making it a positive, though painful, experience is possible.

Your separation is a turning point in your life, and which way you turn is really up to you. You can look forward, face the future with optimism and embrace the new opportunities that separation brings, or you can look back and see only what you've lost. The next sections look briefly at how you can break up yet remain intact during in the process.

For more help, do get yourself a copy of *Divorce For Dummies*, by Thelma Fisher, Hilary Woodward, John Ventura and Mary Reed (Wiley), full of the usual practical advice you expect from For Dummies books, and also a book I wrote for Relate, *How to Have a Healthy Divorce*.

Managing difficult feelings

The more effectively you can manage your emotions, the more comfortable the roller-coaster ride of separation is. You aren't able to avoid going through the stages of grief and having a few extra emotions to boot, but when you can identify and name those emotions and recognise that they're a normal, healthy response, you've made the first step towards managing them healthily.

Getting through the first few weeks, months and perhaps years after a separation can feel like wading through treacle, but doing so does get easier with time. Here's a list of tips you may find helpful to get you through the stickiest patches:

- **Talk.** A problem shared really is a problem halved. Who you talk to doesn't matter – a professional therapist, a trusted friend, a family member or the next-door neighbour. Talking prevents isolation and puts you in touch with the many other people who've been in the same situation.

- **Let yourself feel.** If some days you want to cry, let yourself, and if on others you want to shout, have a good bellow. You need to be real about how you feel and give yourself permission to express your emotions. Keeping powerful feelings bottled up tends to make things much worse and can stop you from moving forward.

✔ **Look after your health.** Don't be tempted to comfort yourself with junk food and slump on the sofa all day, because this just adds to negative feelings. Taking regular exercise and maintaining a healthy diet can help your body and mind feel better.

✔ **Set small goals.** Sometimes you may feel as if you're getting nowhere. Setting yourself small, achievable goals boosts self-confidence. Whether you're getting a chore out of the way, going out for the evening or starting a new work project, goal setting helps you to see that you're moving on.

✔ **Plan ahead.** If you're having one of those days when you think you're never going to get through it, let your imagination go and plan all the things you're going to do when you're finally over this break-up.

✔ **Relax.** Try to take time to relax. Relaxation helps your body to de-stress. You can read a book, watch a DVD, go for a walk or have a soak in the bathtub. If you're an active person, go for a run, work out in the gym, kick a ball around or do some gardening to relax.

✔ **Laugh.** Laughter really is the best medicine. You may not be able to find many things to laugh about right now, but keep watching the comedies and getting your friends to tell you their latest corny jokes. When you laugh, your body releases feel-good chemicals.

✔ **Go out.** Rebuilding a social circle is difficult for anyone after a break-up, but with more and more people separating, it's getting easier. Join a yoga class, darts club, gym or the local Sunday football team. Take up golf or bingo or start a new skill like pottery, plumbing or Portuguese – anything that gets you out and meeting new people.

✔ **Keep a journal.** Many people find help by regularly writing down their thoughts and feelings. Looking back over the weeks and seeing how much you've moved forward is also great.

If you have children, managing your emotions healthily is especially important. Showing that the break-up's a difficult time for you too is important, because you're helping children make sense of their own emotions and allowing them to express them. However, powerful displays of emotion can be frightening to children because they worry that parents may be losing control.

You also need to ensure that you're keeping your emotions separate from the decisions you make about your children. When you're hurting, angry or feeling rejected, or when you're struggling with guilt or low self-esteem, your judgement's often impaired. By all means make the time to cry and shout, but separate those times from the occasions when you have to make decisions that affect your children's future. Take advice from family and friends and ask them to make sure that you're doing what's best for your kids.

Becoming co-parents

As co-parents, you have the task of ensuring that you continue to meet your children's physical and emotional needs. Who ended the relationship and how each of you feels about it doesn't matter; your children's needs must come first. And that means that unless one of you has abused your children, your children need to maintain a healthy relationship with both you and your ex. And the two of you have the responsibility of making that relationship smooth and easy.

Some couples find that their communication improves significantly after they've separated, because without the emotion between them, focusing on the task of parenting is easier. But others may find that their communication problems continue for some time as they try to adjust to their new roles.

Here are some basic rules to ease your communication:

- ✓ **Be calm and courteous.** When you see and speak to each other in front of the kids, for example at handover times or school or family events that you both attend, make sure that you're calm and courteous. Even if deep down inside you hate each other, for your children's sake show them that you can still both behave like rational human beings and treat one another with basic respect and decency.

- ✓ **Don't argue in front of the kids.** Evidence shows that conflict and tension between separating parents damages children, so the easiest way to minimise the damage is to ensure that any potentially contentious conversations don't happen when the children are around. This also avoids the possibility that your children may try to chip in inappropriately or take sides.

- ✓ **Separate conversations about kids from all other conversations.** When you need to discuss the children, make clear that your goal is to reach an agreement for the children's benefit. The children are your mutual agenda and your mutual goal. By agreeing this up front, hopefully both of you can contain any difficult emotions associated with your separation.

- ✓ **Use other resources.** If having a constructive conversation face to face is really difficult, then try the phone or email instead. Many couples find this a much simpler and more stress-free way of communicating, and email has the added advantage of providing each of you with a written copy of what you both said. This can be particularly useful for confirming contact details or financial arrangements about the kids.

✔ **Never use your kids as messengers.** This puts children in an impossible position where they have to remember a message accurately and try to deliver it in a tone that doesn't upset the other parent. They then have to cope with the reaction of the other parent and make a decision about what to do with any spoken or unspoken information they receive, for example when Dad tuts and rolls his eyes and sighs a reluctant 'Okay, tell your mum I said yes.' Acting as a messenger is far too big a responsibility for a child of any age, and with texting, email and the phone, you really have no excuse for it nowadays.

To ensure that you're doing everything you can to make separation as easy as possible for your kids, arm yourself with a copy of Relate's *Help Your Children Cope With Your Divorce*, written by yours truly.

Rebuilding life as a single person

For some, becoming single comes as a huge relief, but others may be dreading that position. The good news is that literally thousands of other single people are out there, so you're definitely not alone. If you embrace this new phase of your life with optimism, you can get loads out of it.

From now on, you're free and independent. You can decide how you spend your time and who you spend it with. Your life's yours to live how you choose. If you've got children and other family commitments and a job, you have to take those responsibilities into account, but you have considerably more freedom and more choices than you had when you were with your ex. That's not to say that your ex was necessarily an unreasonable person who imprisoned you and refused to let you have a life of your own, but over the years, you've inevitably made numerous compromises and concessions to accommodate your differences. That's the way relationships work and that's absolutely fine, but now you have the opportunity to claim back the allowances you made.

Here are just a few advantages of finding yourself a free agent again:

✔ **Reclaiming your free time:** How you spend your spare time is completely up to you, so now's the chance to think about what you may have stopped doing in the past – perhaps a hobby, travelling or letting a friendship slip – which you can now restart. And consider too what you've always fancied doing but never got around to.

✔ **Deepening friendships:** Being single gives you the opportunity to deepen the friendships you have and develop new ones. You may have more time on your hands now than you will ever have again, so make the most of it. The company you keep shapes your life – what shape do you want your life to take in the future? The choice is up to you.

✔ **Making the most of work:** Now you're single, you can work purely for your own benefit. Yes, I know you've still got financial responsibilities, but you can choose your standard of living. Work – whether that's voluntary work, paid employment, part time or full time – is an area of life that can give you a lot of satisfaction. Being single can provide you with an excellent opportunity to focus on your work life and commit more time and more energy to it than you've done before, or take time out and do something completely different.

✔ **Follow a wild dream or ambition:** Today's the beginning of the rest of your life – what do you want to do with it? Your new-found freedom can give you the chance to follow your dreams. What do you fancy: travel, spirituality, relocating, an image change? Becoming a political activist, writer, artist, sculptor, musician? Running a home for stray cats, a B&B, a children's activity centre in a deprived area? Buying a yacht, learning to fly, going bungee jumping? The possibilities are endless.

✔ **Find new love:** Four out of ten weddings in the UK are second marriages, which goes to prove that meeting someone special and falling in love again is perfectly possible. Now may not be the right time for you, but when you're ready you may be able to look for your Mr or Ms Right in countless ways.

No one can tell how long he may be single for. You may meet the new love of your life before you finish reading this book, or a few years down the line. Or you may decide that being single is so satisfying that you don't want to be in another relationship. But one thing's for sure: you're free to decide how you use the extra time that singledom provides.

A relationship breakdown is a significant turning point in anyone's life and brings many new challenges and opportunities. You can choose whether the years ahead are better than the years you're leaving behind, and whether your separation symbolises an ending or a new beginning.

Part V
The Part of Tens

'Gosh, Angela, you really are serious
about getting a divorce!'

In this part . . .

Every *For Dummies* book contains a fun and informative Part of Tens, a burst of short, sharp chapters each containing a list of ten top tips. Here you find ten rules for effective communication, ten ways to fan the flames of passion, ten strategies for avoiding a row and, last but not least, ten 'Great Expectations' for your relationship.

Chapter 16

Ten Ways to Ignite Passion

*P*assion inevitably wanes over the course of a relationship – no matter how in love you are. Periods of stress or tiredness can temporarily dull the flame, and familiarity can mean that getting excited takes more of an effort. The good news is that lighting the spark again is easy, as long as you're both willing to experiment and wander a little out of your traditional comfort zones.

This chapter offers some ideas on how you can turn the heat up a notch. Enjoying a good sex life can help couples survive the tough times and sail through the good ones. But keeping sex interesting and exciting in a long-term relationship takes commitment – commitment to discover together, experiment together and, most importantly, have fun together. (For more detail on sexual relationships, check out Chapters 6 and 7.)

Starting a Fight

'Have you gone completely and utterly crazy?' I hear you ask. Surely a book about improving your relationship should tell you to avoid and resolve conflict, not start a fight? Yes, but this is no ordinary fight. This is a playful, physical fight that's fair and shares the same common objective – sex.

What I'm talking about here is something wonderfully childlike, like a pillow fight or a water fight or a food fight. Or if you prefer to be competitive, how about a tickling contest or a pillow fight? If you're both much too mature and grown up for any of this sort of nonsense, then you can choose a game of tennis or ping-pong instead.

Playing together builds intimacy and a feeling of connection, so it's a great way of building a positive sexual environment. And any fight or competitive game that increases your pulse rate also increases your adrenalin and endorphins and makes you feel excited. So by the time you get around to a bit of naked combat between the sheets, you're both ready for it.

Doing Something Daring

Doing something daring like going on a roller-coaster ride, watching a scary movie or skinny-dipping in the local lake is a great way of giving yourself an adrenalin rush that heightens your body's senses and reflexes and makes you more sensitive to sexual stimulation. From a psychological perspective, you also become more intimate through your shared experience of vulnerability.

You may decide to do something daring every now and again when the fancy takes you, or you may choose to follow a daredevil hobby on a regular basis. How about bungee jumping, motor racing or white-water rafting? Not only do you improve your sex life, you also increase your general fitness and have a lot more to talk about down the pub.

Buying Some Toys

Sex toys have had a bad reputation for far too long. You may come across sleazy toys that do nothing for anyone, but you can also find a lot of good stuff too. Sleek all-body intimate massagers are taking over from the horrible phallic-shaped vibrators of the past, and you can use the new-generation lubes to give a sensual massage, which avoids leaving a sticky mess or an oil slick in the bed. And more products are specifically targeted at couples: his 'n' hers vibrators, loving cushions to help you experiment with sexual positions, and adult games galore.

If you fancy a bit of amateur dramatics, your local high street or online sex shop has a massive range of fancy-dress outfits for different role-play scenarios. And for those of you who find the idea of a little light bondage a turn-on, you have a wealth of accessories to choose from.

The best way to explore the sex toy market is to log on and window shop any of the increasing number of online stores. In the comfort and anonymity of your own home, you can oooh, aahh or even urrgh as much as you like and find out where that bit goes and what that does without embarrassment. You may find, like many couples, that window shopping's all you need to get you in the mood.

Getting Sensual

Sexuality grows from sensuality, so if you want more passion, a good place to start is by becoming more sensual. Many people are guilty of taking their body for granted and forgetting what delights it can provide.

Make a point of loving your skin. When you bathe or shower, pamper your skin, stroke it, remember how good it feels. Or better still, start bathing or showering together and sharing the experience.

Sensual massage can be another excellent way of getting yourselves in the mood. Treat yourselves to some really nice massage oil, light a few candles, put on some smooth tunes and relax and enjoy each other's skin. The rest follows naturally.

If you're new to massage, check out one of the many instruction manuals available or treat yourself to a battery massager. You could also invest in *Massage For Dummies,* by Steve Capellini and Michel Van Welden.

Investing in Erotica

Sometimes a little external input to whet your appetite is helpful. When you're stressed or preoccupied, you often need more to get you in the mood. And for couples who've been together many, many years, sometimes the sheer sight of each other's naked body is no longer enough to light the flame of passion. This is when a bit of erotica (or porn, or romance, or art, or whatever you prefer to call it) comes into its own.

A huge range of erotica is available. Those who prefer visual stimulation can pick up a saucy DVD in a high street rental store or online. Or you may prefer something more artistic such as photography or painting. Those who like to conjure up their own images can choose from a wide variety of written erotica, from magazines and short stories to whole novels where you can pay for yourself to be the star. Or you can download some aural erotica to your MP3 player and snuggle up together with an earpiece each.

Flirting Your Pants Off

Flirting with your partner is a great way of showing him how much you still fancy him and enjoy making love. An appreciative look, a pat on the bum, a nod and a wink and a few phwoars every now and again can revive even the coolest of desires. Flirting may feel odd at first if it hasn't been a normal part of your repertoire, so to avoid arousing suspicion rather than ardour in your partner, start slow and subtle and build up over time.

Talk is also a big part of flirting. Whispering sweet nothings or tender words into your lover's ear doesn't just get him in the mood through suggestion, you're also stimulating the ear lobe with a gentle warm breeze that many find erogenous. And nothing's more erotic on a date than listening to your partner telling you what he wants to do to you when he gets you home.

Start hinting at what's ahead early enough when you're out for dinner together. Not only do you get in the mood, but by skipping dessert and dashing home for a romp, you save money and calories as well!

Trying a New Technique

Hundreds of different stimulation techniques exist for the various male and female erogenous zones. And that's just using your hands. If you add your tongue, mouth, feet or whatever other part of your anatomy you fancy, then the list runs into thousands.

Many couples fall into the comfort trap of only doing what they know works rather than experimenting with different techniques that may provide new, interesting and exciting sensations. Sex can become boring and routine if your goal is only ever to reach orgasm. So take your time on the journey, meander a bit from the well-worn path and discover new delights.

The best way to increase your repertoire is to invest in a good sex guide. Try the new, revived and updated *Joy of Sex* or one of the infamous *The Lovers' Guide* range of DVDs. You could also look out a copy of *Sex For Dummies* by Dr Ruth K. Westheimer and Pierre A. Lehu.

Experimenting with Positions

The *Kama Sutra*, written over a thousand years ago, lists more sexual positions than most of us can ever achieve in a lifetime – not because of the number (a measly 24), but because you need the agility of an Olympic gymnast or a contortionist to achieve most of them.

Times have moved on and now many more-realistic love manuals are on the market, some of which offer over 50 positions – a new one for every week of the year. Some of these positions are still a bit ambitious for mere mortals, but even when you rule out the ones that are dangerous to your health, you have plenty left to play with.

Changing your sexual position can give you a whole new perspective on sex, in every sense of the word. As your bodies touch in different places, you both experience new sensations and maybe see a side of one another you've never seen before!

Shaking Up When and Where

Sex in bed at night can be one of the biggest passion killers out. Most people go to bed because they're tired and want to go to sleep. So, to improve your sex life, change your timing and change your location.

Leaving sex until the dregs of the day can be fatal. If you want to ignite more passion, try reintroducing the quickie in the morning or at lunchtime. Or have sex earlier in the evening, before you stuff your belly with dinner and fall comatose in front of the TV. Changing the time of day can really boost not only your desire but also your physical responsiveness, because your central nervous system hasn't yet started to shut down.

And don't save sex for the bedroom. Sex in different places shakes off the boredom of familiarity and may force you to experiment with new positions. Try sex on the sofa, sitting on a chair, over the kitchen table, against the hall wall, in the shower or the bath, or even in the garden (somewhere the neighbours can't see!).

Changing Your Pants

Feeling sexy is ultimately about how you feel on the inside, but if you know the outside is turning your partner on, you inevitably get caught up in the excitement.

Sexy lingerie is a fantastic way of instantly igniting passion for both partners. Not only does lingerie look good, it often feels good too. The sensual touch of satin and lace, or silk or fur or whatever turns you on, can be totally delicious.

Unfortunately, sexy lingerie on men does little more than raise a giggle in most female partners. The posing pouch just doesn't do the job for most girls. However, if you're still kicking around in the same tired boxers or

Y-fronts of ten years ago, you're really not doing yourself any favours. Chuck them in the bin and go out and treat yourself to something that's more fitting for today's sexy modern man.

If wearing something leaves you feeling silly or slutty rather than sexy, then give that kind of lingerie a miss. Make sure that what you wear makes you feel sexy on the inside as well as looking sexy on the outside.

Chapter 17

Ten Tips for Talking Together

Communicating effectively is one of the most important skills you can develop to make a dramatic improvement in your relationship. Intimacy is built on your ability to share yourself and truly understand your partner, and the best way to achieve that is by talking.

Many couples find that whenever they try to talk, things become tense or strained between them. But with a bit of planning, self-awareness and discipline, those difficulties can become a thing of the past. Here are ten quick tips that can help you get talking. (For a much more detailed discussion on conversation see Chapter 8.)

Be warned: By all means copy these tips out, stick them on your fridge and use them as a point of reference next time you have a conversation, but whatever you do, don't use the tips as ammunition against your partner when he gets something wrong. Commit to working together to make your communication more effective by learning from your mistakes as well as your successes.

Defining Your Objective

Before you open your mouth, make sure that you know why you're doing so. No communication is effective unless you know what you're hoping to achieve by it. Do you want to express your opinion? Discover how your partner thinks and feels about something? Negotiate a compromise on a tricky issue? Discuss ideas to improve your relationship? Or, if you're really honest with yourself, do you just want to let off steam about something?

What your objective is doesn't really matter as long as you have one and you're open and honest about it. If you want your conversation to reach a goal, you first need to define that goal and then share it with your partner. Your first sentence should be something like 'I want to spend some time talking about blah, blah, blah, and make a decision about what to do.' Once you both have the objective clear in your heads, you can much more easily stay on track and work together.

Picking a Good Time

If you're serious about reaching the objective you've set for your conversation, don't ruin your chances of success by ambushing a reluctant partner or choosing a time when either of you is already stressed or tired.

Once you've told your partner that you want to talk, ask when a good time is. Make sure that you're both as relaxed as possible, have plenty of time and can't be interrupted.

If the subject is very sensitive and you know it may be difficult for one or both of you, try going for a walk while you talk. The side-by-side companionship gives you the intimacy that you need, but the lack of face-to-face contact can really help to ease awkwardness.

Sticking to the Subject

When you've finally got around to talking, you can be tempted to grab the opportunity to get everything off your chest. The problem with this approach is that what started off as a constructive conversation becomes nothing more than a dumping ground and a rambling list of thoughts, feelings and issues. So, having defined your objective, stick to it and don't bring up anything that's not directly related to the topic in hand.

Try to keep your conversation in the present and between the two of you. That means not dragging up things from the past or using other people's views to back up your own. Let your thoughts and feelings stand on their own merit. At the end of the day, the only thing that matters is what the two of you want for your relationship, not what happened in the past or what anyone else thinks.

Avoiding Sentences That Begin With 'You'

A conversation can progress much more smoothly when you make a few subtle changes to your language. Starting a sentence with 'You' always points a blaming finger and invites a counter attack, whereas starting with 'I' makes clear that you're stating your opinion, not a fact, and you're owning your feelings rather than blaming your partner.

For example, 'I want you to do more around the house' states a very clear request, whereas saying 'You do nothing around the house' is accusatory and gives no indication of the change that you require. Similarly, saying something like 'I feel angry when you're late' provides a statement of fact and takes responsibility for your feelings, whereas 'You make me angry when you're late' is blaming and more likely to put your partner on the defensive.

Never Saying Never or Always

Unless you want to spend all your time defending your position, ban the words 'always' and 'never' from your vocabulary. When you use a broad generalisation in your argument, you're just asking your partner to find the exception to the rule rather than deal with the issue you're trying to raise.

Saying 'You're always late' or 'You never help' or 'I always make the decisions' or 'I never get any me time' is provocative and almost certainly untrue. Either change your wording to something more realistic like 'You're often late' or 'You rarely help,' or make clear that this is your opinion by saying 'I feel as though I make all the decisions' or 'I don't feel as though I get any me time.'

If the goal of your conversation is to resolve an issue in your relationship or ask for something to change, you need to do everything you can to help your partner empathise with how you feel rather than being forced to defend his position.

Watching Your Shoulds and Shouldn'ts

Unless you honestly believe that you have the right to take the moral high ground and preach to your partner, watch your shoulds and shouldn'ts. Undoubtedly, some things in life we all 'should' and 'shouldn't' do, like eat a healthy diet and not commit murder, but most things are purely a matter of opinion. So, rather than inviting an ethical debate, say 'I want you to . . . ' Or 'I think doing so and so may be good' rather than 'You should . . . ' or 'We should . . . '

Knowing When to Keep Shtum

Everyone knows interrupting is rude, but for some reason politeness often flies out of the window in couple conversations. Even if you're 100 per cent sure that your partner's got nothing else worth saying, keep your gob shut and let him finish. Not only may he surprise you by telling you something you didn't know, but hopefully he extends the same common courtesy to you when you're waffling on.

Constant interrupting is also one of the quickest ways of shutting your partner up permanently. If a person can't make his point without continually having to stop and start, eventually he stops trying.

The most common reason that people don't talk is because they don't believe that their partners ever truly listen. If you want your partner to become a better talker, then first you must become a better listener.

Staying Calm

When people get angry, reason tends to disappear. If you want your communication to be effective, you need to make sure that the dreaded red mist isn't fogging your brain.

The best way to stay calm is to control what's going on in your body. Make sure that you sit in a comfy chair where you can keep your muscles relaxed, breathe deeply and, if necessary, count to ten before you start each sentence. Not only does this help to keep you chilled, it also ensures that your partner doesn't feel intimidated.

If your temper's beginning to rise, stop the conversation immediately. Being angry and expressing your anger is okay, but if one or both of you are going to lose your cool to the point where you say something you may regret, call a halt and reconvene when you're calm again.

If your conversations ever get to the stage of violence between you, then you should seek professional help immediately. Violence or threats of violence are never, ever okay.

Skipping Subtle Sabotage

You can sabotage a conversation in soooo many subtle ways. Showing boredom or contempt by eye rolling, arm folding or yawning. Going silent or expecting mind reading. Launching into a one-sided monologue, repeating yourself, becoming sarcastic or belligerent. Bursting into tears or using some other form of emotional blackmail to take control of the conversation. If you want your conversations to be effective, then make note of the subtle ways in which you try to manipulate what's going on to your favour – and STOP!

If you speak to your partner or act in a way that you'd never dream of doing with your boss, then ask yourself why. Your partner deserves more respect and courtesy than your boss, not less.

Expressing Your Feelings as Well as Your Thoughts

Telling your partner that you think his timekeeping is appalling, that he doesn't spend enough time with you or that you wish he was more interested in sex is only one small part of a conversation. If you want your partner to understand you, and if you want change, then you need to share how you feel as well as what you think. Saying that you feel unvalued when he's late, unloved when he doesn't spend time with you and undesirable when he doesn't want sex explains not just what the problem is, but the effect that the problem is having on you.

Sharing how you feel may make you feel vulnerable, but if you truly want your relationship to improve, that's a risk you have to take.

Chapter 18

Ten Ways to Avoid a Row

In This Chapter

▶ Recognising the triggers behind a row

▶ Stopping an argument before it happens

▶ Diffusing an argument before it escalates

Rows may be an inevitable part of living with another person, but not all rows are inevitable. Some irritations aren't what they seem, and others are best ignored. Deciding when to speak up and when to keep your mouth shut is all about self-awareness. When you become a better observer of your own behaviour, you can be confident that you know what's going on and take appropriate action to deal with it.

You can avoid most arguments by changing your thinking. When your partner does something to annoy you, you can choose either to fuel the battle in your head or to calm it down. And when you do open your mouth to speak, how you manage the conversation to ensure that it doesn't escalate into a full-scale war is up to you.

This chapter offers ten ways to avoid having unnecessary rows. For more information and advice on communication and conflict, take a look at Part III.

Assuming the Best

Misunderstandings cause the vast majority of arguments. You can easily make the mistake of assuming that you know what your partner means when she says something, but the unavoidable truth is that those assumptions are often wrong.

TIP

The best way to avoid an argument is always to give your partner the benefit of the doubt. No matter what you think she said or, more importantly, what you think she meant, assume the best until proven otherwise.

This advice also stands if your partner seems to be acting in an irritated or moody kind of way. Before jumping to the conclusion that she's stressed with you or has some sort of attitude problem, probe what the reason may be. Is she feeling ill or under the weather in some way? Is she preoccupied or worried about something? Or maybe she's feeling angry with someone or something else. Before you jump in the deep end and find yourself drowning alone, ask your partner what's up.

Checking Your Conscience

Before you open your mouth to retaliate to a comment your partner's just made or decide to pick her up on something she's said or done, check your conscience. You can avoid lots of arguments if you clarify your own motivation before you start.

Defensiveness gets you nowhere, but unfortunately it's a very common motivation for arguments. You know you're being defensive if, on examining your conscience, you realise you're trying to avoid one of the following:

- ✔ Apologising for something
- ✔ Backing down or compromising on an issue
- ✔ Facing up to something you've done wrong
- ✔ Forgiving your partner for something she's done

 When you feel defensive, you're more likely to misinterpret what your partner's saying or doing. Rather than assuming the best (see the previous section), you become sensitive and overreact, thinking that your partner's having a dig at you. Alternatively, you may find yourself starting a fight over something relatively trivial in order to detract attention away from the issue that you're avoiding. The classic example of this is the person who goes ballistic at her partner for reading the email that exposes an affair.

Checking Your Environment

A common cause of unnecessary arguments is sensitivity due to external factors. Whenever you feel down or anxious, whatever the reason, your tolerance of other people tends to get lower. The minor irritations that you normally put up with without any comment suddenly become unbearable. So if your partner seems to be particularly irritating or annoying, before challenging her, check that your sensitivity hasn't changed because of external pressures.

Ask yourself:

- Am I more tired or stressed than usual?
- Am I under more pressure from work or anxious about something else?
- Am I feeling unwell?
- Am I angry with something or someone else?

If your answer to all these questions is no, maybe your partner's under more external pressure than usual. Give her the benefit of the doubt and check the situation out before you get stressed with her.

Being Adult

If you want to avoid an argument, then the best position to be in is an adult one – not acting like a condescending or critical parent or a whining, sulking, stroppy, bullying child, but a reasonable, rational, warm-hearted adult.

Childlike behaviour is great if you're feeling playful or creative with your partner, but if contention is in the air, childishness makes it ten times worse. Below are some telltale signs that you're not acting your age:

- Calling your partner names
- Being stubborn
- Saying 'I don't care' or 'So?' or 'It's not my fault'
- Slamming doors and stomping around
- Sulking
- Refusing to talk at all

Or, if you're the kind of person who becomes all high and mighty and self-righteous in an argument, then perhaps you go into a parenting stance rather than staying as an equal adult. A parenting style is belittling, critical, disapproving, punishing or questioning.

When the heat is on and you feel an argument brewing, be an adult. Adults are calm and rational and avoid confrontation. The goal of an adult is to reach a mutually agreeable resolution by sharing their opinions, listening to the views of the other person and negotiating a compromise.

Owning Your Feelings

Telling your partner (or anyone else for that matter) that she 'made' you feel something is like a red rag to a bull. The statement is blaming, avoids responsibility and is also fundamentally untrue.

You're responsible for your own feelings. If your partner is late home from work, this may evoke anger in you. But she didn't 'make' you angry. You may as easily have felt anxious (has something happened?) or relieved (you only just got in yourself) or concerned (she really needs a break from overtime) or suspicious (is she really working late?). You can have many different feelings, all of which are within your control.

Blaming your partner for your feelings puts her in the position of defending herself rather than addressing the issue. Calmly stating and owning your feelings helps you both to discuss what needs to change rather than argue about who's to blame.

Finding a Code Word

This is a very simple technique for avoiding an argument and one that works especially well if one or both of you struggle to articulate your feelings in times of stress. If you know that the tension is mounting between you but you really, really don't want to have an argument, then a code word is the perfect solution.

Agree a word that when you say it means 'let's not do this, let's stop now'. Obviously, you need to choose a word you don't commonly use in your vocabulary, or life can get very confusing, so think of something obscure but memorable. Common favourites that I've heard over the years are bananas, coconuts (I guess any tropical fruit may do), donkey or crocodile. The word you pick really doesn't matter, as long as you make it mean 'stop'.

Doing Something Practical

Sometimes the only way to avoid a train crash is to get off the train. If the atmosphere between you is so thick with tension you need a knife to cut through it, then get up and do something else. That may mean going for a walk, getting a chore done, watching a film or getting some space on your own – anything that breaks the status quo and forces the two of you into a different position.

In the counselling room, I sometimes suggest that a couple simply swap seats. Suddenly they see the world and each other from a different angle and the looming storm cloud of a row shifts.

Deciding whether to do something different together or alone really is up to each of you and the severity of the approaching row. It also depends on how you use the time. Your objective is to do something that distracts you emotionally and psychologically, so if you're going to spend time alone sulking or chuntering about your grievances, then you're better off doing something together.

Everyone's different, so your partner may need time alone to cool down, while you prefer to distract yourself as a couple. If this describes your situation, then agree a compromise where your partner gets an agreed time to herself and then you come back together to do something.

Agreeing to Disagree

Choose your battles wisely. You don't need to argue about everything, and some things really are best left unsaid. Some arguments go on and on and on simply because one person wants to prove she's right, when in reality that just doesn't matter.

Here are three common types of arguments that you never need to have:

- **Memory rows:** 'It was Wednesday.' 'No it wasn't, it was Thursday.' 'No, it was definitely Wednesday.' 'Well, I know for a fact that it was Thursday.' Aarrgh – stop. The day of the week doesn't matter. Stop arguing over who's got the better memory and get on with the conversation.

- **Matters of taste:** 'Golf's a boring sport.' 'No it's not, not if you know how to play.' 'Well, I've always found it boring.' 'Maybe that's because you don't know how to play.' 'Or maybe you're just a boring person and that's why you don't find it boring.' Children, children, please stop. This is just a matter of taste. A matter of personal opinion. Neither of you is right or wrong, so you have nothing to argue about.

- **Different styles:** 'You should write a list, then you can't forget things.' 'I hate writing lists, you know I find them too constricting.' 'That's why you're so disorganised.' 'Only to a control freak like you.' People have different ways of doing things, and 99 per cent of the time the result is the same. If your partner has different methods and routines than you do, this isn't a character fault, merely a character difference.

Sometimes you can agree to disagree inside your head without ever opening your mouth. You simply bite your tongue, take a deep breath and smile. At other times, you may have to remind each other that being different is okay.

Using the Big Brother Technique

This is a brilliant way of making sure that you either avoid a row altogether or at least conduct it in a calm and civilised manner. Basically, all you have to do is imagine that you're in the Big Brother house and millions of people are watching you. The viewers include your parents, your kids, your friends and your boss. They're judging you and deciding whether you should be evicted.

You may be amazed by how much you say and do when you think no one's watching you. When you're alone with your partner, you can easily try to justify your behaviour or blame her. But if you think the world's watching, the usual cognitive distortions don't work. Now you think before you speak and you do everything you can to portray yourself as the loving, caring, understanding partner whose only desire is a harmonious home and a happy spouse. Try it – it works.

Using Humour

Last and by no means least, make a joke, have a laugh, see the funny side of things. Humour's a fantastic way of defusing a difficult situation – as long as the joke isn't at your partner's expense, of course.

Laughing at yourself, as individuals as well as a couple, is a skill that helps you ride the storms of life together. Humour puts things into perspective and draws you closer to each other in your shared humanity. So when all else fails, laugh.

Chapter 19

Ten Great Expectations for Couples

● ●

In This Chapter

▶ Defining the expectations that strengthen your relationship

▶ Being realistic but hopeful

● ●

Have you heard the opinion that the problem today is that people expect too much from their relationships? Well, I think that's rubbish. Nothing's wrong with having high expectations as long as your partner shares them and as long as they're realistic.

This chapters shares ten great realistic expectations for couples. If you're expecting your relationship always to be happy and to meet all of your physical, emotional and intellectual needs, then I'm sorry, you're going to be disappointed. But if your expectations are that you're committed to each other, love each other, develop and grow together and work through life's difficulties when they arise, then you can look forward to living happily ever after.

Expecting Your Relationship to Improve

Never underestimate the power of positive thinking. If you expect your relationship to improve, then you have significantly more chance of achieving that. But if you expect your relationship to fail, then you're almost certain to be right.

When you expect your relationship to improve, your motivation goes up and you find yourself doing everything you possibly can to make it work and fulfil your expectation. You start to notice all the things, however small, that are steps in the right direction. You also find yourself focusing on your partner's good points and the strengths in your relationship rather than the negatives and the weaknesses.

Expecting to Be Loved

Knowing that your partner loves you is essential for a successful relationship. But even more important is knowing that you're loved. To be loved by someone is an active process, not just an emotional feeling. When you know you're loved, you see your partner as someone who always has your best interests at heart. When your partner challenges you, he does so because he's thinking about your growth. When he gets upset, that's because he values your opinion. When he gets angry, he's showing that he cares about the quality of your relationship.

Expecting to be loved shows that you have positive self-esteem and good self-confidence. Consequently, you're less likely to doubt and challenge your partner and more likely to feel secure within the relationship.

The more you expect to be loved, the more you feel loved. So until your partner does something that was very obviously meant to hurt you, assume that you're loved.

Expecting to Discover Difficult Things about Each Other

Most relationships start off as a fairytale romance with both of you believing that you've found the answer to your dreams. Unfortunately, reality kicks in after a while and you're forced to realise that your partner isn't perfect.

As time goes on, you may well discover some aspects of your partner's character or behaviour that you don't like. That may be something relatively trivial like the way he eats his food, or it may be something more significant like the lack of respect he shows his parents. The issue may be something that has a direct impact on your relationship, such as his habit of withdrawing into silence for days when he's stressed, or the difficulty of living with something your partner has done in the past.

But before you chuck in the towel, remember that your partner is almost certainly discovering some uncomfortable truths about you too.

Hollywood has a lot to answer for in setting up expectations of the perfect romantic partner. In the real world, you must accept imperfections and painful pasts and be willing to love each other just the same.

Expecting to Discover Even More Difficult Things About Yourself

Getting into an intimate relationship is like living with a mirror right in front of you. Everything you do, good and bad, reflects back at you, either directly through conversation or confrontation, or indirectly through the reactions and responses you evoke in your partner. Getting close to someone inevitably means finding out more about yourself. And some discoveries you may prefer not to make.

You may discover that you tend to be short tempered, unaffectionate, insensitive or moody. Or that you're difficult to live with because you're so untidy or such a control freak. Maybe you have an irritating laugh or snore, or you're a terrible cook, a bad time keeper or a scary driver. When you're alone, these weaknesses may stay gloriously hidden, but in a relationship everything's exposed.

Knowing about a fault gives you a chance to fix it, so wherever possible use your discoveries to your advantage and change. If you discover things that you really can't change, then both you and your partner have to find ways to live with these parts of you.

Expecting Your Relationship to Change

A relationship's not a static commodity but a living, evolving and growing entity. Sometimes your relationship feels fantastic, a source of comfort and joy, and occasionally it feels terrible and you wonder what on earth you're doing with your partner. And you experience many varying degrees of highs and lows in between.

This is the normal ebb and flow of a relationship, and as long as you always get more highs than lows, you're doing just fine. Accepting the rough with the smooth is a valuable lesson for every aspect of life.

The quality of your relationship also changes. At first, when you're madly in love, you may want to spend every waking moment together and you can't bear to be apart. But as this phase wears off, so does the urgency, and you find yourselves feeling more relaxed about the time you spend together. As more time passes, you probably find yourselves wanting to spend more time with friends or doing things alone. This doesn't mean that your relationship isn't as strong as it used to be, just that it's evolving.

Trying to hang on to the past or go back to how things used to be never works. You must always be ready to move forward and embrace each stage of your relationship as it changes and matures.

Expecting Sex to Get Better and Better

The myth that sex is best when you first get together is just that, a myth. Sex may be more passionate and urgent then, but it's often a bit lacking in the knowledge and skills department.

As your relationship grows and you get closer and closer, you can expect your sex life to get better as well. As you get to know one another's bodies and feel more confident and comfortable sharing what you like, you find that not only does your performance improve, your intimacy does too. Sex loses any of its early awkwardness and you enjoy more openness and eroticism.

If you expect sex to get better, then you feel more motivated to make sure that it does. With a shared commitment to grow and develop together and to fight against complacency and routine, you can look forward to many, many years of fun.

Expecting to Be Bored Sometimes

Boredom's a really annoying and tiring fact of life. In the early stage of a relationship, being together is all you need to make your life complete. But as you continue your joint journey, you find that your relationship isn't enough to satisfy all your needs and you have to do other things as well.

When you're feeling bored with your partner or bored with your relationship, you can be tempted to wonder whether you'd be happy with someone else. And, of course, the truth is that you may be, at least for a short while. But in time, that relationship would surely also become boring unless you commit to doing something about it.

To avoid boredom, you need to work together at keeping yourselves and your life interesting. Take up new hobbies and interests, separately and alone, to ensure that you have plenty to talk about.

Don't expect your partner to be your social entertainer and the answer to all your needs and desires. No relationship can ever live up to this, and thinking like this leaves you moving from relationship to relationship and feeling permanently unfulfilled.

Expecting to Have Doubts Sometimes

Because people and relationships can change so much, times are bound to occur when you sense a nagging doubt in the pit of your stomach that your relationship isn't okay. When that happens, listen and take heed, but whatever you do, don't panic.

Having relationship doubts is part of being human. Doubts can be triggered in all sorts of ways: an article in a magazine, listening to a friend's story, something that's recently happened within your relationship, or the resurfacing of an issue that you're struggling to resolve. Whatever the trigger may be, use the opportunity to reflect on your relationship and take stock of where you are.

If you have problems in your relationship that you need to address, then do so. But if, on reflection, you can't identify anything wrong, redirect your energy to focusing on the positives in your relationship and forget it.

You're bound to doubt your relationship at times. But that absolutely does not mean that you have a problem – your doubts are just a symptom of living in an uncertain world.

Expecting to Face Tough Times Together

The storms of life can be particularly harsh at times and, sadly, few relationships come through unscathed. The true strength of a relationship is often tested when times are tough – during bereavements, health problems, redundancy, financial difficulties or family crises.

Tough times are an opportunity to lean on each other and become closer. You have a chance to discover more about yourself and about each other. This is a time to find new strengths and new reserves of humour and intimacy.

When you find yourselves going through a tough time, make sure that you pull together. Continue to prioritise your relationship and both give and receive support. Couples who can ride through these storms together inevitably come through stronger and closer than ever before.

Expecting to Be Together, Forever

Divorce and separation are commonplace today, so trusting in the longevity of a relationship can be difficult. But commitment isn't about having any guarantees, it's about making a decision that you're going to stay together, for better and for worse.

Unfortunately, not all relationships work out, but that's no reason to think that yours is going to be one of the casualties. The more you expect to be together forever, the harder you work at resolving any problems when they arise, and the more effort you make to create a relationship that you both cherish till death you do part.

Appendix

Relationship Resources

● ●

Here you can find some additional resources to help you improve your relationship. And if all else has failed, you'll also find people and places to turn to if your relationship has come to the end of the line. In addition you'll find resources to help you in specific areas of your relationship life such as parenting, second families and retirement as well as help with emotional struggles such as anxiety, depression, anger and jealousy.

Self-help Books

These books are particularly useful as both general reads and as reference works when you need another perspective on your relationship. They contain top-notch information and are written in user-friendly styles. I've grouped them under five main headings.

General relationship

After the Affair; How to Build Love & Trust Again by Julia Cole (Vermillion)

Love is Never Enough; How Couples can Overcome Misunderstandings, Resolve Conflicts & Solve Relationship Problems through Cognitive Therapy by Aaron T Beck (Harper Collins)

Make Love Work For You; The Essential Guide for Career Couples by Julia Cole (Hodder & Stoughton)

Stop Arguing, Start Talking; The 10 Point Plan for Couples in Conflict by Susan Quilliam (Vermillion)

The 7 Principles for Making Marriage Work by John M. Gottman and Nan Silverman (Three Rivers Press)

Divorce and separation

Divorce For Dummies by Thelma Fisher, Hilary Woodward, John Ventura and Mary Reed (Wiley)

Help Your Children Cope with Your Divorce by Paula Hall (Vermillion)

How to Have a Healthy Divorce: A Step-by-Step Guide for Anyone going through Separation or Divorce by Paula Hall (Vermillion)

Too Good to Leave, Too Bad to Stay; A Step-by-Step Guide to Help You Decide Whether to Stay or Get Out of Your Relationship by Mira Kirshenbaum (Michael Joseph)

Parenting

Babyshock: Your Relationship Survival Guide by Elizabeth Martin (Vermillion)

Getting Your Little Darlings to Behave by Sue Cowley (Continuum)

Get Out Of My Life, But First Take Me and Alex into Town; A parents Guide to the New Teenager by Tony Wolf and Suzanne Franks (Profile Books)

Parenting For Dummies by Helen Brown (Wiley)

Step Families: Living Successfully with Other People's Children by Suzie Hayman (Vermillion)

Better sex and sexual problems

Out of the Shadows; Understanding Sexual Addiction by Patrick Carnes (Hazelden)

Sex in Loving Relationships by Sarah Litvinoff (Vermillion)

The New Male Sexuality; The Truth about Men, Sex and Pleasure by Bernie Zilbergeld (Bantam)

The New Joy of Sex by Alex Comfort and Susan Quilliam (Mitchell Beazley)

Women without Sex; The Truth about Female Impotence and Other Sexual Problems by Catherine Kalamis, (Self-help direct)

Emotional wellbeing

Addiction and Recovery For Dummies by M. David Lewis, Brian F. Shaw, Paul Ritvo and Jane Irvine (Wiley)

Anger Management for Dummies by W. Doyle Gentry (Wiley)

Boosting Self Esteem for Dummies by Rhena Branch and Rob Willson (Wiley)

Jealousy; Overcoming Common Problems by Paul A. Hauck (Sheldon Press)

Loving Yourself, Loving Another The Importance of Self-Esteem for Successful Relationships by Julia Cole (Vermillion)

Managing Anger; Simple Steps for Dealing with Frustration and Threat by Gael Lindenfield (Thorsons)

Overcoming Anxiety For Dummies by Elaine Iljon Foreman, Laura Smith and Charles Elliott (Wiley)

Overcoming Depression For Dummies by Elaine Iljon Foreman, Laura Smith and Charles Elliott (Wiley)

Advice and Support

These organisations all maintain useful websites full of valuable information on relationships issues:

- ✔ **The Association for the Treatment of Sexual Addiction and Compulsivity** (ATSAC: www.sexaddictionandcompulisivity.org) provides support and information for anyone affected by sexual addiction.

- ✔ **The British Association of Counselling and Psychotherapy** (BACP: www.bacp.co.uk) provide a register of private counsellors and psychotherapists who can work with a wide range of problems.

- ✔ **The British Association of Sexual and Relationship Therapy** (BASRT, www.basrt.org.uk) provides online advice on sexual problems and a register of private therapists who specialise in relationship and sexual problems.

- ✔ **DivorceAid** (www.divorceaid.co.uk) is an independent group of professionals providing all round advice and support on every aspect of divorce and separation. Also provides resources for children and teenagers.

- ✔ **Parent Line Plus** (www.parentlineplus.org.uk) provides advice and support on a range of parenting issues and also have a 24/7 helpline.

- ✔ **Pink Therapy** (www.pinktherapy.com) is the UK's largest independent therapy organisation working with gender and sexual minority clients.

- ✔ **Relate** (www.relate.org.uk) is the UK's largest counselling service for couples and individuals with sexual or relationship difficulties. Also provides services for young people and families.

- ✔ **Respect** (www.respect.uk.net) provides information and help for perpetrators of domestic violence.

- ✔ **The Relationship Specialists** (www.TheRelationshipSpecialists. com) is an independent website providing online advice for relationship and sexual problems run by a team of accredited therapists.

- ✔ **Women's Aid** (www.womensaid.org.uk) is a national domestic violence charity that provides support, advice and temporary accommodation to women and men affected by violence or abuse.

Index

• B •

• C •

• D •

• F •

• G •

• H •

new baby and issues for, 240
overcoming problems about, 196–198
rota for, 197–198
understanding each other's perspective, 196–197
humour
during arguments, 170, 324
after ending a relationship, 301
during illness or disability, 255
importance of, 71
incorporating in your relationship, 72

• *I* •

'I don't know' (communication block), 148
'I love you', actions saying, 12, 14–15
ignorance (communication block), 148
illness
aging and, myths about, 257
caring for each other during, 255
keeping the dynamic equal with, 254
role changes with, 254
shock, loss, and anger with, 253
terminal, coping with, 254
important and urgent things, prioritising, 67–68
'in love'. *See also* romance
arguments to rekindle feeling of, 185
chemistry of, 51, 86–87, 88
falling again, 87–90
'loving' versus, 22
phase of relationships, 10, 51, 53, 94
remembering why you fell in love, 90–92
short-term nature of, 51, 87
inadequacy
fear of, 178
feelings with depression, anxiety, or addiction, 224
indifference
ending a relationship due to, 294
as relationship wrecker, 19
as sign of drifting apart, 80
infertility, 239
information updates (communication type), 28
inhibition, lowered by arguments, 185
initiation, sexual, 103, 131
in-laws, 27, 182, 240

insecurity. *See also* anxiety; jealousy
arguments triggered by, 179
as natural in relationships, 216
safety affair due to, 266
integrity, trust in partner's, 283
intellectual intimacy, 26. *See also* intimacy
intention, trust in partner's, 283
intercourse
painful, 118
sex versus, 108
Internet
advice and support resources, 333–334
platonic affairs over the, 266
interpreting, empathy shown by, 158
interrupting (communication block), 149, 316
intimacy. *See also* friendship; sex
arguments to avoid, 183–184
assumptions as dangers to, 78
building, 60–61
commitment and effort required for, 26
communication needed for, 43
curiosity as aid to, 78–79
cyber-affairs due to lack of, 266
definitions of, 25
facets of, 26
as indicator of relationship health, 65
maintaining a sexual connection, 127–128
planning pastimes for, 72
questionnaire assessing, 29, 31
in sexual growth plan, 103
vulnerability strengthening, 74–75
intimate sharing (communication type), 28
Irvine, Jane (*Addiction and Recovery For Dummies*), 226, 333
isolation, 224

• *J* •

jealousy
about partner's affair, 268
admitting feelings of, 222
changing the environment, 221
components of, 217
emotions heightened by, 217
further help for, 333
helping a jealous partner, 222–223
irrational, signs of, 219

• L •

• M •

• N •

• O •

• P •

• T •

• U •

• V •

• W •

• Y •

FOR DUMMIES®

Do Anything. Just Add Dummies

UK editions

BUSINESS

Starting a Business FOR DUMMIES

978-0-470-51806-9

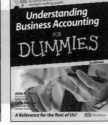

Understanding Business Accounting FOR DUMMIES

978-0-470-99245-6

Lean Six Sigma FOR DUMMIES

978-0-470-75626-3

FINANCE

Investing FOR DUMMIES

978-0-470-99280-7

Tax FOR DUMMIES

978-0-470-99811-3

Sorting Out Your Finances FOR DUMMIES

978-0-470-69515-9

PROPERTY

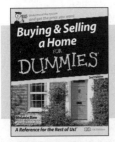

Buying & Selling a Home FOR DUMMIES

978-0-470-99448-1

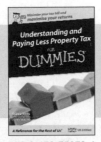

Understanding and Paying Less Property Tax FOR DUMMIES

978-0-470-75872-4

DIY & Home Maintenance ALL-IN-ONE FOR DUMMIES

978-0-7645-7054-4

Backgammon For Dummies
978-0-470-77085-6

Body Language For Dummies
978-0-470-51291-3

British Sign Language
For Dummies
978-0-470-69477-0

Business NLP For Dummies
978-0-470-69757-3

Children's Health For Dummies
978-0-470-02735-6

Cognitive Behavioural Coaching
For Dummies
978-0-470-71379-2

Counselling Skills For Dummies
978-0-470-51190-9

Digital Marketing For Dummies
978-0-470-05793-3

eBay.co.uk For Dummies,
2nd Edition
978-0-470-51807-6

English Grammar For Dummies
978-0-470-05752-0

Fertility & Infertility For Dummies
978-0-470-05750-6

Genealogy Online For Dummies
978-0-7645-7061-2

Golf For Dummies
978-0-470-01811-8

Green Living For Dummies
978-0-470-06038-4

Hypnotherapy For Dummies
978-0-470-01930-6

Available wherever books are sold. For more information or to order direct go to
www.wiley.com or call +44 (0) 1243 843291

13902_p1

FOR DUMMIES®

A world of resources to help you grow

UK editions

SELF-HELP

978-0-470-01838-5

978-0-7645-7028-5

978-0-470-75876-2

HEALTH

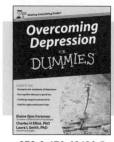
978-0-470-69430-5

978-0-470-51737-6

978-0-470-71401-0

HISTORY

978-0-470-99468-9

978-0-470-51015-5

978-0-470-98787-2

Inventing For Dummies
978-0-470-51996-7

Job Hunting and Career Change
All-In-One For Dummies
978-0-470-51611-9

Motivation For Dummies
978-0-470-76035-2

Origami Kit For Dummies
978-0-470-75857-1

Personal Development All-In-One
For Dummies
978-0-470-51501-3

PRINCE2 For Dummies
978-0-470-51919-6

Psychometric Tests For Dummies
978-0-470-75366-8

Raising Happy Children For
Dummies
978-0-470-05978-4

Starting and Running a Business
All-in-One For Dummies
978-0-470-51648-5

Sudoku for Dummies
978-0-470-01892-7

The British Citizenship Test
For Dummies, 2nd Edition
978-0-470-72339-5

Time Management For Dummies
978-0-470-77765-7

Wills, Probate, & Inheritance Tax
For Dummies, 2nd Edition
978-0-470-75629-4

Winning on Betfair For Dummies,
2nd Edition
978-0-470-72336-4

**Available wherever books are sold. For more information or to order direct go to
www.wiley.com or call +44 (0) 1243 843291**

13902_p2

FOR DUMMIES

The easy way to get more done and have more fun

LANGUAGES

978-0-7645-5194-9

978-0-7645-5193-2

978-0-471-77270-5

MUSIC

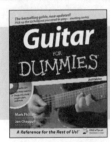
978-0-7645-9904-0

978-0-470-03275-6
UK Edition

978-0-7645-5105-5

SCIENCE & MATHS

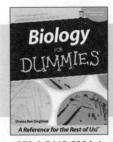
978-0-7645-5326-4

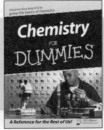
978-0-7645-5430-8

978-0-7645-5325-7

Art For Dummies
978-0-7645-5104-8

Baby & Toddler Sleep Solutions For
Dummies
978-0-470-11794-1

Bass Guitar For Dummies
978-0-7645-2487-5

Brain Games For Dummies
978-0-470-37378-1

Christianity For Dummies
978-0-7645-4482-8

Filmmaking For Dummies, 2nd
Edition
978-0-470-38694-1

Forensics For Dummies
978-0-7645-5580-0

German For Dummies
978-0-7645-5195-6

Hobby Farming For Dummies
978-0-470-28172-7

Jewelry Making & Beading For
Dummies
978-0-7645-2571-1

Knitting for Dummies, 2nd Edition
978-0-470-28747-7

Music Composition For Dummies
978-0-470-22421-2

Physics For Dummies
978-0-7645-5433-9

Sex For Dummies, 3rd Edition
978-0-470-04523-7

Solar Power Your Home For Dummies
978-0-470-17569-9

Tennis For Dummies
978-0-7645-5087-4

The Koran For Dummies
978-0-7645-5581-7

U.S. History For Dummies
978-0-7645-5249-6

Wine For Dummies, 4th Edition
978-0-470-04579-4

**Available wherever books are sold. For more information or to order direct go to
www.wiley.com or call +44 (0) 1243 843291**

13902_p3

FOR DUMMIES®

Helping you expand your horizons and achieve your potential

COMPUTER BASICS

978-0-470-27759-1

978-0-470-13728-4

978-0-471-75421-3

DIGITAL LIFESTYLE

978-0-470-25074-7

978-0-470-39062-7

978-0-470-17469-2

WEB & DESIGN

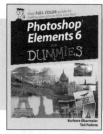

978-0-470-19238-2

978-0-470-32725-8

978-0-470-34502-3

Access 2007 For Dummies
978-0-470-04612-8

Adobe Creative Suite 3 Design Premium
All-in-One Desk Reference For Dummies
978-0-470-11724-8

AutoCAD 2009 For Dummies
978-0-470-22977-4

C++ For Dummies, 5th Edition
978-0-7645-6852-7

Computers For Seniors For Dummies
978-0-470-24055-7

Excel 2007 All-In-One Desk Reference F
or Dummies
978-0-470-03738-6

Flash CS3 For Dummies
978-0-470-12100-9

Mac OS X Leopard For Dummies
978-0-470-05433-8

Macs For Dummies, 10th Edition
978-0-470-27817-8

Networking All-in-One Desk Reference
For Dummies, 3rd Edition
978-0-470-17915-4

Office 2007 All-in-One Desk Reference
For Dummies
978-0-471-78279-7

Search Engine Optimization For
Dummies, 2nd Edition
978-0-471-97998-2

Second Life For Dummies
978-0-470-18025-9

The Internet For Dummies, 11th Edition
978-0-470-12174-0

Visual Studio 2008 All-In-One Desk
Reference For Dummies
978-0-470-19108-8

Web Analytics For Dummies
978-0-470-09824-0

Windows XP For Dummies, 2nd Edition
978-0-7645-7326-2

Available wherever books are sold. For more information or to order direct go to www.wiley.com or call +44 (0) 1243 843291

13902_p4